T0303919

ROUTLEDGE LIBRARY EDITIONS:
THE ECONOMICS AND BUSINESS OF
TECHNOLOGY

Volume 49

TECHNOLOGICAL CHANGE, DEVELOPMENT AND THE ENVIRONMENT

TECHNOLOGICAL CHANGE, DEVELOPMENT AND THE ENVIRONMENT
Socio-Economic Perspectives

Edited by
CLEM TISDELL AND PRIYATOSH MAITRA

Routledge
Taylor & Francis Group

LONDON AND NEW YORK

First published in 1988 by Routledge

This edition first published in 2018
by Routledge
2 Park Square, Milton Park, Abingdon, Oxon OX14 4RN

and by Routledge
711 Third Avenue, New York, NY 10017

Routledge is an imprint of the Taylor & Francis Group, an informa business

British Library Cataloguing in Publication Data
A catalogue record for this book is available from the British Library

ISBN: 978-1-138-50336-6 (Set)
ISBN: 978-1-351-06690-7 (Set) (ebk)
ISBN: 978-1-138-47639-4 (Volume 49) (hbk)
ISBN: 978-1-351-10609-2 (Volume 49) (ebk)

Publisher's Note
The publisher has gone to great lengths to ensure the quality of this reprint but
points out that some imperfections in the original copies may be apparent.

Disclaimer
The publisher has made every effort to trace copyright holders and would welcome
correspondence from those they have been unable to trace.

TECHNOLOGICAL CHANGE, DEVELOPMENT AND THE ENVIRONMENT

Socio-Economic Perspectives

EDITED BY

CLEM TISDELL AND

PRIYATOSH MAITRA

ROUTLEDGE
London and New York

First published in 1988 by
Routledge
11 New Fetter Lane, London EC4P 4EE

Published in the USA by
Routledge
in association with Routledge, Chapman & Hall, Inc.
29 West 35th Street, New York, NY 10001

British Library Cataloguing in Publication Data

Technological change, development and the
    environment: socio-economic perspectives.
    1. Technological development. Socioeconomic
aspects
    I. Tisdell, C.A. (Clement Allan)
    II. Maitra, Priyatosh, *1930-*
303.4'83

ISBN 0-415-00447-0

Library of Congress Cataloging-in-Publication Data

ISBN 0-415-00447-0

Printed and bound in Great Britain by
Biddles Ltd, Guildford and King's Lynn

CONTENTS

TABLES

FIGURES

PREFACE

This volume highlights the interconnectedness of
technological change, economic development, the
state of the environment, population and social
change. In so doing, it provides a comprehensive
overview of technological change and development
patterns relevant to both less developed and
developed countries. Contributions are written
from varied perspectives by a group of international economists from five different continents.
Contributions vary in nature. Empirical, analytical
and philosophical approaches are all represented as
well as case studies, for example, of Bangladesh,
China, India, Australia, New Zealand, South Africa
and the United Kingdom. Past events as well as
future prospects are considered. An outline of the
contributions is given in Chapter 1 so we shall not
repeat this here. Those concerned either with
current issues or with long-term fundamental
questions about economic development and growth or
with rising populations and technological change
will find much interest in this volume.

Contributions to this book are based upon
papers which were originally presented to three
sessions of the Fourth World Congress of Social
Economics held in Toronto, Canada, in August, 1986.
These sessions were organized by the editors of
this volume but the Congress itself was organized
by the International Institute of Social Economics,
Hull, England. We wish to thank Professor Barrie
Pettman, Director of this Institute, for providing
us with this opportunity.

During 1987, the original Congress papers were
revised by contributors in the light of comments by
discussants and participants at the Congress, as
well as later feedback so as to make them suitable
for presentation in book form. We would like to

take this chance to thank all of those who have contributed to this revision process.

Also thanks are due to Jenny Hargrave, Lorraine King and Kath Kirkby for assisting in manuscript production, to Wanda Lis for the artwork production, to Richard Dear for computer systems assistance and to Sitha Kahagalle for completing the task of final word-processing and typescript preparation.

Clem Tisdell   Priyatosh Maitra
University of Newcastle   University of Otago

Chapter One

TECHNOLOGY: A FACTOR IN DEVELOPMENT AND
SOCIO-ECONOMIC AND ENVIRONMENTAL CHANGE

Clem Tisdell

INTRODUCTION

New technology (its availability and application)
is of extraordinary importance as a factor in
economic growth and development, as a determinant
of the nature and structure of society and as a
contributor to changes in environmental quality.
Its importance in these respects, though now widely
recognized by economists and social scientists, has
not been and is not always fully appreciated. The
contributions in this volume are intended to
underline its pervasive influence both in less
developed countries (LDCs) and developed economies.
    It has been suggested that the major reason
for the commencement of sustained economic growth
in the eighteenth century in Great Britain was not
high levels of savings and capital accumulation but
new inventions and their application (Dean, 1955).
Blum et al. (1967) have argued that in almost every
developed country of today sustained economic
growth has followed adoption of a new technology
and that this adoption has often been a precursor
to rising levels of capital accumulation and
economic growth. All these writers argue strongly
against the hypothesis that in order to obtain a
take-off of economic growth, it is necessary
initially for a country to achieve a high rate of
savings and capital accumulation as, for example,
proposed by Rostow (1952). It is argued that this
is neither a necessary nor a sufficient condition
for sustained economic growth. Recent studies
support this point of view (see for example,
Kenwood and Lougheed, 1982). It is also clear that
in developed countries, qualitative factors (such
as improved technology) have been more important
than quantitative factors, (such as increases in

1

the quantity of capital) as apparent sources of
growth in Gross Domestic Product (GDP) in recent
decades (Cf. Denison, 1962).

If one accepts the critical importance of
technological change as a factor in economic
growth, this leads onto further questions. Not all
of these are answered in this volume but many are
addressed. They include the following: To what
extent can we expect the socially most appropriate
technology to be developed in a society and
applied? What controls (degree of free choice) do
nations and individuals have over the application
of technology? Is the range of technologies
developed and actually applied in the best interest
of nations and societies, especially LDCs, and if
not, why not? How is the nature of the family,
family life and of work likely to be affected by
new technologies both within the home, and the
workplace, for example, by the increased
availability of information-intensive goods and
machines and telecommunication facilities? Can we
predict the likely characteristics of future
technologies, what are they likely to be and what
social consequences can be expected from them? Do
LDCs face particular obstacles to economic
development because of their later start and their
reliance on imported technology? What environmental problems and social adjustment problems may
be encountered as a result of the emergence of new
technologies which increase man's control over or
effect on nature and which also lead to the
relative rise and fall of different industries?
Let me indicate how these matters are addressed in
this book.

THE CONTRIBUTIONS

The next five chapters (Chapters 2-6) concentrate
on the role of new technology in the development
(or underdevelopment) of less developed nations
(especially India, Bangladesh and China) whereas
most of the remaining chapters are focussed on the
social and industrial consequences of new
technology in more developed nations such as the
United Kingdom, Australia and New Zealand.
However, some contributions are not country-
specific but are general, and even those that refer
to the experience of particular nations have wider
applications as pointed out by their individual
authors.

It may be useful to readers to have an overview of the individual contributions to this volume, and I shall now provide that. However, I wish to emphasize that a brief overview is by necessity selective. It is a personal interpretation and cannot do full justice to the individual contributions. Each reader must in the end interpret the individual contributions. Nevertheless, an initial guide may prove of value for orientation purposes.

In Chapter 2, Priyatosh Maitra argues that India has failed to develop in the main because as a consequence of past British territorial imperialism, it was not able to develop its own indigenous technology (which it would have most likely done as an independent nation in order to cope with the pressure of its rising population) and has become dependent on imported foreign technology. It has not recovered from its experience under imperial control and still remains heavily dependent on imported technology from developed countries (the Centre) even though technically it has the power to cut itself off from such imports. He believes that India is only likely to achieve economic development, or at least lasting economic development, if it develops its own technology independently of the Centre. While Maitra uses Marxian-type analysis, he criticizes a number of Marxist interpretations of India's development experience.

Alauddin and Tisdell consider in Chapter 3 the experience of Bangladesh in adopting 'Green Revolution' technologies in its agriculture. Those technologies have been 'spearheaded' by developed nations through CGIAR (Consultative Group for International Agricultural Research). While in Bangladesh's case, the use of those technologies has resulted in a tremendous increase in food production, Bangladesh has become increasingly unable to sustain its rising population from its own food production and has become more dependent on imports of food, of technology and of inputs required for agricultural production. In addition, doubts are raised about the ecological possibility of sustaining its past growth rates of food production. Nevertheless, Bangladesh's predicament might have been worse in the absence of its use of 'Green Revolution' technologies.

Nripesh Podder takes an optimistic view in Chapter 4 of the benefits to mankind of new technology and disagrees with Maitra's thesis that

3

the dependence of a nation such as India on foreign technology is a prime factor in underdevelopment, that is, an important element contributing to economic backwardness (Cf. Tisdell, 1987). He argues that on the whole import of technology from abroad should be welcomed as a means of improving human welfare in recipient countries.

Joseph Remenyi suggests (Chapter 5) that more attention should be given to improving institutional mechanisms for developing appropriate agricultural technology for LDCs. In the past, developed countries have tended to take a dominating role (even through CGIAR) in providing assistance to LDCs for the development of new agricultural technologies, for example, in determining research priorities and in directing actual research. He suggests that a partnership is likely to be more beneficial and that the operation of the Australian Centre for International Agricultural Research (ACIAR) might prove to be a useful model to emulate (Cf. Tisdell, 1986).

For a period of time, China followed a path of technological and economic autarky which it abandoned with its adoption of the Four Modernisation principles for the 1976-85 ten-year economic programme. As Hsu O'Keefe points out in Chapter 6, China now needs to develop and become more familiar with economic technologies for better evaluating new technologies and choosing between technologies available from abroad. She illustrates China's requirement for economic evaluation of technologies by considering problems of choosing between alternative urban transportation systems and projects in China requiring different transport technologies.

In developed countries, there has been a long-term tendency for the terms of trade to move against agriculture, partly because rapid technological progress has increased agricultural supply, and demand for agricultural produce is relatively inelastic. Consequently, employment in the agricultural sector has fallen in most developed countries and continues to do so. This has been associated with considerable structural adjustment and change in rural societies. This is especially evident in Australia, which has been much disadvantaged by the protective agricultural policies of industrialized nations. Warren Musgrave outlines in Chapter 7 the adjustment problems that have been experienced by the Australian rural sector paying particular attention

4

to the emergence of rural poverty. He suggests that the Australian experience is also relevant to that of other countries (e.g., Canada).

At a general level, Khan and Zerby use cluster analysis in Chapter 8 to consider the association between technological change and social welfare. Indices of technological change and technological effort for 126 countries are compared by them with selected indicators of social welfare or social development. Their evidence suggests that the association between the two factors is not a close one. However, this conclusion must be regarded as a tentative one, given the difficulties of obtaining appropriate technological and social indicators.

Chisholm raises a different issue in Chapter 9, namely the prospect that economic development and continuing use of resources employing new technology may prove ecologically or environmentally unsustainable. To some extent, this possibility is mentioned by Alauddin and Tisdell in relation to agricultural resource use in Bangladesh, but for Chisholm's contribution it is the prime focus. He pays particular attention to the implications for rational decisions of irreversible use of natural resources when uncertainty exists about the future value of these resources.

Chapters 10-13 and to some extent 14, concentrate on social and sociological implications of new technologies, especially Third Wave technologies (Toffler, 1981, 1979) such as those associated with the growth of the electronics industry, telecommunications and information-intensive technologies.

Darton and O'Neill make use in Chapter 10 of U.K. survey data to identify patterns of changing consumption within the home. They examine new technology that can be used within the house and identify various social implications of it, e.g., the increasing tendency of individual family members to engage in individualistic rather than group-leisure activities in the home, an increasing tendency of individuals to spend their leisure-time in the home rather than outside.

Peter Hall explores the question in Chapter 11 of whether technical advances in telecommunication and associated technology such as computer technology, are likely to change work patterns fundamentally. In particular, is there likely to be a substantial increase in the number of people

working from home? What factors are likely to
influence the decision to work from home? He
demonstrates that the answers to these questions
are not as simple as they may seem to be at first
sight.
     Advances in electronics, telecommunications
and computing equipment have had a substantial
impact on technology in the banking industry. In
Chapter 12, Hazel Suchard considers the attitudes
and reactions of bank employees to such changes in
South Africa. In Chapter 13, Rae Weston and Alan
Williams examine the socio-economic impact of
technological change in banking for Australia and
New Zealand. They consider its human resource
consequences, note that appropriate banking
technologies may become more consumer-determined in
the future than in the past as deregulation of
monetary and fiscal services proceeds and believe
that banking culture and organizational structure
will undergo considerable changes as a result of
the continuing introduction of new electronic
technologies.
     Jacobus Doeleman debates in Chapter 14 the
issue of social determinism in relation to new
technology. To what extent is society able to
choose at all? Are technologies the result of
historical events beyond the control of societies?
Even if societies have some choice, individuals may
have little or no choice in using technologies
because of externality phenomena - a possibility
which Doeleman illustrates, for instance, by
reference to the availability of transport systems
based on the car, and the decision of an individual
to own a car.
     Rias van Wyk reviews in Chapter 15 standard
methods which have been used by economists to
identify sources of economic growth and finds them
wanting particularly in suggesting prognoses for
future technological change. He suggests that a
more direct approach to technological forecasting
is needed, namely a general theory of technology -
'eine allgemeine Technologie', in order to properly
understand and manage technology. Taking this
point of view, he outlines an approach to
'technological analysis' which is used to identify
technological trends and outlines how these might
be measured. He suggests research possibilities
which could, as he claims 'lead to a new level of
understanding of technology and the measurement of
its impact on society'.

CONCLUDING OBSERVATIONS

Scientific and technological change has a wide impact on society from both economic and sociological viewpoints (Cf. Bell, 1973; Tisdell, 1981). The diversity of its effects are well illustrated by the contributions to this volume, which also raise several policy and social philosophy issues. Indeed, as is to be anticipated, when dealing with such a complex subject, some contributors hold conflicting views about the consequences of technological change, for example when it depends on import of foreign technology, and therefore their work suggests different policy conclusions. In order to provide appropriate background and comparison, alternative interpretations and hypotheses as put forward in the literature are reviewed as part of most contributions. It is hoped that the diversity of contributions and perspectives in this volume, dealing as they do with the common theme of technology as a factor in economic and social development, will prove to be an asset.

NOTE

1. I wish to thank Dr. Priyatosh Maitra for his helpful suggestions for this chapter.

REFERENCES

Bell, D. (1973) **The Coming Post-Industrial Society: A Venture in Social Forecasting**, Basic Books, New York

Blum, J., Cameron, R. and Barnes, T.G. (1967) **The Emergence of the European World**, Routledge and Kegan Paul, London

Dean, P. (1955) 'The Implications of Early National Income Estimates for the Assessment of Long-Term Economic Growth in the United Kingdom', **Economic Development and Cultural Change**, 4, pp 3-38

Denison, E.F (1962) **Survey of Economic and the Alternatives before Us**, Committee for Development, New York

Kenwood, A.G. and Lougheed, A.L. (1982) **Technological Diffusion and Industrialisation Before 1914**, Croom Helm, London

Rostow, W.W. (1952) **Process of Economic Growth**, Norton, New York

Technology: A Factor in Development

Tisdell, C.A. (1987) 'Imperialism, Economic Dependence and Development: A Brief Review of Economic Thought and Theory', **Humanomics**, **3**, pp. 6-29

Tisdell, C.A (1986) 'International Scientific Co-operation, Technology Transfer and Aid: ASEAN countries, Australia and New Zealand', **Prometheus**, **4**, pp. 111-127

Tisdell, C.A. (1981) **Science and Technology Policy: Priorities of Governments**, Chapman and Hall, London

Toffler, A. (1981) **The Third Wave**, Pan, London

Toffler, A. (1979) **Future Shock**, Pan, London

Chapter Two

POPULATION GROWTH, TECHNOLOGICAL CHANGE AND ECONOMIC
DEVELOPMENT - THE INDIAN CASE, WITH A CRITIQUE OF
MARXIST INTERPRETATION

Priyatosh Maitra

INTRODUCTION

This chapter involves a critique of Marxist
interpretation of the nature and causes of
persistence of underdevelopment in terms of
population growth and technological change, using
India as a case study.

In most works on technological change, effects
of population growth have been ignored or considered
as a negative factor. One important reason might be
that since modern technological change began to
evolve as a result of the use of modern science in
the process of production in the late nineteenth
century in the United Kingdom and later in the
European countries, population growth in the West
began to slow down and has continued to do so. High
economic growth with rapidly expanding foreign trade
caused the demand for labour to exceed its supply
and necessitated technological change from an
extensive to an intensive phase of industrial
growth. Rapid technological change since then has
fostered the processing of human resources into
human capital.

Thus it is that, in all works on the role of
technological change in the Third World,
quantitative growth of population is considered as
the greatest hindrance to development. In those
economies, in the modern sector, technological
sophistication has been going on at an appreciable
rate but is failing to create any linkage effects
between this dynamic sector and the stagnating
sector. To overcome problems of poverty, overpopulation and unemployment, most development models
advocate, on the one hand, increased doses of
technology transfer to raise productivity, and on
the other, vigorous measures to combat population

9

growth. The results to date in terms of growth and
sophistication have been remarkable. But in terms
of development of dynamic structural change,
reduction in poverty and underemployment, they have
been extremely frustrating and disappointing.

Recently, the policy of eradication of poverty,
famine, underemployment and so on, known as the
policy of meeting 'basic needs', has become the
major objective of development planning (Streeten et
al., 1981; Sen, 1983; Griffin, 1978), again
ignoring inter-related problems of technological
change and population growth, except in a negative
sense. Marxist approaches also suffer from the same
limitation. Today basic needs models too ignore
this question of the nature of technological change
(Maitra, 1986, Ch. 2).

Technology is defined here as a method of using
science in production determined by the economic
systems (feudal, capitalist and socialist). Two
assumptions are often made about technology: First,
that as far as economics is concerned, it is a
parameter of the system and determined by scientists
and technologists. Secondly that technology is
neutral with respect to history, class, country and
factor endowments and technological change takes
place with the development of technological
knowledge. Faults that appear in development
patterns occur, not because of the nature of
technology itself, but due to its misuse: say, for
example, due to faulty institutional factors
(Stewart, 1978, pp. xi, 32–38).

These assumptions suit perfectly a capitalist
economic system. Paradoxically, in Marxist
socialist systems today, borrowed technology from
capitalist countries plays the most vital part in
socialist plans for development. This surely
contradicts Marx's concept of production and
technology to be discussed later.

K.E. Boulding (1983, p. 7) wrote:

> One can argue that science based technology was
> not very important before about 1860:
> ... The so-called industrial revolution in
> England in the eighteenth century was built
> largely on development from medieval
> technology. Even the steam engine owed nothing
> to thermodynamics, nor did the railway. From
> about 1860 however, we do detect an almost
> exponential explosion of science based
> technology, beginning perhaps with the chemical
> industry.

Population, Technology, Development

During the industrial revolution traditional
technology evolved from an extensive growth phase of
utilizing growing human resources more productively,
through increased division of labour and large-scale
organization of production, to the intensive phase
when demand for labour began to exceed its supply as
a result of rapid growth and capital accumulation.
This phase is characterized by the use of modern
science in the process of production to substitute
labour by capital and increase efficiency to face
competition in the local and international markets.
In this process human resources of yesterday have
been developed into the human capital of today.

INDIA - ITS DEVELOPMENT IN A HISTORICAL CONTEXT

The intensive growth phase in India was introduced
from overseas, and is not a natural product of the
evolution in India of the first phase of extensive
growth. It did not get the opportunity to be
initiated internally, although the Indian economy
was well known in the past for its prosperous
prototechnology phase.
India's underdevelopment, in the sense we
understand it today, began with its colonization and
domination by the British capitalist economy. This
capitalist colonization of India resulted in
distortion of the course of India's economic life
culminating in underdevelopment. India had been
colonized before by many foreign feudal powers and
its massive wealth plundered by these powers. But
these feudal colonizations had left India's own
feudal economy and prosperous commerce little
affected for obvious reasons. Exploitation of one
feudal economy by another cannot bring about any
fundamental change in mode and method of economic
production and economic structure, other than that
the exploited country is impoverished. But when an
industrial economy dominates a feudal economy to
serve its own economic interests it invariably
introduces new products, and new methods and modes
of production that destroy the historical course of
indigenous economic development, destabilizes factor
endowments, diverts the social mind from its
historical course and thus inhibits development of
its own technology that would form the basis of the
relationship between production and society. When a
new but alien technology with a fundamentally
different objective of production developed in
different historical circumstances, is introduced

11

into another country, with the help of political
power, it gradually destroys the potential
indigenous force of social and economic development
of the latter. In such a situation, introduced
production is divorced from the society.

Marx and many other authors praised the high
level of human resources of the pre-British India:
"The great mass of the Indian people possesses a
great industrial energy; is well fitted to
accumulate capital and remarkable for a mathematical
clearness of head, and talent for figures and exact
sciences" (Marx, 1953b, p.390). But the society's
need for the harnessing of these resources in
production is conditioned by its own historical
force; that is, only when the pressure of population
on existing resources, technology and economic
organization reaches a critical point, does change
become inevitable in a human society. In those
days, pressure of population on existing resources
could have brought about these changes as the
Industrial Revolution in England proved. In spite
of the development of modern science in Europe long
before the Industrial Revolution, it has not been
used in economic production until the historical
condition of growing population pressure prepared
the ground for it and supplied the resources for its
use in technological and economic change.

Plundering of resources from a country, whether
by a foreign feudal or capitalist country, does not
make the former underdeveloped but it undoubtedly
makes it poorer. But a poorer economy meant in
those days low population growth and poorer health
which retarded technological change. Underdevelopment is caused and perpetuated by the
destruction of productivity of indigenous technology
even if in its place, a much higher level of
productivity through the transfer of capital, skill,
education and technology is introduced from outside
thereby enhancing the wealth of the country. Vera
Anstey wrote about the pre-British Indian economy:

> Up to the eighteenth century, the economic
> condition of India was relatively advanced, and
> Indian methods of production and of industrial
> and commercial organization could stand
> comparison with those in vogue in any part in
> the world. A country which has manufactured
> and exported the finest muslins and other
> luxurious fabrics and articles, at a time when
> the ancestors of the British were living an
> extremely primitive life, has failed to take

part in the economic revolution initiated by
the descendants of those same wild barbarians
(Anstey, 1952, p.5).

Paul Baran (1957, p.277) also quoted Anstey in his
work to support his arguments for India's failure to
initiate its own industrial revolution due to
exploitation by Britain and not due to lack of
population pressure of the time on India's
prototechnology.
    To understand the nature of underdevelopment in
India as seen from Marxist perspectives, we would
have to discuss Marx's views on the relationship
between production and society and between
population growth and technological change and
examine how Marx and later Marxists tried to explain
the development of underdevelopment in India and
other Third World countries. Some Marxists believe
that sufficient development of capitalism in India
is a basic condition for industrial development and
the growth of class contradiction that would
ultimately end capitalism and establish socialism.
They do not understand that imported capitalism
could not have these effects. It is difficult to
deny that in spite of the tremendous growth of
modern capitalist industries in India from the late
19th century in general, and the 1950s in
particular, India is still an underdeveloped
economy. Modern industries in India have been
growing at the rate of 6-10 percent per annum,
capital formation as a proportion to total GNP, is
nearly 20 percent, which is 4 to 5 times higher than
the proportion during the late 19th century in
industrial England. Growth of highly skilled people
has been spectacular in recent times and India is
regarded as having the third largest pool of high
skills in the world. India is also considered as
one of the 10 most industrialized nations in the
world. India's industrial production consists of a
wide variety of manufacturers including the most
sophisticated consumer durables and computer
technology. India is the sixth nuclear power and
the fourth space power in the world. But
paradoxically all this has happened with little
change in its economic structure, with 75 percent of
the population in primary activities, only 11
percent of the labour force in industry, including
small-scale traditional industries, a 36 percent
literacy rate and nearly 50 percent of total
population below India's poverty line. This is a
gloomy picture of India's economy after more than

13

one hundred years of modern industrial growth. It also clearly shows that India's modern sector has not evolved in its own soil. Imported capitalism is not expected to generate the dynamic force that ultimately destroys itself as Marx thought.

The nature of India's underdevelopment in terms of Marxist perspectives needs to be discussed in the context of Marx's concept of the relationship between production and society, population growth and industrial technological change. According to Marx the growth of industrial capital, the prime force behind modern economic development is essentially a function of the interaction between human resources and natural environment. Two phases (extensive and intensive) of industrial growth in England during the Industrial Revolution had been greatly influenced by the population growth patterns and economic growth. These aspects need serious attention today to understand the persistence of underdevelopment of India despite substantial industrial growth. An examination of Marx's views on the introduction of Western capital to India, and of latter Marxists on the persistence of underdevelopment will follow with a brief note on technological change and social consciousness at the end.

MARX, PRODUCTION AND SOCIETY

According to Marx, the existence of living human individuals and their consequent relation to the rest of nature, that is, the environment is the primary basis of human society. The physical nature of humans and the natural environment in which they find themselves, are the natural basis of human life, modified by human action and changing human consciousness and control of nature. Production is definite form of expressing life which is a reflection of the relation between man and nature. Thus, production is a definite mode of expressing life. What individuals are, therefore, is closely linked to the most fundamental way of expressing life, their production - what and how they produce (Marx and Engels, 1976, pp. 31-32).

Marx writes that

... Because of the simple fact that every succeeding generation finds itself in possession of the productive forces acquired by the previous generation, which serve it as the raw material for new production, a coherence arises in human history, a history of humanity takes shape (Marx and Engels, 1982, p.518).

Marx writes elsewhere,

all history must be studied afresh, the conditions of existence of the different formations of society must be examined individually before the attempt is made to deduce from them the political, civil law, aesthetic philosophic, religious etc. view corresponding to them" (Marx and Engels, 1955, p.416).

In Marx's view, therefore, productive forces are not objective facts external to human consciousness and activity. They represent rather the social organization of human consciousness and human activity.

It is useful to consider here Marx's views on population as far as they are relevant to our present discussion. While discussing the method of political economy, Marx writes in the Grundrisse (1971, p.33) it seems to be the correct procedure to commence with the real and the concrete, the actual prerequisite; in the case of political economy, to commence with population which is the basis and the author of the entire productive activity of society. Then he proceeds to say that population is an abstraction if we leave out, for example, the classes of which it consists. The classes again are but an empty word unless we know what they are based on such as wage labour, capital, etc. These imply in their turn exchange, division of labour, capital, etc.

However, it is to be noted here that the quantity of population has always been the determining factor in production until industrial capitalism reached the second stage of capital accumulation (that is, the intensive-growth stage) when it needed 'quality' labour. During pre-industrial days production was essentially dependent on the quantity of manual labour – the main source of production. In the past when the population growth was small, it was difficult to increase output by manipulating nature. With the gradual growth of population, it was possible to operate an increasing division of labour resulting in increasing production. This has happened in the UK since the mid-eighteenth

15

century which marked the beginning of the agricultural revolution.

Marx's main concern was the growth of capital- ism and as such class relationships and class contradiction played the dominant role in his discussion of industrial growth. But economic inequality or class emerges when there is an increased output - a direct result of an increased supply of labour during the pre-industrial period and early days of the industrial revolution. Increased pressure of population on resources requiring technological and organizational changes augmented output and thereby, the amount of economic surplus. This increased population served as an expanding market, and as a source of division of labour helped increase output and thus bourgeois surplus. Thus the expanding market stimulates in due course capital accumulation and capital intensity of production.

Marx says of technology in Capital, Vol.1, that "Technology discloses man's mode of dealing with nature, the process of production by which he sustains his life and thereby also lays bare the mode of formation of his social relations and of mental conceptions that flow from them" (Marx, 1960, p.372). This relation between production and society determines the nature and process of indigenous technological change.

Thus the use and development of a technological system is dependent on the particular form of social formation. That is why, in Marx's view, the scope of using machinery would be completely different in a communist society from that in a free enterprise economy.

Lastly, Marx writes about the growth of industrial capital:

> ... the capitalist mode of production is based on the dominion of man over nature. Where nature is too lavish, she keeps him in hand, like a child in leading strings, she does not impose upon him any necessity to develop himself. It is not the tropics with their luxuriant vegetation, but the temperate zone, that is the Mother Country of Capital.... It is the necessity of bringing a natural force under the control of Society, economising, or appropriating or subduing it on a large scale by the work of man's hand, that first plays the decisive part in the history of industry (Marx, 1907, pp. 563-64).

POPULATION GROWTH AND TECHNOLOGICAL CHANGE FROM
EXTENSIVE GROWTH TO INTENSIVE GROWTH PHASE

Marx's main concern being the analysis of dynamics
of capitalism, he discusses the effect which
economic growth has on population on two separate
assumptions. The first is that capital accumulation takes place without technical progress; it is
the period of manufacture proper based on the division of labour. This is what is called 'extensive
growth', that is, the expansion of the economy by
using labour more productively through increased
division of manual labour in an enlarged organization by amassing more plant and more workers to
produce more of the same output in the same way.
This period of manufacture is followed by the
period of factory production based on improved
techniques and mechanical power, known as the
'intensive growth' period. According to Marx, it
entails more output and a higher ratio of capital
to labour in investment, that is, the increasing
organic composition of capital (Marx, 1906, p.613).

Marx argues that sooner or later a point must
be reached at which the requirements of accumulation begin to surpass the customary supply of
labour and therefore, a rise of wages takes place.
As a consequence, at least for a while the wage
rate continues to rise as long as it does not
interfere with the progress of accumulation, or
accumulation slackens in consequence of the rise in
the price of labour because the stimulus to gain is
blunted (Marx, 1960, Vol.III, Ch.15, p.264). When
this happens, demand for labour tends to decline,
reducing wage rates and thus restoring profit
rates. But this did not happen in the nineteenth
century. Rather rapid economic growth, stimulated
by an ever expanding international market of manufactured goods, maintained a high demand for labour
in excess of the supply of labour (population
growth in the UK was rapid and proceeded at the
rate of 1.0 - 1.6 per cent per annum until 1910 -
while the economic growth and capital accumulation
growth rates were around 2 per cent and 5 per cent
respectively). A high economic growth, implying a
high profit rate, made it possible for the intensive growth process to begin. Improved techniques
of production resulted in a rising organic composition of capital. That was the only way to out-
compete the others in the free enterprise capitalist economy and to increase output at a lower wage
cost. As Marx observes, "no capitalist ever

17

voluntarily introduces a new method of production, no matter how much more productive it may be, and how much it may increase the rate of surplus value, so long as it reduces the rate of profit" (Marx, 1953, p.103).

According to Marx, the capitalist does not care how his capital outlay is divided between variable capital (or wages) and constant capital (Marx, 1904, pp. 12-13). An increase in the relative cost of variable capital, that is, the cost of labour, would create an incentive to economize as long as it raises the rate of profit. This explains how the population growth pattern during the process of the industrial revolution influenced patterns of technological change from labour-intensive to increasingly capital-intensive processes. According to Marx, the organic composition of capital remains unchanged during the accumulation of capital, so that a definite mass of means of production constantly needs the same mass of labour power to set it in motion. Obviously, the demand for labour then rises in proportion to the growth of capital. At this stage of labour-using industrial growth, the accumulation of capital caused the demand for labour to exceed its supply despite the fact that population is growing at a high rate. This is the period when the organic composition of capital remained constant. With the increased demand for labour in excess of the supply of labour, wages began to rise, the organic composition of capital began to increase, that is the ratio of capital to labour began to rise. According to Marx, with a rising ratio of capital to labour in investment, demand for labour will fall causing unemployment and misery. This was inevitable if capitalism was confined to only one country, but with expanding international trade the internationalization of capitalism had already set in with the consequent increase in demand for labour exceeding its supply. Exports of industrial goods at first, followed by industrial capital to other countries by pioneering capitalist countries saved these countries from misery. Whereas in due course, capital and technology importing Third World countries, like India, began to face an increasing pressure of population caused by a falling death rate and the problems of disguised unemployment. The former was the result of effects of imported medical technology and not due to better food, shelter and clothing, which occurred in the UK at the time of industrial growth. The latter problem of surplus labour was caused by lack of demand for labour by imported industry. Industrial growth in the West by that time had reached the stage of intensive growth.

The process of industrialization was a result of increased pressure of human resources on the environment, structure of society and technology of production. The increased pressure of population fulfilled the basic condition, that is, created an urge for exploring the mysteries of nature, bringing it under man's control, and for introducing science into the process of production. During the earlier systems, population growth rate being negligible had very little impact on existing technology and therefore on social and economic structure. On the other hand, the earlier systems were also not conducive to population growth because of the conditions of life, that is, because life was at the mercy of nature. Output was not sufficient to feed a large population, neither was its supply steady. Hence natural disasters, malnutrition and epidemics were constant companions of the poor masses of the population who were deprived of their due share of output by feudal rulers of the time. With a small increase in population in the course of time, the growing pressure of population on existing resources and structure led to piecemeal changes first, and ultimately to fundamental changes, in technology; this process brought about changes in organization of production, and thus a process of agricultural revolution leading to the industrial revolution. This process made possible an increase in the amount of surplus value and accumulation of capital in the hands of the capitalist class. The rapid increase in population and productivity that followed provided an expanding scope for utilizing the accumulated capital through division of labour and a larger market for products in a private enterprise economy. The population growth pattern played a vital role in the evolution of capitalist industrialization from artisanal workshop through manufacture system to factory production. Marx's views that as labour power grows together with population, science masters natural forces for mankind to a greater extent every day, could be advanced as a support for the above.

According to Marx, it is man's changing needs as they become articulated in the sphere of production that determine the direction of scientific progress.

Population, Technology, Development

Without the presence of this fundamental condition of population pressure on environment, other changes mentioned would not have occurred in society and the emergence of surplus value or surplus labour and of its class ownership was impossible. The main productive force in this process was the increasing pressure of population.

MARX, MARXIST ECONOMISTS AND UNDERDEVELOPMENT OF INDIA

This section deals with the underdevelopment of India in terms of Marx's prediction that "the Western bourgeoisie by the rapid development of all instruments of production by the immensely facilitated means of communication draws all even the most barbarian nations into civilisation" (Marx, 1957). But Western capitalism failed to produce a cumulative cycle of investment leading to the "regeneration of India's economy" as predicted by Marx. Latter Marxists, however, have tried to explain the causes of the failure in different terms. These are: (1) removal or expropriation of the affected countries' previously accumulated surplus (Baran, 1957; Frank, 1971, 1978); (2) unequal exchange between developed and underdeveloped countries. Thus, the improved living standard of the working class of the developed countries is paid for by the underdeveloped countries (Immanuel, 1972); (3) not by simple exploitation but by insufficient exploitation (Kay, 1975). (4) The basis of backwardness cannot be attributed to the capitalist character of its economy and its integration with the world capitalist system, but rather to the lack of capitalist development and the persistence of feudal forms of agriculture (Fernandez and Ocampo, 1974). These explanations suffer from one important missing link – the adverse effects of technology and capital transfer from the centre to peripheries in building the capitalist sector in underdeveloped countries. Capitalist industrialization in its initial stage (that is, when technology was simple and labour and the organizations of production were characterized by free and perfect competition among factors of production, among buyers and sellers, etc.) was expected by Marx to play the important role of regenerating another economy (for example, British capital, technology and labour in France or Germany in the mid-nineteenth century) wherever it was

20

transferred. But that effect could not be expected of capital and technology transferred from capitalist countries, when the capitalist process of production became increasingly capital-intensive and the organization of production oligopolistic.

The problem of underdevelopment was scarcely dealt with in classical Marxist writing of the nineteenth century. This is not unexpected, as the phenomena of development and underdevelopment, in the sense it is understood today, was hardly dis- tinguishable at that time (Furtado, 1976, p.6; Maitra, 1980). However, history shows that under the impact of the spread of Western capitalism, the indigenous process of development in colonies and other affected countries has been stunted since the late nineteenth century. The economic history of India before it was introduced to Western capital- ism shows that she had elaborate agricultural techniques; efficient proto-industries and complex social organizations. Population pressure at that time (population growth rates varied between 0.1 to 0.2 per cent), however, was not enough to induce change in the prevailing agricultural organizations and to transform techniques and to start an indus- trial revolution as it did in the UK. In the case of Latin American and western African countries (the population growth of latter countries was seriously impaired by the slave trade), population was reduced by colonial powers, thereby affecting the course of natural development from their proto-technology stage. Hobsbawm wrote that the technological problems of the early industrial revolution were fairly simple, requiring merely a sufficiency of men with ordinary literacy, familiar with simple mechanical devices and the working of metals, practical experience and initiatives. Little initial investment was required to use new techniques, and their expansion could be financed out of accumulated profits. Industrial development was within the capacity of the multiplicity of small entrepreneurs and skilled traditional artisans (Hobsbawm, 1969, p39).

Hobsbawm ignores an important fact of history in that most underdeveloped countries, particularly India in the eighteenth and nineteenth centuries, also had skilled traditional artisan classes and entrepreneurs, sufficient mercantile capital (the Indian merchant class supplied huge finances to the East India Company), and rich cottage and small-scale industries. But the growth of population and its pressure on resources were not enough to lead to the kind of industrial change that took place in England at the comparable period. And then came the impact of technology transfer from the West when their technology had reached its intensive phase.

Marx grew up during the process of the Industrial Revolution in England and the Marxist theory as presented in the Communist Manifesto (1848) dealt directly but briefly with the spread of capitalism throughout the world and appeared to anticipate not underdevelopment but development. For instance, Marx wrote:

> When you have once introduced machinery into the locomotion of a country, which possesses iron and coals, you are unable to withhold it from its fabrication... The railway system will, therefore, become, in India, truly the forerunner of modern industry (Marx, 1973, pp.323-341).

Thus, it appears that Marx thought that the spread of the "reproductive power", that is, industrialization, was inevitable in India as a result of investment by British capitalists. There is no doubt about the fact that there was some growth of modern industries in this period, mainly confined to light consumer goods production, railways and communication, and cash crop production. But this growth absorbed a negligible proportion of the labour force and led to the destruction of India's own technology. The proportion of the non-agricultural labour force was about 26-30 percent before the introduction of modern industries (Bagchi, 1976).

However, Marx also pointed out that the process would not benefit the masses directly, as all the English bourgeois may be forced to do will neither emancipate nor materially mend the social condition of the mass of the people, depending not only on the development of the 'reproductive powers', but on their appreciation by the people. But what they will not fail to do is to lay down the premisses for both. As we have noted, however, the premisses laid down were not historically rooted to the past of the countries concerned and therefore they failed to spur these countries to dynamic industrial development.

It is well known today that the process also had an indirect effect on retarding the development of indigenous technology, forces of regeneration and industrialization. The process of industrialization that was introduced into France and Germany, for example, from the UK in the nineteenth century, had the effect of fully-fledged industrial development. Population pressure resulting from their own economic growth, unlike in India today, led to changes in agrarian organization and production relations, and thereby prepared them for industrial development. Secondly, the industrial capital and skill introduced from the UK was simple and labour absorbing at that time and thus it helped in utilizing the human resources released from the shackles of feudalism and laid down the foundations for industrial development.

It is to be noted here, that capitalism then was at its nascent stage and production process was largely based on increasing productive utilization of labour resources. Perfect competition and small scale operation characterized economic activities and organization of production. But in the subsequent stage of monopoly capitalism, capital-intensive technology and large-scale organization evolved to meet growing international markets for manufacturing goods, production was which confined to a handful of countries. Marx's confident prediction that "We may safely expect to see ... the regeneration of that great and interesting country [that is, India] as a result", unfortunately did not materialize. Even today, over 70 percent of the total population are still dependent on underdeveloped agricultural sectors for a living. It is true that a very limited but highly sophisticated modern sector has been created. The introduction of Western industrial capitalism obviously had neither the objective nor the effect of developing human resources, contrary to Marx's expectation.

When capitalism reached the stage of imperialism because of its inner contradiction resulting from its inevitable urge for survival and expansion, Lenin wrote that the export of capital influences, greatly accelerates, the development of capitalism in these countries to which it is exported. While, therefore, the export of capital may tend, to a certain extent, to arrest development in the capital-exporting countries, it can only do so by expanding and deepening the further development of capitalism throughout the world (Lenin, 1934, p.107). There is no doubt about the fact that capitalism introduced to India from overseas countries has been confined to a very

23

negligible proportion of the total population and of the economy.

According to Marxists, by exporting capital and technology in its mature stage, Western capitalism has been able to export its own misery and unemployment to importing underdeveloped countries and thus, it has been able to lessen the state of increasing misery in its economies as predicted by Marx. It is also not borne out by the evidence as claimed by Lenin that the export of capital will slow down development in capital-exporting countries. Instead, it is largely responsible for full employment and the prosperity under monopoly capitalism in the West and for the widening gap between developed and underdeveloped nations. Rapidly increasing capital intensity of production needs ever expanding markets. Capitalist countries by exporting capital have made importing underdeveloped countries perpetually dependent on them, first for finished consumer goods, then capital and technology as well as markets for their finished products. Developed capitalist countries constitute today only about 30 percent of all nations of the world and supply more than 90 percent of world manufactures. And so long as this dependence continues to dominate the relationship between developed industrial nations, socialist nations (dependent on Western technology) and Third World countries, capitalism in the industrialized countries will never face any serious threat to its survival and expansion.

According to Baran (1957), India had been prevented from developing and regenerating as a result of introduction of such industrialization. India experienced only the destruction of its traditional economy and society and after that nothing but "the chronic catastrophe of the last two centuries" (Baran, 1957, p.48). According to Baran, the removal of a large share of accumulated capital was responsible, for "... had the amount of economic surplus that Britain has torn from India been invested in India, India's economic development to date would have borne little similarity to the actual sombre record" (Baran, 1957, p.42).

Baran's view in connection with the failure of Western capitalists' presence in Asia, Africa and Latin America to create a cumulative process of capitalist development there was that either they found "established societies with rich and ancient cultures" or "the general conditions and in particular the climate were such as to preclude any mass settlement of Western European arrivals .... consequently, the Western European visitors rapidly determined to extract the largest possible gains from the host countries, and to take the loot home" (Baran, 1957, p.44). This is Baran's view of the first phase of capitalist exploitation of Asia, Africa and Latin American countries. Most Marxists are in complete agreement with his exploitation theory. What makes an economy underdeveloped is the destruction of its technology and human resources and distortion of its own course of history through the introduction of foreign technology. Western capitalism reached the stage of monopoly capitalism in the early twentieth century which was also reflected in its capital-intensive sophisticated technology.

Concerning the impact of Western capitalism on colonies when it reached the next stage of monopoly capitalism and imperialism, Baran wrote that "the rule of monopoly capitalism and imperialism in the advanced countries and economic and social backwardness in the underdeveloped countries are immediately related, represent merely different aspects of what is in reality a global problem" (Baran, 1957, p.47).

Baran's analysis is seriously limited by the absence of two very important factors: (1) he did not consider the level of technology introduced in India, and its ineffectiveness in utilizing more productively its domestic resources. Regeneration of India could have taken place as Marx predicted provided the industrial investment resulted in more productive use of human resources of India, thereby laying down the premiss for regeneration; (2) no consideration has been given to the question of the source of investment in Baran's analysis. When the source of capital investment is foreign and not domestic (that is, it is not a result of more productive utilization of domestic labour resources), then the capital investment cannot have the desired effect of regeneration of the country. The share of capital formation in India today is 20 percent of GDP compared to 5 percent in the UK in the 1850s, which had tremendous dynamic effects because its source was indigenous. In India, it has led to the building up of an island of modern capitalism which is not rooted to its history, and it has acted as the greatest hindrance to the growth of the indigenous reproductive power and the regeneration of the country. This is evident today in all Third World countries whether they receive aid from capitalist West or from socialist blocks and whether the surplus generated in this process of investment is withdrawn or reinvested. China's economic record during the 1950s and early 1960s when a massive transfer of capital and technology from the USSR took place is also not encouraging. These experiences belie the thesis of Baran and other Marxists.

However, Baran accepts the fact that capitalism forced the diversion of some of this economic surplus to the improvement of their systems of communications, to the building of railroads, harbours and highways, providing thereby, as a by-product, the facilities needed for profitable production and a "powerful impetus to the development of capitalism". But, according to Baran, "this development was forcibly shunted off its normal course, distorted and crippled to suit the purpose of Western imperialism". In other words, Baran thinks that had there been no removal of surplus from these countries and instead, had there been reinvestment of these surpluses, these economies could have been transformed into reproductive (i.e., industrialized) ones as Marx predicted. But the question remains — could industrialism or capitalism, a product of external economic forces and history imposed from outside, lead to regeneration, even if surplus produced in the process was reinvested. Another intriguing question involving the earnings from exports of products of Western investment in these countries is whether investment of these export earnings in the form of imports of consumer goods or even capital goods could lead to development. Apparently it has not done so. I will discuss this question later. Consider the views of A.G. Frank, A. Immanuel, S. Amin and G. Kay.

Frank (1971, p.32) has taken a stand in this respect which is more or less identical with that of Baran. He interpreted the process as the metropolis (developed economies-present author) expropriates economic surplus from its satellites (that is, underdeveloped economies) and appropriates it for its own economic development. The satellites remain underdeveloped for lack of access to their own surplus and as a consequence of the same polarization and exploitative contradiction which the metropolis introduces and maintains in the satellite's domestic structure. The combination of these contradictions reinforces

26

the processes of development in the metropolis and underdevelopment in the even more dependent satellites. This is one side, though a very important side of the picture, which, however, is seriously limited by the absence of the exposition of the most basic aspect of this process of polarization between rich and poor nations. Frank's analysis does not indicate anything about the effects of foreign technology and capital which embody stored labour, knowledge and needs of a different country.

Supporting the view that exploitation of colonies by Western capitalism is the basic factor responsible for the failure of industrialization leading to the regeneration of these countries as predicted by Marx, Immanuel focuses on trade as a mechanism of exploitation of underdeveloped countries by developed countries. Immanuel's thesis (Immanuel, 1972) is that the underdeveloped countries are exploited through unequal exchange. The developed countries sell commodities to the underdeveloped countries at prices that exceed values and buy from them commodities at prices below values, so that every transaction between the two sets of countries involves a drain of value out of the underdeveloped countries and thus reduces the pace of accumulation there. This is Immanuel's thesis in the narrower sense. In a broader sense, Immanuel claims that the improved living standards of the working class in the developed countries are paid for, in part at least, by the underdeveloped countries. Immanuel's thesis that the working class in the industrialized countries has benefitted from such exploitation in terms of a higher level of living and full employment conditions, may be advanced as a support to Marx's prediction of the increasing misery of the working class when it is considered globally. Because of the transfer of capital and technology resulting from the rapid growth of trade and foreign investment, fuller employment and relative affluence for the working class in the developed countries have been possible but at the cost of increasing impoverishment of the labour force in underdeveloped countries. But this is one side of the picture. The important questions that the unequal exchange thesis would raise are: Would equality in exchange have led to the development of underdeveloped countries? What kind of goods would have been exchanged? Would those imported goods have been suitable to India's economic

27

development? Could the imported inputs create sufficient demand for labour to justify higher wages?

Samir Amin (1974) has followed Baran and Frank in defining underdevelopment as the process taking place within the global context of capital accumulation and dependence for the periphery economies. It is precisely the absence of auto-centric expansion in the dependent economies that has characterized their accumulation process. An economy experiencing auto-centric accumulation must at least have one sector to produce the means of production (the capital goods sector) and then one producing the mass consumption goods to feed workers employed in both sectors. Marx developed the famous 'two department schema' for the study of capitalist accumulation in an essentially auto-centric structure. Amin then uses Marx's Unequal Exchange Theory which has been developed by Immanuel in his explanation of the phenomenon of underdevelopment as mentioned earlier.

Amin distinguishes between values and prices in his analysis following Immanuel. According to Amin, a large number of the export commodities of the underdeveloped countries are produced with modern technology so that the productivity of labour in the periphery and the centre is equalized for these commodities. He says further that the wages of underdeveloped countries are much lower than those of the metropolis even for equal labour productivity. Under such conditions, the rate of exploitation of labour is much higher in the periphery economies. This is also the conclusion of Immanuel.

Kay's position (Kay, 1975, pp.34-35) is somewhat different. According to him, development of colonies has been thwarted because capitalist exploitation was not sufficient enough. He elaborates his point thus: underdevelopment is explained as the result of capital expanding from its homelands in the form of merchant capital which drew surplus value out of the underdeveloped countries without being able to revolutionize the mode of production. Furthermore, when an attempt was made at such a revolution in the period after the last war through a strategy of industrialization, it could only reinforce the conditions of underdevelopment that already existed. In other words, imported capitalism cannot revolutionize the mode of production as discussed earlier.

It might be noticed that there are two sets of argument: (1) one regards exploitation and removal of surplus produced by Western investment as being responsible for Third World underdevelopment and the rapid development of the West; (2) the other relies on unequal exchange - resulting in the exploitation of the working class of underdeveloped countries.

If we are to explain why Marx'x prediction did not materialize, it will help in explaining the limitations of the thesis of Baran, Frank, Immanuel and Kay.

It is well known that the introduction of modern industry, particularly railways, into the colonies, did not unleash forces of regeneration and a cumulative cycle of investment in underdeveloped countries. However, such introduction in the mid-nineteenth century in Western Europe (for example, Germany and France) revolutionized modes of production leading to development.

There is no doubt about the fact that exploitation and looting of precious metals and other resources from colonies at the mercantile stage has impoverished their economies, and thus deprived them of vast resources that could have been used to transform them into reproductive countries when the need arose with the increasing pressure of population on existing resources. In this way, technology and more productive machines could have evolved indigenously and produced the regenerative effects. (1) The modern industries and railways which were introduced into India by the "English millocracy" were products of investment of surplus resulting from the increased productivity generated by the Industrial Revolution in the UK. Needless to say, these were not the results of increased productivity of India's indigenous resources, and therefore, the capitalist investment from outside has failed to generate a cumulative cycle of investment in India. It had created only an island of so-called "modern" sector completely isolated from the local economy. (2) Investment in the production of cash crops thus had very little relation with the evolution of the local economy and did not cause the transformation of India into a reproductive country initially.

This is the first stage of English investment in India. Exports were not products of indigenous capital and labour; the technology and capital came from abroad, which had little effect in terms of transforming India into a reproductive country.

Population, Technology, Development

The second stage is marked by the investment
of capital goods to produce consumer goods. In
fact, as history shows, modern producer goods and
manufacturing industries began to grow, slowly in
the latter part of the nineteenth century and
rapidly since the 1950s. But this had not led to
the regeneration and transformation of India into a
reproductive country, because of the reasons stated
above. One important point to be noted here is
that these investment resources and productivity
were not generated indigenously, and hence had no
linkage effects. Even if profits that were earned
through exports were reinvested (in fact, according
to recent studies, a large portion was reinvested)
it would not have led to what Marx or Baran
expected to have happened. This is not happening
today in spite of reinvestment of profits. The
reason is that the imports of consumer goods and
capital goods earned as export earnings and their
use within India's economy could not have diffusion
effects resulting in cumulative investment effects,
because of non-indigenous sources of origin of
capital and technology that were used.
    There is no doubt about the fact that British
capital (for example, the railways) introduced in
the Western European countries in the
mid-nineteenth century became the forerunner of
modern industry in Europe. But European countries
earned capital, machineries, railways and so on,
through exports of their domestic product produced
by their own inputs and thus raised the level of
income of all factors of production. This helped
them to absorb the foreign capital and technology
which was labour-using and not labour-dispensing as
it is today, and avoid the perpetuation of an
island of imported modern sector surrounded by a
vast and expanding sea of underdeveloped
traditional sector. Exports of cash crops from
India were financed from overseas, were not a
result of India's own economic growth and their
export led to diffusion of income in the society.
    These schools of Marxists did not take into
consideration the fundamental aspect related to the
question of the source of investment (that is,
whether it is generated indigenously or externally)
and the level of technology. If the industrial
investment was the result of surpluses produced
within the economy by natural and human resources
through their interaction, as happened in the UK
and in other European countries, investment of that
surplus would have created the desired effect.

30

Industrial investment of the period under reference
in India and other underdeveloped countries, in
so-called "modern" activities such as crop
plantation, railways and communications, etc., was
undertaken not to meet the need of local economy,
neither was it a result of increased productivity
of domestic resources. The surplus that was
invested in these economies was generated
elsewhere. Capitalism in the nineteenth century
could produce the effects of regeneration as
envisaged by Marx if it had resulted from or in the
evolution of the domestic economy.

Then we should also take note of the effects
of changes in technology. This is very important
in the sense that when Western capitalism reached
the stage of monopoly capitalism and imperialism as
depicted by Baran and Frank, capital and technology
became increasingly labour-dispensing. When these
types of capital and technology were supplied to
the underdeveloped countries by the Western
industrialized countries, they had very limited
effects in terms of absorbing labour resources of
former countries and thus failed to produce any
effects of their regeneration.

CONCLUSION

Economists regard contacts between industrialized
and non-industrialized nations as resulting in the
transfer of capital, modern goods, technology and
modern attitudes to self, family and society which
facilitate economic development.

Marxist economists think that what today's
less developed countries need for their development
is quite simply a good dose of capitalism to
destroy feudal structures and to organize the
accumulation of the material pre-conditions of
socialism (Mahler, 1980, p.57).

About the effects of transplanted capitalist
development Brookfield wrote: "the middle class, so
far from being progressive, enterprising and
expanding [Marx praised the progressive role of
this class in the development of human society in
the nineteenth century] is tied to foreign
consumption patterns; [and therefore to a
technology and production not rooted to the soil of
these societies] policies designed to strengthen
the middle class, reinforce the ruling class and do
not lead to any diffusion of development"
(Brookfield, 1975, p.157). These classes act as a

de facto intermediary for continued foreign economic penetration and domination.

These classes in the present international set-up will have little incentive to develop traditional prototechnology into industrial technology, as was done by the bourgeois or middle class - a product of the indigenous capitalist development in the UK in the nineteenth century. All economic records of underdeveloped countries show that they have achieved tremendous economic growth since 1960s. But the vast majority of the population has been deprived of the effects of such growth and as in India, nearly 50 percent of the total population still lives below the official poverty line.

To develop economically, culturally and politically, these economies essentially need the advancement of their traditional technology. This claim does not imply, however, that these economies should have to go back to the 'wooden plough' age. It is not possible to go back to the past technology today for two basic reasons: (1) the level and organization of social consciousness of these people, and their knowledge of an environment and production is sufficiently high because of the historical evolution of these societies; (2) their number is now large enough, relative to the past, which properly organized and harnessed, with their present level of social consciousness could generate a force that could develop their traditional technology into industrial technology to suit their present needs and resources (Maitra, 1986).[1]

NOTE

1. I am indebted to K.P. Cochran, Economics Department, North Texas State University, C. Tisdell, University of Newcastle, N. Podder of University of N.S.W., and E. Bairam and A.K. Dasgupta, Otago University, for valuable comments on the earlier paper on which this chapter is based.

REFERENCES

Amin, S. (1974) **Accumulation on a World Scale**, Monthly Review Press, New York
Anstey, V. (1952) **The Economic Development of India**, Longman, London
Bagchi, A.K. (1976) 'De-Industrialisation in

India', **The Journal of Development Studies,**
12, 2, pp.132-50

Baran, P. (1957) **The Political Economy of Growth,**
Monthly Review Press, New York

Boulding, K.E. (1983) 'Technology in the
Evolutionary Process' in S. Macdonald, et al.
(eds) **The Trouble with Technology,** Francis
Pinter, London, pp.4-10

Brookfield, H. (1975) **Interdependent Development,**
Methuen, London

Fernandez, R.A. and Ocampo, J.F. (1974) 'The Latin
American Revolution: A Theory of Imperialism
not Dependency', **Latin American Perspectives,**
6, Spring, p.36

Frank, A.G. (1971) **Capitalism and Underdevelopment**
in Latin America, Pelican, Harmondsworth

Frank, A.G. (1978) **Dependent Accumulation and**
Underdevelopment, Macmillan, London

Furtado, C. (1976) **Economic Development of Latin**
America, Cambridge Press, Cambridge

Griffin, K. (1978) **International Inequality and**
National Poverty, Macmillan, London

Hobsbawm, E. (1969) **Industry and Empire,** Pelican,
Harmondsworth

Immanuel, A. (1972) **Unequal Exchange,** Monthly
Review Press, New York

Kay, G. (1975) **Development and Underdevelopment,**
Macmillan, London

Lenin, V.I. (1934) **Imperialism, The Highest Stage**
of Capitalism, Lawrence & Wishart, London

Maitra, P. (1980) **The Mainspring of Economic**
Development, Croom Helm, London

Maitra, P. (1986) **Population, Technology and**
Economic Development, Gower, London

Mahler, V.A. (1980) **Dependency Approaches to**
International Political Economy, Columbia
University Press, New York

Marx, K. (1904) **A Critique of Political Economy,**
Kerr, London

Marx, K. (1906) **Capital,** Vol.I, Kerr, Chicago

Marx, K. (1907) **Capital,** Vol.II, Kerr, Chicago

Marx, K. (1953a) 'Relative Surplus Population under
Capitalism' in R.L. Meek, **Marx and Engels on**
Malthus, Lawrence and Wishart, London

Marx, K. (1953b) 'The Future Results of the British
Rule in India', in K. Marx and F. Engels, **On**
Britain, Progressive Publishers, Moscow

Marx, K. (1957) **The Communist Manifesto, The**
Revolution of 1848, Penguin, Harmondsworth

Marx, K. (1960) **Capital,** Vol.I and Vol.II, Foreign
Language Publishing House, Moscow

Population, Technology, Development

Marx, K. (1971) **Grundrisse**, London
Marx, K. (1973) **Surveys from Exile**, Penguin, London
Marx, K. and Engels, F. (1955) **Selected Correspondence**, Progressive Publishers, Moscow
Marx, K. and Engels, F. (1976) **Collected Works**, Lawrence Wishart, London
Marx, K. and Engels, F. (1982) **Selected Works**, Progressive Publishers, Moscow
Sen, A. (1983) 'Goods and People', Plenary Session Paper, **Proceeding of 7th Congress of International Economic Association**, Madrid, pp.138-147
Streeten, P. (with Burke, S.J., Haq, M.L., Hicks, N. & Stewart, F.) (1981) **First Things First: Meeting Basic Needs in Developing Countries**, Oxford University Press, New York
Stewart, F. (1978) **Technology and Underdevelopment**, Macmillan, London

Chapter Three

NEW AGRICULTURAL TECHNOLOGY AND SUSTAINABLE FOOD
PRODUCTION: BANGLADESH'S ACHIEVEMENTS, PREDICAMENT
AND PROSPECTS

Mohammad Alauddin and Clem Tisdell

INTRODUCTION

Domestic food production has increased tremendously
in Bangladesh as a result of its adoption of new
agricultural technologies associated with the
'Green Revolution'. Unfortunately, however, Lester
Brown's comments that such technology "is literally
helping to fill hundreds of millions of rice bowls
once only half full" (Brown, 1970) does not apply
to Bangladesh (Cf. also Remenyi; Chapter 5 in the
present volume). In fact its expanding food
production has not kept pace with population growth
and Bangladesh has become increasingly dependent on
imported foodgrain. More rice bowls are now
half-filled or not quite half-filled! In addition,
indications are that the growth rate of food
production in Bangladesh is tapering off and that
sustaining the growth rates of recent years is
becoming ecologically more difficult. Furthermore,
as a result of its change in agricultural
technology (to higher 'tech' production),
Bangladesh has become more dependent on foreign
technology and imports of inputs required to
maintain agricultural production. This dependence
could also threaten the sustainability of
Bangladesh's economic growth. While we do not wish
to be pessimistic, there is cause for concern. Let
us detail some of the issues involved.
    Sustainability of per capita food production
preoccupied classical economists such as Malthus
(1798) and Ricardo (1817) and it is of widespread
current concern to many. For example, the **World
Conservation Strategy** (IUCN, 1980) argues that if
economic growth or development is to be successful,
it must be sustainable. Also FAO (1984) sees
difficulties in sustaining food production into the

next century, particularly given anticipated population growth rates for many less developed countries. Numerous institutions and individuals now argue that sustainable economic development is desirable. This sustainability is likely to require, among other things: (a) sustainable ecological systems on which economic production ultimately relies (IUCN, 1980; Thibodeau and Field, 1984); (b) economic exchange that can be sustained if the country engages in international trade to a significant extent (Tisdell and Fairbairn, 1984); and (c) a socio-political structure that does not have within it the seeds of its own collapse (Cf. Douglass, 1984). Thus the policy focus for economic development has shifted to some extent to stressing the importance of sustainability of ecosystems and socio-economic and environmental factors on which agriculture relies.

Some economists as opposed to some ecologists see no particular virtue in a sustainable economic system or what in many cases amounts to a steady-state or stationary equilibrium for an economy. On the basis of the discounted present value criterion used by many economists (for example, Krutilla and Fisher, 1975) a productive system that is not sustainable may be preferred to the one that is. The issues are complex (Tisdell, 1983a; 1985a; 1985b) and are not debated here (see also Chisholm, Chapter 9 in this volume).

Here the main focus is on the prospects for sustainability of foodgrain production in Bangladesh and the identification of factors which could influence this sustainability, including technological change and population trends. Bangladesh's situation is not unique in the world and it , therefore, provides a useful case study of sustainability problems faced by developing countries. Its food sustainability problem parallels, for example, the situation of some African countries and so makes its case of additional interest.

Given our interest in the sustainability of food production, the production characteristics of agricultural systems are of particular interest. Gordon Conway (1986) suggests that alternative agricultural techniques should be assessed on the basis of their influences (a) on the level of yields; (b) on the variability of yields and incomes; (c) on the sustainability of agricultural production; and (d) on the distribution of income. A technique which results in higher yields, less variability of incomes, sustainable production and a more equal distribution of income is more desirable than the one without such character- istics. In practice, however, one technique rarely dominates another in terms of all of these characteristics. In such cases, difficult social choices and conflicts arise. Nevertheless, despite the limitations of Conway's test (Tisdell, 1985c), the characteristics mentioned by him are relevant in evaluating agricultural techniques. It is interesting that he includes sustainability as an important consideration, even though the concept of sustainability allows several interpretations (Tisdell, 1985a).

Douglass (1984) pays particular attention to alternative meanings of agricultural sustain- ability. He claims that there are three different concepts in current use: (1) sustainability as food self-sufficiency; (2) sustainability as steward- ship; and (3) sustainability as community. We shall consider each in turn.

The food self-sufficiency concept is a rather mechanical one. If a nation can meet current or future projected demands for food from its own agricultural resources, its demands are considered to be sustainable. Tests for this type of sustainability often hinge on whether or not a country has a net dependence on imported food.

The stewardship concept of sustainability appears to have a number of strands to it. One view seems to be that it is unwise to push yields using non-renewable resources such as artificial fertilizers beyond levels that can be maintained by the use of renewable resources alone. For one thing, the use of non-renewable resources may damage or deplete the renewable resource-base e.g., life-support systems, so that future production is irreversibly restricted. Or another possibility is that "too rapid application of non-renewable resources may cause a society to raise population and consumption levels unsustainably, leading eventually to a crisis breakdown of natural systems as they attempt to maintain the living levels to which they are accustomed" (Douglass, 1984, p.13).

The sustainability of community concept is also complex but is espoused by some 'alternative life-style' groups. It encompasses views on man's duty towards nature, the desirability of a fair distribution of income and full participation in the social-political systems of the community. Cooperation with nature rather than the domination

Technology, Sustainable Food Production

of it are considered most desirable. Social
structures which take power away from local farming
communities and impersonalize them (such as
capitalistic farming companies with headquarters
distant from a farming community) are seen as a
threat to the community and to a sustainable
economic order in harmony with nature (Cf. Tisdell,
1983b).
Douglass says that

> ... reserving some of their harshest
> judgements for modern agricultural technology
> for its spread to the Third World countries,
> alternative agriculturalists and others have
> developed evidence that the patterns of land
> tenure, market structure, and government
> policies which are found in many developing
> countries favour large land owners at the
> expense of peasants in the harvest of benefits
> from the new seed-fertilizer innovations, and
> this fact, they contend, is yet again
> destabilizing to rural communities. (Douglass,
> 1984, pp.19-20)

With this backdrop in mind, let us now
consider the main characteristics of growth and
change in the Bangladeshi economy. This will
provide a setting for us to assess the sustainability of food production in Bangladesh in terms
of various concepts of sustainability mentioned
above.

GROWTH AND CHANGE IN THE BANGLADESH ECONOMY:
BACKGROUND

Bangladesh is one of the most densely populated
countries in the world and is often regarded as
the test case for development (see, for example,
Faaland and Parkinson, 1976). The economy of
Bangladesh is dominated by its agricultural sector
(including livestock, forestry and fishery). This
sector accounts for half of its Gross Domestic
Product (GDP) and nearly 75 percent of its labour
force is employed in agriculture. Bangladesh's
exports consist, in the main, of agricultural
commodities, primarily jute and jute goods even
though remittances by Bangladeshi workers abroad
(especially from the Middle East) have added
significantly to the country's export earnings in
recent years (BBS, 1984b, p.425). Bangladesh's

economy rests on a narrow base of natural resources and lacks diversification. Large-scale manufacturing contributes about 6 percent and construction and housing contributes no more than 19 percent of the GDP (BBS, 1984b, p.571). Bangladesh has no known major mineral and energy resources excepting natural gas.

During the last three decades (early 1950s to early 1980s), GDP has more than doubled but so has population and so has its density per square kilometre. While the contribution of agriculture to GDP increased by more than 60 percent in this period, its growth lagged behind population growth and growth of GDP. Hence, the non-agricultural contribution to GDP more than quadrupled during the same period. The share of non-agricultural sectors in the GDP has increased steadily while there has been a secular decline in the relative share of agriculture in GDP. Value added by the manufacturing sector increased from less than 4 percent in the early 1950s to about 11 percent in the early 1980s (Alauddin and Mujeri, 1981, p.238; BBS, 1984b, p.571). Production by the tertiary sector grew relatively rapidly. Nevertheless, overall growth in GDP has been sluggish due to slow growth in agricultural value added, because agricultural value added is the main component of Bangladesh's GDP (see, for example, Alamgir and Berlage, 1974, pp.161-167,172; BBS, 1979, p.340; BBS, 1984b, pp.570,690; EIU, 1976, pp.17-18; EPBS, 1969, p.120).

In the period under consideration, the population of Bangladesh increased from 43.3 million to 93.6, that is, by 116 percent. Hence per capita GDP in Bangladesh in the early 1980s was only marginally higher than three decades earlier. The growth rate of its population remains high at 2.32 percent (BBS, 1985b, p.71). This creates a continuing poverty problem for Bangladesh.

Against this background, let us apply the self-sufficiency approach to Bangladesh and then consider prospects for maintaining growth in food production, taking into account limits to agricultural practices that have effectively expanded food production in the past in Bangladesh. This leads to a consideration of whether Bangladesh's food production is ecologically sustainable given (a) its increasing dependence on new ('modern') agricultural technology, (b) its reliance on foreign technology and (c) its dependence on imports of inputs required for 'modern agriculture'. In short, we consider Bangladesh's prospects for providing itself with an adequate and sustainable food supply using modern agricultural technology.

TRENDS IN FOODGRAIN PRODUCTION AND IMPORT

Foodgrain production is central to the agricultural economy of Bangladesh. In recent years over 83 percent of the gross cropped area has been cropped with rice and wheat (BBS, 1984b, pp.217-218, 255). About 80 percent of the total cultivated land is allocated to rice which accounts for about 93 percent of cereal production even though wheat as a foodgrain is gaining in importance.

Table 3.1 presents Bangladeshi data on production of rice and wheat (**RICEP** and **WHEATP**), which is used as a proxy for foodgrain production, import of the grains (**IMPORTF**), offtake from government stock (**OFFTAKEF**), total per capita consumption, per capita consumption from domestic sources, as well as per capita domestic production (**PERCAPIT**, **DOMPERCP** and **DMPRDPHD**) and the percentage of imported foodgrains as a proportion of total available foodgrains (**IMPRAVL**). In aggregate terms, domestic food production has more than doubled during the last three decades. There has been moderate growth in rice production and a spectacular expansion in the production of wheat. From less than 25 thousand tonnes in the early 1950s, wheat production increased to more than 1000 tonnes in recent years. Since the introduction of the seed-fertilizer-irrigation technology in the late 1960s, foodgrain production has increased by 27 percent due to a 19 percent increase in rice output and a phenomenal 1000 percent rise in wheat production.

However, one gets a completely different picture if foodgrain availablity per capita is considered. Total foodgrain available for consumption is defined as domestic production less 10 percent deduction for seed, feed and wastage plus imports.[1] Overall per capita foodgrain available for consumption (**PERCAPIT**) has not increased on the whole. In fact, the domestic component of foodgrain availability per capita (**DOMPERCP**) shows a declining tendency as does the domestic production per capita (**DMPRDPHD**). This implies that during the last three decades Bangladesh has been unable to produce sufficient

Table 3.1

Table 3.1: Domestic Production, Availability and Import Intensity of Foodgrains, Bangladesh 1950-51 to 1982-83

Year	RICEP	WHEATP	IMPORTP	OFFTAKEF	PROCUREF	AVLFOOD	PERCAPIT	DOMPERCP	IMPRAVL	DMPRDPHD
1950	7460.7	20.4	144.28	193.049	66.043	6860.00	158.429	155.496	2.103	172.774
1951	7147.6	23.2	94.49	254.012	19.305	6688.43	150.640	145.354	1.413	161.505
1952	7452.8	24.4	289.57	243.851	15.241	6958.09	153.262	148.226	4.162	164.696
1953	8377.0	24.1	202.19	111.765	26.417	7646.34	164.085	162.253	2.644	180.281
1954	7711.0	26.6	50.80	81.284	127.006	6918.12	145.034	145.992	0.734	162.214
1955	6486.6	22.6	172.73	50.802	0	5909.08	117.946	116.932	2.923	129.924
1956	8315.8	23.8	599.47	124.974	0	7630.61	149.620	147.169	7.856	163.522
1957	7720.2	22.8	684.82	98.557	33.530	7033.73	135.004	133.756	9.736	148.618
1958	7032.5	25.5	473.48	169.680	33.530	6488.35	122.191	119.627	7.297	132.919
1959	8617.8	29.2	621.82	194.065	200.161	7776.20	143.472	143.585	7.996	159.539
1960	9672.2	32.9	709.20	204.225	24.385	8914.43	161.493	158.235	7.956	175.817
1961	9617.2	39.6	414.55	259.092	26.417	8923.79	157.386	153.283	4.645	170.314
1962	8869.7	45.1	1459.04	721.393	10.160	8734.55	150.078	137.858	16.704	153.175
1963	10623.7	35.0	1018.08	451.125	4.064	10039.90	168.172	160.684	10.140	178.538
1964	10500.0	34.6	350.54	755.906	13.209	10221.80	166.751	154.668	3.429	171.853
1965	10500.6	35.6	937.81	961.180	94.492	10349.30	167.735	153.688	9.062	170.765
1966	9575.4	59.3	1117.65	1101.390	3.048	9769.58	153.852	136.555	11.440	151.728
1967	11458.7	62.5	1035.55	659.414	22.353	11006.10	168.947	136.791	9.407	176.435
1968	11543.8	107.4	1136.96	1085.140	9.144	11562.10	177.055	156.043	9.833	173.381
1969	12004.7	120.8	1571.82	1375.730	6.096	12282.60	177.238	157.474	12.797	174.971
1970	11143.2	132.8	1164.19	1338.130	6.096	11480.40	161.696	142.935	10.142	158.817
1971	9931.3	136.9	1715.09	1762.840	0.160	10814.00	148.953	124.811	15.860	138.679
1972	10091.4	91.4	2800.33	2660.010	5.080	11819.50	159.077	123.345	24.285	137.050
1973	11109.1	110.7	1692.73	1754.710	72.139	12500.40	163.618	141.595	13.541	157.327
1974	11287.3	116.8	2599.05	1785.190	129.038	11919.80	152.819	131.586	21.804	146.206
1975	12762.6	218.5	1468.19	1694.770	355.616	13022.10	162.980	146.220	11.275	162.467
1976	11752.6	259.1	807.16	1473.270	324.119	11959.70	146.206	132.158	6.754	146.842
1977	13695.9	347.5	1634.82	2029.040	581.179	14406.90	168.303	148.839	11.605	167.783
1978	13662.4	493.8	1180.45	1814.660	360.696	14194.50	165.824	148.318	8.318	165.376
1979	12740.2	823.0	2871.35	2440.540	269.252	14378.20	163.947	139.189	19.970	154.655
1980	13881.2	1092.3	1078.03	1550.490	1043.480	13983.20	155.541	149.902	7.709	166.557
1981	13630.0	967.4	1245.67	2068.670	301.766	14904.80	162.717	143.427	8.358	159.364
1982	14215.5	1095.3	1870.54	1936.580	192.03	15524.30	165.858	147.219	12.049	163.577

Note: 1950 refers to 1950-51 (July 1950 to June 1951) etc. RICEP and WHEATP respectively refer to production of (cleaned) rice and wheat. IMPORTP is import of rice and wheat. OFFTAKEF is offtake of foodgrains from government stocks. PROCUREF is internal procurement of food. AVLFOOD is defined as production of food less 10 percent deduction for seed, feed and wastage plus OFFTAKEF less PROCUREF. The above named variables are measured in thousands of tonnes. PERCAPIT, DOMPERCP and IMPRAVL are per capita availability of total and domestic foodgrains and imported foodgrains as percentage of available foodgrains from all sources. DMPRDPHD refers to per capita domestic food production. PERCAPIT, DOMPERCP and DMPRDPHD are measured in kilograms.

Source: Production. Adapted from BBS (1976, pp.1-2,4-7,8-10,12-15,26-29; 1979, pp.168-171; 1980, pp.20-25, 30-31, 33-34, 36-37, 46-52; 1982, pp.233, 235-236, 240-241; 1984a, pp.39,42; 1984b, pp.249-252,255); BRRI (1977, p.89); World Bank (1982, Tables 2.5 and 2.6). Import: Alamgir and Berlage (1973, pp.45; EPBS (1969), pp.120-121); and Alamgir (1980, p.221). Offtake: Alamgir and Berlage (1973, p.45); BBS (1978, p.379; 1984b, p.691). Internal procurement: Alamgir and Berlage (1973, p.45); BBS (1984b, p.691).

<u>food to maintain the per capita food consumption of</u> <u>its growing population</u> and per capita food consumption has declined marginally.

For centuries Bangladesh was self-sufficient in food but in the last few decades, it has become a net importer of foodgrains. Its agricultural production is erratic because of considerable year to year climatic variability (BBS 1984b, p.248) and fluctuations in its domestic food production are as a rule compensated for by variations in grain imports (**IMPORTF**), as can be seen from Table 3.1. From an average (based on three years) of 147 thousand tonnes of imports per year in the early 1950s foodgrain imports reached an average of 1.4 million tonnes in the early 1980s. Measured in per capita terms, imports increased from 3.3 kgs. to 15.4 kgs. during the period. In some years imports have exceeded 2 million tonnes and have been well over 1.5 million tonnes in a number of years in the last two decades. Trends in the import intensity of Bangladeshi food consumption are highlighted by considering food imports as a percent of total available food for consumption (**IMPPRAVL**). This percentage increased from less than 2 percent in the early 1950s to an average exceeding 10 percent in the last decade. In other words, <u>Bangladesh now</u> <u>imports more than 10 percent of its food require-</u> <u>ments</u>.

Figure 3.1 illustrates the growing imbalance between Bangladeshi demand for food and its supply from domestic sources and Figure 3.2 shows the increasing import intensity of foodgrain supplies. Trends in per capita food consumption (**PERCAPIT**), per capita food consumption from domestic sources (**DOMPERCP**), and per capita domestic food production (**DMPRDPHD**) are indicated by the following linear regression equations:

$$\textbf{PERCAPIT} = 146.94 + 0.5901T \quad\quad\quad (3.1)$$
$$(R^2 = 0.1870, \ t = 2.677)$$

$$\textbf{DOMPERCP} = 146.18 - 0.0163T \quad\quad\quad (3.2)$$
$$(R^2 = 0.0074, \ t = 0.480)$$

$$\textbf{DMPRDPHD} = 162.43 - 0.1181T \quad\quad\quad (3.3)$$
$$(R^2 = 0.0074, \ t = 0.480)$$

The statistical fit of these regression lines is, however, poor. To the extent that any inferences can be drawn from them, they suggest that per capita foodgrain consumption shows a very

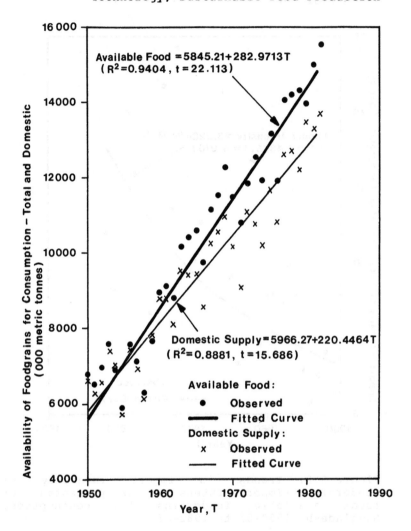

Figure 3.1: Trends in total available foodgrains (Available Food) and foodgrains from domestic production (Domestic Supply), Bangladesh, 1950–51 to 1982–83.

slight upward trend. On the other hand, the domestic per capita food production (and availability of food per capita for consumption from domestic sources) possibly show a very slight downward trend. To the extent that increased per capita food consumption has been achieved in

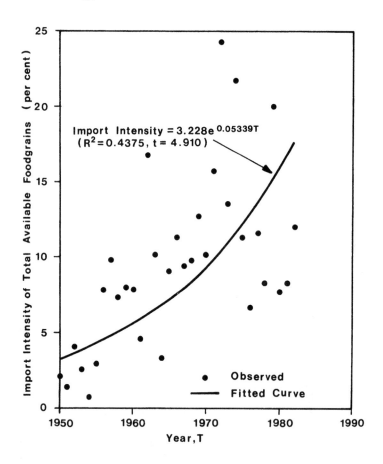

Figure 3.2: Trends in import intensity of foodgrains (Import Intensity) as percentage of total available foodgrains for consumption, Bangladesh, 1950-51 to 1982-83.

Bangladesh, it has been achieved by increased dependence on imported foodgrains. While the 'Green Revolution' in Bangladesh has greatly expanded food supply, per capita gains are being thwarted by population increases even though the latest census report shows some decline in the growth rate of population.[2]

In reality, however, Bangladesh's food-import dependence is much higher than demonstrated above in terms of its direct dependence on imported foodgrains. Account must be taken of the import of

44

inputs required for domestic food production, for example, chemical fertilizers, irrigation machinery, agro-chemicals and so on, as well as the import intensity of inputs critical to domestic production of some of the agricultural inputs, such as nitrogenous fertilizer. These factors are taken into account later in this chapter.

EXPANDING FOODGRAIN PRODUCTION IN RESPONSE TO POPULATION PRESSURE

Bangladesh's initial response to increased population pressure was to bring additional marginal land under cultivation, that is, to extend cultivation. Its subsequent response was to intensify cultivation. Net cultivated area (NCA), that is the area cultivated only once during the year, increased from about 8.0 million hectares in the late 1940s to about 8.4 million hectares on average throughout the 1950s and by the early 1960s, it reached a little over 8.5 million hectares (EPBS 1969, p.41). As can be seen from Table 3.2, the upward trend in net cultivated area continued until the end of the 1960s when it reached a peak of 8.8 million hectares. Since the 1970s, net cropped area has shown clear signs of decline. Even though net cultivated area increased marginally to 8.6 million hectares in the early 1980s, it was still lower than that in the late 1960s so that in the intervening period some land was 'lost' from cultivation. Gross annual cultivated area (GCA), that is, net cultivated area plus area cultivated more than once during the year, remained stagnant at around 10.5 million hectares in the 1950s and rose to about 13.0 million hectares by the late 1960s. By the earlier part of the 1980s it increased to a little over 13.2 million hectares. Both net and gross cultivated land per head of population (NCAPHD and GCAPHD) have declined monotonically over the years, the fall in the former being more rapid than that for the latter. The trends in gross and net cultivated land in aggregate as well as per capita terms can be specified by the regressions given in equations 3.4 to 3.7. Overall, net cropped area and gross cropped area have expanded but net cropped area and gross cropped area per head have declined at a decreasing rate with the passage of time.

45

Table 3.2: Net and Gross Cultivated Area, Net and Gross Land-man Ratio, Foodgrain Yield per Gross and Net Cropped Hectare, Bangladesh, 1950-51 to 1982-83

Year	NCA	GCA	NCAPHD	GCAPHD	INTENSITY	GYFDT	NYFDT
1950	8.313	10.623	.192	.245	127.788	919.732	1175.31
1951	8.375	10.836	.189	.244	129.385	868.767	1124.05
1952	8.461	11.122	.186	.245	131.450	885.085	1163.45
1953	8.453	11.249	.181	.241	133.077	938.985	1249.57
1954	8.481	11.141	.178	.234	131.364	891.840	1171.56
1955	8.277	10.506	.165	.210	126.930	821.454	1042.67
1956	8.278	10.491	.162	.206	126.734	1020.760	1293.64
1957	8.218	10.492	.158	.201	127.671	940.598	1200.87
1958	8.044	10.216	.151	.192	127.001	883.465	1122.01
1959	8.326	10.715	.154	.198	128.693	1003.710	1291.71
1960	8.442	11.166	.153	.202	132.267	1088.870	1440.22
1961	8.475	11.086	.149	.196	130.808	1130.510	1478.80
1962	8.457	11.208	.145	.193	132.529	1016.740	1347.48
1963	8.532	11.403	.143	.191	133.650	1175.810	1571.47
1964	8.540	11.548	.139	.188	135.222	1135.190	1535.04
1965	8.742	11.955	.142	.194	136.754	1152.130	1575.57
1966	8.544	11.752	.135	.185	137.547	1053.780	1449.44
1967	8.801	12.723	.135	.195	144.563	1155.930	1671.06
1968	8.751	12.600	.130	.188	143.984	1179.630	1698.47
1969	8.807	13.290	.127	.192	150.903	1162.110	1753.66
1970	8.644	12.292	.122	.173	142.203	1123.330	1597.41
1971	8.244	11.400	.114	.157	138.282	1068.230	1477.18
1972	8.434	11.752	.114	.158	139.341	1044.390	1455.26
1973	8.489	11.907	.111	.156	140.264	1201.860	1685.77
1974	8.320	11.589	.107	.149	139.291	1154.490	1608.11
1975	8.485	12.013	.106	.150	141.579	1238.650	1753.68
1976	8.274	11.727	.101	.143	141.733	1196.270	1695.50
1977	8.374	12.623	.100	.151	150.740	1331.130	2006.55
1978	8.418	12.888	.098	.151	153.100	1312.460	2009.38
1979	8.447	12.940	.096	.148	153.190	1280.510	1961.63
1980	8.562	13.160	.095	.146	153.702	1373.720	2111.43
1981	8.584	13.208	.094	.144	153.868	1327.910	2043.22
1982	8.610	13.316	.092	.142	154.657	1378.730	2132.31

Note: 1950 is 1950-51 (July 1950 to June 1951) etc. **NCA** and **GCA** respectively are millions of net and gross cropped hectares. **NCAPHD** and **GCAPHD** respectively are net and gross cropped hectare per capita. **INTENSITY**=[(GCA/NCA)x100]. **GYFDT** and **NYFDT** are kgs. of foodgrain per gross and net cropped hectare respectively. **NYFDT**=[GYFDTxINTENSITY]/100.
Source: Based on Table 3.1 and Alamgir and Berlage (1974, pp.161-167,172); BBS (1979, pp.166-167,340; 1984a, p.31; 1984b, pp.570,690); EPBS (1969, pp.40-41, 120).

NCA = 8.3746 + 0.0054T   (3.4)
$$(R^2 = 0.0902, \ t = 1.753)$$

GCA = 10.4592 + 0.0791T   (3.5)
$$(R^2 = 0.6904, \ t = 8.315)$$

ln**NCAPHD** = −1.6496 − 0.0235T   (3.6)
$$(R^2 = 0.9896, \ t = 54.260)$$

ln**GCAPHD** = −1.4234 − 0.0174T   (3.7)
$$(R^2 = 0.9284, \ t = 20.045)$$

Consider now the intensification response. New technology (designed to intensify cultivation practices), was introduced in several phases: It commenced with the distribution of chemical fertilizers and the introduction of modern-irrigation in the early 1960s. High yielding varieties (HYVs) of rice and wheat, suitable for growing during the dry (rabi) season were introduced in the late 1960s. Subsequently rice strains were introduced which were suitable for the rainy (kharif) season. Kharif foodgrains consist of aus and aman rice crops while rabi foodgrains consist of boro rice and wheat crops. Table 3.3 provides relevant data on three components of the new technology since the late 1960s. The first three columns (**PRKHA, PRRABIHA, PRFDHA**) respectively refer to percentage of kharif, rabi and overall foodgrain area under HYV cultivation, and **PRFDI, IRKHP** and **IRRBP** refer respectively to percentage area irrigated of total, kharif and rabi foodgrains. **FPHA** refers to quantity of chemical fertilizers in kgs. of nutrients per gross cropped hectare. By 1980-82 (average for the years 1980-81, 1981-82 and 1982-83), over 26 percent of total foodgrain area had been brought under HYV cultivation compared to less than 2 percent during 1967-69 (average for the years 1967-68, 1968-69 and 1969-70). During this period the quantity of chemical fertilizers applied rose from just over 9 kgs. of nutrient per hectare of gross cropped area to over 33 kgs. Nearly 70 percent of the dry season rice area is now under HYV cultivation. Practically all the wheat area is under HYV cultivation and over 16 percent of the rainy season foodgrain area is under HYV cultivation. The proportion of the foodgrain area irrigated increased from about 8 percent in 1969-70 to over 13 percent in 1980-82.

During the 1950s cropping intensity (**INTENSITY**) remained stagnant at around 130

47

Table 3.3: Intensity of Modern Input Use,
Bangladesh Agriculture, 1967-68 to 1982-83

Year	PRKHA	PRRABIHA	PRFDHA	PRFDI	FPHA	IRKHP	IRRBP
1967	0.044	9.207	0.686	NA	7.898	NA	NA
1968	0.097	16.513	1.648	NA	8.499	NA	NA
1969	0.309	24.315	2.618	8.725	9.908	20.787	79.213
1970	1.268	32.566	4.720	10.174	11.771	15.866	84.134
1971	3.592	33.293	6.779	10.304	10.170	13.869	86.131
1972	7.223	41.780	11.140	10.863	15.459	13.839	86.161
1973	10.874	52.621	15.772	11.583	14.890	16.297	83.703
1974	9.088	55.483	14.946	13.103	11.371	14.173	85.827
1975	9.908	56.266	15.651	12.100	17.626	12.450	87.550
1976	8.729	59.952	13.904	10.474	20.343	15.294	84.706
1977	9.723	59.837	16.069	12.145	26.941	13.234	86.766
1978	11.861	64.331	18.694	12.225	25.804	14.419	85.581
1979	14.139	71.688	22.735	13.229	28.794	15.733	84.267
1980	15.818	75.254	25.368	13.334	31.955	17.897	82.103
1981	15.587	76.990	25.845	13.904	30.171	19.450	80.550
1982	16.921	80.850	28.161	14.885	37.945	19.333	80.667

Note: 1967 refers to 1967-68 (July 1967 to June 1968) etc.
PRKHA and PRRABIHA respectively refer to percentages of
kharif (rain-fed rice, aus and aman varieties) and rabi (dry
season, boro rice and wheat) area under HYV cultivation.
PRFDHA represents percentage area under HYV foodgrains. FPHA
is fertilizer (kgs. of nutrients) applied per hectare of
gross cropped area. IRKHP and IRRBP are percentages of kharif
and rabi foodgrain area irrigated in total irrigated area. NA
means not available.
Source: Based on data from BBS (1979, pp.162,212;1982,
pp.206,209,213;1984a, pp.31,33;1984b, pp.225).

percent. Throughout the entire period of the 1960s,
cropping intensity increased slowly but steadily.
The incidence of multiple cropping has increased
significantly in recent years. For example, the
area triple cropped (annually) expanded from around
480 thousand hectares to 670 thousand between the
mid 1960s and early 1980s (BBS, 1978, p.113; 1985a,
pp.833-835). By the early 1980s, the intensity of
cropping rose to over 150 percent. The behaviour of
intensity of cropping over the years is depicted in
Figure 3.3.
        What implications do the changes in cropping
intensity and cultivated area have for foodgrain

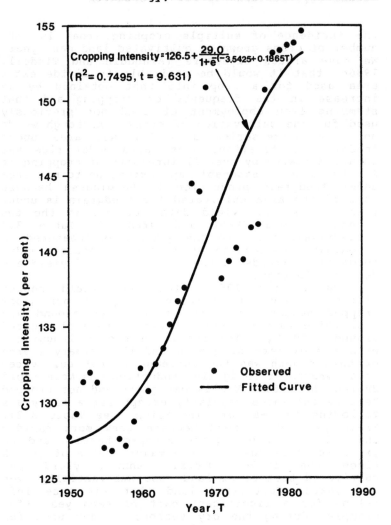

Figure 3.3: Trend in cropping intensity, Bangladesh, 1950–51 to 1982–83.

yield per hectare? This can be considered by distinguishing between two types of yields. These are: Yield per hectare of gross area cropped under foodgrains (**GYFDT**) and yield per hectare of net area under foodgrain cultivation (**NYFDT**).

One of the most important effects of the 'Green Revolution' has been to increase the intensity of cultivation or cropping by increasing the incidence of multiple cropping, that is, the number of crops grown on cultivated land each year. We have argued elsewhere (Alauddin and Tisdell, 1986c) that it would be desirable to divide extra area used for a crop into that obtained by an increase in the frequency of cropping and that stemming from employment of land not previously used for the cultivation of crops. Although we do not have time-series data for net area under foodgrain cultivation, gross area under rice and wheat, deflated by overall intensity of cropping is likely to be a reasonable approximation to net area under foodgrain production in Bangladesh because most of the area cultivated for foodgrain is under these crops. The yield data set out in the two columns headed **GYFDT** and **NYFDT** in Table 3.2 respectively refer to the quantities (measured in kilograms) produced per gross and net hectare under foodgrains. Trends in the two measures of yield are depicted in Figure 3.4.

During the 1950s, foodgrain yield showed little tendency to increase and yield per gross cropped hectare remained stagnant at around 920 kgs. while that per net cropped hectare fluctuated around 1200 kgs. The foodgrain sector languished with a slow rate of growth and the primary source of this growth was the increase in net cultivated area. Growth of foodgrain production was more rapid during the 1960s. Yields per gross and net cropped hectare increased regularly except for a few years following the War of Liberation (see Table 3.2). Yield per net cropped hectare grew more rapidly than the yield per gross cropped hectare and so yield increase has been the major source of growth since the 1960s. Overall annual yield per cultivated hectare of land rose substantially over the years. Cultivated land that was once left fallow for a significant part of each year (for example, during the dry season) is now used for crops such as wheat or dry season rice varieties. This is an important way in which the new varieties have added significantly to agricultural production. The major contribution of the 'Green Revolution' to increased agricultural output in Bangladesh may lie more in its contribution to increased productivity of already cultivated land through multiple cropping rather than in its contribution to extension of the area of cultivated land or to increased yields from single cropping even though seasonal yields have also

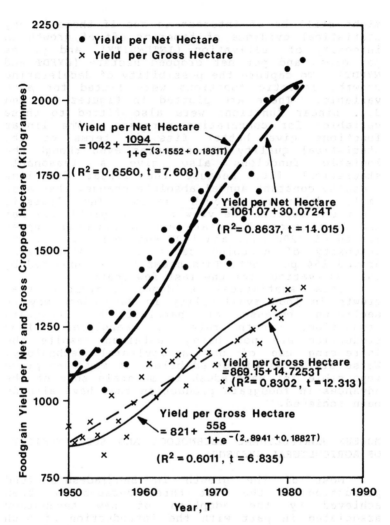

Figure 3.4: Trends in foodgrain yields per hectare of net and gross cropped area, Bangladesh, 1950-51 to 1982-83.

shown an upward trend since the introduction of modern agricultural technology.

The important question that arises at this stage is whether recent growth rates in Bangladesh's food production can be sustained. Are past trends likely to continue? While one needs to be cautious about extrapolating past trends, it might still be of interest to see if there is any statistical evidence of tapering off of growth in intensity of cultivation (**INTENSITY**), and yields per gross and per net cropped hectare (**GYFDT** and **NYFDT**). To capture the possibility of decelerating growth, logistic functions were fitted for each variable. These are plotted in Figures 3.3 and 3.4. Linear functions were also fitted to these variables for comparative purposes. The linear functions give better fits in terms of the statistical quality of estimates even though the logistic functions also give a reasonable statistical fit. Because the linear functions indicate constant annual absolute change, they also imply declining growth rates. The logistic functions support the view that the yields per net and gross cropped hectare are approaching upper limits of 2200 kgs. and 1400 kgs respectively. The intensity of cropping seems to be stabilizing around 154 per cent. This seems to be supported by the observations for the last few years.

This statistical evidence indicates that growth in food availability in Bangladesh may be declining because of barriers to foodgrain production. Growth rates of Bangladeshi food production are not being sustained despite the increasing use of new agricultural technology. Worse still, as discussed below, it may even prove impossible for Bangladesh to maintain some of the advances in foodgrain production that have already been achieved.

MODERN AGRICULTURAL TECHNOLOGY AND SUSTAINABILITY OF AGRICULTURAL SYSTEMS

Most of the growth in Bangladesh's food production in the last three decades has been achieved by the adoption of new technology associated in part with the introduction of high yielding crop varieties. Biochemical technologies have played a dominant part in this growth (Diwan and Kallianpur, 1985;1986). Opinions of scientists and agricultural economists vary widely as to the extent that high levels of production based on such modern technology can be sustained. Conway (1986) believes that on the whole modern agricultural technologies provide less sustainability for production than traditional methods. On the other hand, Schultz (1974), citing experience on the drylands of the United States, argues that modern

52

technologies have led to agricultural systems that are environmentally more sustainable than in the past. It may be unwise, however, to generalize from a limited number of cases for there are variations in modern technologies and in the environmental conditions under which they are applied, and so results may differ depending on particular conditions present (Tisdell, 1985c).

Yet it is clear that we cannot assume that high production levels which may be achieved by the use of modern technologies are sustainable. The possibility of such production being unsustainable deserves to be considered seriously. This requires us to be alert for signs of such non-sustainability and where appropriate to adopt scientific and social measures to counteract these trends or reduce their adverse impact on welfare.

Increased intensity of cultivation has been a key element in the use of modern agricultural technology in Bangladesh. Even though cultivation intensity is already high in many districts, hydrological conditions make it possible to further increase intensity, especially by extending cultivation during the rabi (dry) season. For instance, during the 1984-85 rabi season only 35 percent of the net cultivable area was actually used (see MPO, 1985). However, the realization of this requires effective expansion of irrigation facilities. Furthermore, increased cropping intensity depends critically on growing period of crops. This suggests a need for biological innovations so that varieties possessing wider adaptability and shorter growing periods are developed. But there may be limits to the extent to which intensification can be used to increase food production. Over-intensification e.g., triple cropping in a year, may reduce overall yields by creating deficiencies of important soil nutrients like zinc and sulphur[3]. This matter and related long-term effects, mentioned below, require continuing study by agricultural research bodies (Cf. Alauddin and Tisdell, 1986a; Gill, 1983).

Soil structure can be changed by increased frequency of cultivation. Soil may lose organic content (humus), deteriorate physically, become more subject to erosion and lose its water absorption and aeration properties, all of which may reduce yields. The use of agrochemicals can reduce species diversity, upset ecological balances and stimulate the development of pest populations (M. Ahmed, 1986, p.91; M.F. Ahmed, 1986, p.44;

Technology, Sustainable Food Production

Biggs and Clay, 1981, p.330; Hayami and Ruttan, 1985, p.297) once again limiting yields. Irrigation can also have an adverse impact on ecology and environment. It can result in saline soils (see, for example, Sinha, 1984, p.181). M. Ahmed (1986, pp.47-48) claims that the withdrawal of ground water in the dry season has lowered the ground water table beyond suction limits in the northern part of Bangladesh and has disrupted the drinking water supply system based on hand-pump tubewells. Furthermore, agricultural production has become increasingly dependent on man-made chemicals most of which are derived from non-renewable resources. This could create additional problems as discussed in the next section.

DEPENDENCE ON FOREIGN TECHNOLOGY AND IMPORTED INPUTS

The use of modern agricultural technology by Bangladesh has made it increasingly dependent on foreign technology and knowhow. Taking this into account, Bangladesh has become more food-dependent on foreigners than is suggested by its need to import an increasing proportion of its grain supplies.

Modern seed-fertilizer-irrigation technology is highly import-intensive. Bangladesh now depends heavily on the foreign supply of chemical fertilizer, pesticides and fungicides as well as irrigation equipment. Data set out in Table 3.4 clearly indicate the extent of import dependence of Bangladesh for the inputs critical to augmenting domestic food production. Bangladesh primarily produces two types of nitrogenous fertilizer, urea and ammonium sulphate (AS), and one type of phosphatic fertilizer, triple super phosphate (TSP). Bangladesh depends heavily on external supply for other non-nitrogenous fertilizers like muriate of potash (MP), hyperphosphate (HP) and NPK. The production of TSP is entirely based on imported rock phosphate, and Bangladesh has not been able to secure a long-term source of supply of phosphate rock for TSP production (Alamgir, 1980, p.211) even though Bangladesh produces most of its nitrogenous fertilizer from domestic natural gas.

While in its production of nitrogenous fertilizers (urea and AS), Bangladesh does not import its basic raw materials (natural gas), it is very import dependent (at least indirectly) for

Table 3.4: Imports of Modern Agricultural Inputs, Bangladesh, 1973-74 to 1982-83. Fertilizers in 1000 tonnes gross weight and chemicals and irrigation equipment in million taka c.i.f.(cost, insurance, freight)

	Fertilizers				Chemicals	Irrigation		
Year	Urea	TSP	MP	Others	Pesticides	DTW	STW	LLP
1973	0	97.13	41.25	10.87	105.50	289.10	7.10	110.80
1974	142.25	48.16	7.01	35.46	118.70	508.50	8.80	343.40
1975	72.34	222.72	37.39	0	21.90	266.70	44.50	0
1976	10.97	20.83	9.96	0	35.00	146.70	54.60	78.00
1977	260.31	114.61	37.49	0	67.80	203.40	13.10	27.20
1978	353.79	191.52	78.03	0	76.00	57.00	35.20	0
1979	286.32	215.81	60.05	11.28	80.60	NA	492.50	6.90
1980	62.99	224.55	42.67	19.30	152.80	162.40	171.30	83.20
1981	254.00	184.00	26.00	0	147.70	174.80	293.20	89.60
1982	43.00	208.00	44.00	9.00	NA	NA	NA	NA

Notes: 1973 means 1973-74 (July 1973 to June 1974) etc. DTW, STW and LLP respectively represent Deep and Shallow Tubewells and Low Lift Pumps. NA means not available.
Source: Based on data from BADC (1978 p.14;1979 p.8;1980 p.9;1981 p.9;1984 pp.1-2); BBS (1985a, pp.867-871).

several other materials and inputs required to manufacture nitrogenous fertilizer. An examination of Bangladesh's interindustry input-output structure indicates that sectors such as other chemicals and transport service are important suppliers of inputs to the Fertilizer sector and these sectors are heavily dependent on imported inputs like petroleum, machinery, chemicals and so on for the production of their output (see, for example, BPC, 1980, pp.50-53).

A recent study (Alauddin and Tisdell, 1986b) shows that, along with many other industries in Bangladesh, fertilizer production involves higher capital-labour ratios in terms of techniques used than seem appropriate given the total factor composition of the economy. It is possible that Bangladesh's dependence on import of capital equipment and/or the dependence on foreign technology (required for industrial manufacture of inputs necessary for agriculture) will continue to grow as it tries to augment domestic food production (Cf. Maitra, 1980 and Chapter 2 of this book).[4]

Technology, Sustainable Food Production

CONCLUDING COMMENTS

Our analysis indicates that Bangladesh is failing
to produce sufficient food to sustain its growing
population and is, therefore, becoming increasingly
dependent on imported foodgrains. This periodically
strains the already low foreign exchange reserves
of Bangladesh and adds to its problems of
development planning.[5] Nevertheless, Bangladesh has
substantially expanded its food production in the
last three decades, initially by extending the
margin of cultivation and in the last decade and a
half mainly by increasing the intensification of
agricultural production using techniques associated
with the 'Green Revolution'. The growth rate in its
crop yields and the rate of increase in the
intensity of cropping seem to be tapering off.
However, it is far from clear whether intensive use
of arable land has gone as far as to irreversibly
restrict future production or to make for a level
of production that will be ecologically
unsustainable or even non-sustainable from an
economic or social point of view. Thus the
sustainability consequences of modern agricultural
technology (in both Conway's and Douglass' sense)
is still uncertain for Bangladesh.

The restoration of Bangladesh's supply-demand
food balance depends critically on a significant
reduction in population growth and on an increase
in yield per hectare. Given the present low
productivity in agriculture, the potential for
increased yield is substantial (FAO, 1984). This
requires optimum doses of fertilizer, adequate
irrigation as well as higher intensity of cropping.
A further complication is the decrease in net
cultivated area over the years. With population
pressure mounting, net cultivated area may decrease
even further because of higher demand for housing
and urbanization. With the prospect of declining
area of cultivable land, there will be further need
to increase intensity of cropping. But as mentioned
earlier there may be ecological limits to the
degree of intensification that is sustainable.

In a wider context, Bangladesh, along with
other countries, may encounter problems in the long
run in sustaining agricultural productivity because
of loss of genetic diversity, ecological damage due
to application of agro-chemicals and from its
dependence on chemical products, for example,
fertilizers and pesticides produced from
exhaustible and non-renewable resources. Another

difficulty for Bangladesh is that increased food production using modern techniques tends to raise its dependence on imported technology and imported inputs.

It still remains uncertain whether the new agricultural technology introduced into Bangladesh will result in a higher production per capita being sustained than in the recent past. Continuing concern about the sustainability issue is not misplaced. Biological deterioration of ecological and agricultural ecosystems and human population growth combined with greater socio-economic interdependence may threaten sustainability of Bangladesh's food production in the future.

NOTES

1. Net availability of foodgrains for consumption = Gross production less 10 percent for seed, feed and wastage less internal procurement plus offtake from government ration distribution. Offtake from government ration distribution is made up of imports and internal procurement and carry-over from previous year.

2. High import intensity of foodgrains does not necessarily imply non-sustainability. Japan imports a sizeable proportion of its foodstuff. However, Japan's balance of payments position is fundamentally different from Bangladesh's. While the former can pay for its food imports from export of manufactured goods, the latter has hardly any such scope. For Bangladesh, its difficulty is that its imports are difficult to sustain (Cf. Tisdell and Fairbairn, 1984).

3. A recently conducted field survey by us in a village in the northwestern district of Rajshahi in Bangladesh, found farmers reporting use of fertilizers containing zinc on the advice of agricultural research workers. This was also confirmed in the course of an interview with a soil scientist at the Bangladesh Rice Research Institute (BRRI). Jones (1984, p.199) reported zinc and sulphur deficiency caused by more intensive cultivation in the Dhaka district of Bangladesh.

4. One needs also to consider the substantial costs involved in heavy dependence on imported technology. Apart from requirements of foreign exchange, technologies (fertilizers, pesticides and insecticides and irrigation machinery) materially transferred to countries with characterstics different from those in the country of origin is

unlikely to perform in the way it has performed in the area to which it is indigenous. Even though agrochemicals may be applicable to a wide range of environmental conditions, one needs to consider a number of factors more or less unique to agricultural innovations. Differences in ecological conditions influenced by geophysical and climatic variables have a critical influence on the performance of agricultural innovations in farmers' fields. This highlights the importance in agriculture of diversity or heterogeneity in environmental conditions.

5. Our conclusions are based on official data which have limitations (see for example, Boyce, 1985) and, therefore, must be qualified.

REFERENCES

Ahmed, M. (1986) "The Use and Abuse of Pesticides and the Protection of Environment", pp.89-95 in BMOE, **Protection of Environment from Degradation, Proceedings of South Asian Association for Regional Cooperation (SAARC) Seminar 1985,** Bangladesh Ministry of Education, Science and Technology Division, Dhaka

Ahmed, M.F. (1986) "Environmental Degradation", pp.42-49 in BMOE, **Protection of Environment from Degradation, Proceedings of South Asian Association for Regional Cooperation (SAARC) Seminar 1985,** Bangladesh Ministry of Education, Science and Technology Division, Dhaka

Alamgir, M. (1980) **Famine in South Asia,** Oelgeschlager, Gunn & Hain, Cambridge, Massachusetts

Alamgir, M. and Berlage, L.J.J.B. (1973) "Estimation of Income Elasticity of Demand for Foodgrain in Bangladesh from Cross Section Data: A Skeptical View", **Bangladesh Economic Review,** 1, pp.25-58

Alamgir, M. and Berlage, L.J.J.B. (1974) **Bangladesh National Income and Expenditure 1949-50 To 1969-70,** Bangladesh Institute of Development Studies, Dhaka

Alauddin, M. and Mujeri, M.K. (1981) "The Strategy of Agricultural Development in Bangladesh: Past and Present", **Bangladesh Journal of Political Economy,** 5, pp.235-253

Alauddin, M. and Tisdell, C. (1986a) "Bangladeshi and International Agricultural Research:

Administrative and Economic Issues", **Agricultural Administration**, 21, pp.1-20

Alauddin, M. and Tisdell, C. (1986b) "Inappropriate Industries and Inefficient Resource-Use in Bangladesh: Some Evidence from Input-Output Analysis", **Socio-Economic Planning Sciences**, **20**, pp. 135-143

Alauddin, M. and Tisdell, C. (1986c) "Decomposition Methods, Agricultural Productivity Growth and Technological Change: A Critique Supported by Bangladeshi Data", **Oxford Bulletin of Economics and Statistics**, 48, pp.353-372

BADC (1978) **Annual Report 1977-78**, Bangladesh Agricultural Development Corporation, Dhaka

BADC (1979) **Annual Report 1978-79**, Bangladesh Agricultural Development Corporation, Dhaka

BADC (1980) **Annual Report 1979-80**, Bangladesh Agricultural Development Corporation, Dhaka

BADC (1981) **Annual Report 1980-81**, Bangladesh Agricultural Development Corporation, Dhaka

BADC (1984) **Annual Report 1982-83**, Bangladesh Agricultural Development Corporation, Dhaka

BBS (1976) **Agricultural Production Levels of Bangladesh, 1947-72**, Bangladesh Bureau of Statistics, Dhaka

BBS (1978) **Statistical Pocket Book of Bangladesh, 1978**, Bangladesh Bureau of Statistics, Dhaka

BBS (1979) **Statistical Year Book of Bangladesh 1979**, Bangladesh Bureau of Statistics, Dhaka

BBS (1980) **Year Book of Agricultural Statistics of Bangladesh, 1979-80**, Bangladesh Bureau of Statistics, Dhaka

BBS (1982) **Statistical Year Book of Bangladesh 1982**, Bangladesh Bureau of Statistics, Dhaka

BBS (1984a) **Monthly Statistical Bulletin of Bangladesh**, March 1984, Bangladesh Bureau of Statistics, Dhaka

BBS (1984b) **Statistical Year Book of Bangladesh 1983-84**, Bangladesh Bureau of Statistics, Dhaka

BBS (1985a) **1983-84 Year Book of Agriculutral Statistics of Bangladesh**, Bangladesh Bureau of Statistics, Dhaka

BBS (1985b) **1984-85 Statistical Year Book of Bangladesh**, Bangladesh Bureau of Statistics, Dhaka

Biggs, S.D. and Clay, E.J. (1981) "Sources of Innovation in Agricultural Technology", **World Development**, **9**, pp.321-336.

Boyce, J.K. (1985) "Agricultural Growth in Bangladesh, 1949-50 to 1980-81: A Review of

Evidence", **Economic and Political Weekly**, 20, pp.A31-A43

BPC (1980) **The Structure of the Bangladesh Economy: An Input-Output Analysis**, Background papers of the Second Five Year Plan of Bangladesh, Volume I, Bangladesh Planning Commission, Dhaka

Brown, L. (1970) **Seeds of Change**, Praeger, New York

BRRI (1977) **Workshop on Ten Years of Modern Rice and Wheat Cultivation in Bangladesh**, Bangladesh Rice Research Institute, Joydevpur

Conway, G.R. (1986) **Agroecosystem Analysis for Research and Development**, Winrock International, Bangkok

Diwan, R.K. and Kallianpur, R. (1985) "Biological Technology and Land Productivity: Fertilizers and Food Production in India", **World Development**, 13, pp.627-638

Diwan, R.K. and Kallianpur, R. (1986) **Productivity and Technical Change in Foodgrains**, Tata McGraw-Hill, New Delhi

Douglass, G.K. (1984) "The Meanings of Agricultural Sustainablility", pp.3-29 in Douglass, G.K (ed.), **Agricultural Sustainability in a Changing World Order**, Westview Press, Boulder, Colorado

EIU (1976) **Quarterly Economic Review of Pakistan, Bangladesh and Afghanistan**, Annual Supplement, Economist Intelligence Unit, London

EPBS (1969) **Statistical Digest of East Pakistan, No. 6**, East Pakistan Bureau of Statistics, Dhaka

Faaland, J. and Parkinson, J.R. (1976) **Bangladesh: The Test Case of Development**, C. Hurst & Co, London

FAO (1984) **Land Food and People**, Food and Agricultural Organization, Rome

Gill, G.J. (1983) "Agricultural Research in Bangladesh: Costs and Returns", Bangladesh Agricultural Research Council, Dhaka

Hayami, Y. and Ruttan, V.W. (1985) **Agricultural Development: An International Perspective**, The Johns Hopkins University Press, Baltimore

IUCN (1980) **World Conservation Strategy: Living Resources Conservation for Sustainable Development**, International Union for the Conservation of Nature and Natural Resources, Glands, Switzerland

Jones, S. (1984) "Agrarian Structure and Agricultural Innovations in Bangladesh: Panimara Village, Dhaka District", pp.194-211 in Tim P. Blyss-Smith and Sudhir Wanmali (eds.), **Understanding Green Revolutions: Agrarian Change and Development Planning in South Asia,** Cambridge University Press, Cambridge

Krutilla, J.V. and Fisher, A.C. (1975) **The Economics of Natural Environments,** Resources for the Future, Washington, D.C.

Maitra, P. (1980) **The Mainspring of Economic Development,** Croom Helm, London

Malthus, T.R. (1798) **An Essay on the Principles of Population,** Macmillan, London (reprinted for the Royal Economic Society, 1926)

MPO (1985) **National Water Plan Project: Draft Final Report,** Master Plan Organization, Dhaka

Ricardo, D. (1817) **Principles of Political Economy and Taxation,** E.P. Dutton & Co., New York (Everyman's edition, 1911)

Schultz, T.W. (1974) "Is Modern Agriculture Consistent with a Stable Environment?", pp.235-242 in **The Future of Agriculture: Technology, Policies and Adjustment,** Papers and reports, 15th International Conference of Agricultural Economists, Oxford Agricultural Economics Institute, Oxford

Sinha, S. (1984) "Growth of Scientific Temper: Rural Context", pp. 166-190 in Gibbons, M., Gummett, P. and Udgaonkar, B. (eds.) **Science and Technology Policy in the 1980s and beyond,** Longman, London

Thibodeau, R. and Field, H. (1984) **Sustaining Tomorrow: A Strategy for World Conservation and Development,** University Press of New England, Hanover

Tisdell, C. (1983a) "An Economist's Critique of the World Conservation Strategy with Some examples from Australian Experience", **Environmental Conservation, 10,** pp.43-52

Tisdell, C. (1983b) "Conserving Living Resources in Third World Countries: Economic and Social Issues", **International Journal of Environmental Studies, 22,** pp.11-24

Tisdell, C. (1985a) **Sustainable Development: Conflicting Approaches of Ecologists and Economists and Implications of LDCs,** Research Report or Occasional Paper, No. 122, Department of Economics, University of Newcastle, N.S.W.

Tisdell, C. (1985b) "The World Conservation Strategy, Economic Policies and Sustainable

Resource-Use in Developing Countries", **Environmental Professional**, 7, pp.102-107

Tisdell, C. (1985c) "Economics, Ecology, Sustainable Agricultural Systems and Development", **Development Southern Africa**, 2, pp.512-521

Tisdell, C. and Fairbairn, I.J. (1984) "Subsistence Economies, and Unsustainable Development and Trade: Some Simple Theory", **Journal of Development Studies**, 20, pp.227-241

World Bank (1982) "Bangladesh: Foodgrain Self-Sufficiency and Crop Diversification" (Annexes and Statistical Appendix), Report #3953-BD, World Bank, Washington, D.C.

Chapter Four

TECHNOLOGY AND ITS TRANSFER TO LESS DEVELOPED ECONOMIES

Nripesh Podder

INTRODUCTION

Technological changes in any economy arouse intense social interest mainly due to their possible effects on the labour market, and since most, if not all, changes are considered to be labour-saving or capital-intensive, the debates over such changes are often quite spirited. The controversy over the choice of an appropriate technology in a less developed country creates even more animosity if the country happens to be overpopulated by any definition. The plethora of public opinions seems to be sufficiently polarized with respect to the basic issue. While one group is completely opposed to the introduction of any modern labour-saving technology, for the other, the latest technology is the only choice for rapid growth. The first group seems to argue that for an overpopulated country the appropriate technology should be labour-using and not labour dispensing. This proposition is apparently quite reasonable. But we must then investigate what is meant by labour-using technology or if at all such a thing exists.

The main aim of this chapter is to clear up some common misunderstandings about the meaning of technological change. The other equally important aim is to demonstrate the impracticability and the self-defeating character of the proposition that for the sake of the evolution of the most suitable technology that is based on the specific factor endowment of a less developed economy, all modern and imported technology should be completely banished and the country should be kept in total technological isolation.

The next section of this chapter gives a brief history of technological change in human society and thereby unfolds its actual meaning and implications. It is my view that the meaning of technological change cannot be completely understood without some basic knowledge of engineering thermodynamics. The third section discusses the causes of technological change, and critically examines the Marxian approach. The fourth section shows the inevitability of the global diffusion of new technology. It also makes a modest attempt to explain why the basic problems of physical existence still persist in many less developed countries in spite of comparatively prolonged efforts of development planning. The fifth section critically examines Priyatosh Maitra's thesis that the failure of developmental efforts of many Third World countries is due to the importation of the latest technology. The last section makes some concluding remarks.

A BRIEF HISTORY OF TECHNOLOGICAL PROGRESS

Since the dawn of civilization relentless efforts have gone into devising ways to extend human capabilities. The extension of human capabilities is essential for man's domination over nature which he can utilize to increase his productivity. Human capabilities could be extended either by an extension of the senses or by the control of or the command over nonhuman sources of energy. The invention and the use of tools in production were the first step towards this goal. Many would even argue that the use of tools is the main distinguishing feature of a human from other animals, although his power of reasoning and his creative faculty, perhaps are of no less importance.

The early tools increased human productivity mainly by making use of the mechanical advantage provided by the wheel, the lever and the pulley. It is probably one of the earliest scientific insights that the operation of a tool depends on two essential inputs namely, the driving force and the guiding intelligence. The early tools were simple in design and they entirely depended on human or animal muscle as the source of their driving force and on human brain as the exclusive source of their guiding intelligence. Henceforth, in this chapter we shall refer to this guiding intelligence as information. Although the human brain has been considered to be adequate as the

64

source of information until recently, it was soon
realized that man's physique as the source of
driving energy for the tools was subject to severe
limitations and those, therefore, put a relatively
low ceiling to the level of material prosperity
that could be achieved per head no matter what
variety of tools were used. The human brain as the
source of information was not considered to be
subject to any limitation at this stage of technological .development. Therefore, in his search for
nonhuman sources of energy, man made a significant
step forward by the domestication of wild animals.
The harnessing of animal muscle power as the substitute or the complement of human muscle power
significantly increased per capita productivity and
the practice continues to this day. Nevertheless,
with rising aspirations it was found to be quite
inadequate even for the socially accepted minimum
comforts of life. Of course in the days of tribal
warfare and slavery one human group dominated
another in order to use the slave muscle power to
produce useful goods and services for the
conquerors. The slave society was in fact
dependent on the stage of development in which the
slave was capable of producing a surplus over and
above the subsistence of the slave. It is well
documented in history that many civilizations like
the Roman civilization were based on slavery.

The search for other sources of energy,
however, continued relentlessly. The next major
development in technology is probably the discovery
of natural forces like wind and water flows and the
invention of appropriate tools that could utilize
those forces in productive tasks. The examples of
these are abundant even in the contemporary world.
The use of these natural forces were obviously
limited by their availability as well as their
somewhat unpredictable character. Even the use of
all these were considered to be inadequate due
mainly to rising expectations.

However, the period just before the so-called
Industrial Revolution is characterized by a
significant phenomenon which resulted in an
enormous increase in the per capita productivity.
This could be described as the development and the
introduction of <u>organizational technology</u>. This
was the emergence of the factory system of
production in which specialization and division of
labour was possible. The importance of
specialization and division of labour can be best
described by Adam Smith's famous example of the pin

factory. With the same labour and capital the production of pins could be increased from 10 to 4000 just by introducing a different order in which the productive activities are organized. It is indeed a quantum leap.

A technological invention is nothing but the invention of a new tool designed to perform a specific task in a way different from ones known hitherto. When the new invention is commercially introduced in the actual production process it is called an innovation in economic terminology. The tool always embodies some specific knowledge which could be appropriately described as knowhow. Obviously, the design of a tool will depend on the type of energy source by which it is supposed to be driven. Therefore, the knowledge and availability of different energy sources and their relative costs are of crucial importance in designing a tool. It is well known in history that the knowledge of the energy sources have gradually progressed with the progression of civilization. It is also a matter of history that mankind has virtually exhausted some sources of energy that were in limited supply. However, it is important to keep in mind that a tool designed to be powered by human muscles is characteristically different from one designed to be driven by some kind of fossil fuel. At this point I must mention that I shall use the word machine to describe a tool when it is powered by some nonhuman source of energy although some people would use the word machine when the tool becomes sufficiently large or complex.

The use of fire as a source of energy was probably known to man at the very early stage of human civilization and except for its use in cooking and keeping warm, fire has been used in certain tasks like metal smelting for a long period of history. By the technique of transforming fire or heat into useful work, I specifically mean mechanical motion which is what is needed to drive a machine. The invention of techniques to transform heat into mechanical motion marks the beginning of the Industrial Revolution in the eighteenth century. Fire was used to transform water into steam which, in turn, was used to drive a steam engine which could be employed in various productive activities. In the process, the tools became sufficiently complex and bigger in size and capacity to be designated as machines. Initially wood was used as the fuel in the steam engine but

the rate of use of wood soon outstripped its
supply. The discovery of hydrocarbon in the form
of coal at this juncture provided a relatively
unlimited supply of fuel for the steam engine and
also for making steel to construct steam engines.
The supply of fuel was further extended by the
discovery of the liquid form of hydrocarbon, i.e.,
petroleum.

The discovery and the use of fossil fuel
revolutionized production technology. Historians
mark this stage at which mankind truly became the
exploiter of nature instead of being only part of
it. Fossil fuel removed the constraint on the size
and on the capacity of the machine designed for
producing virtually any commodity or service. At
the same time, it liberated the human operator of
the machine from the drudgery of physical labour
and gave him the command over a relatively
unlimited amount of energy. With a minimal
physical labour required to operate machines, the
human operator's role in production was virtually
reduced to be simply the supplier of information.
This phenomenon marks the separation of skill from
physical labour in production. Also, the skill of
a craftsman gradually started to be replaced by the
skill in operating the machine. In the process the
level of affluence reached a point unprecedented in
history.

Two hundred years since the beginning of the
Industrial Revolution has seen continual improvements in the design of machines and the utilization
of new forms of energy. As wood, coal, gas,
petroleum and atomic energy came into use in
production either sequentially or simultaneously,
the design of the machines changed not only to
utilize newer forms of energy but also with respect
to their thermodynamic efficiency[1]. In simpler
terms the situation can be explained as follows:
Production of goods and services requires work. In
thermodynamics, work is synonymous with energy.
If we call the work done in the course of actual
production useful work then alternative machines
can be compared by the quantity of energy used by
each to perform the same task. Obviously, the
machine that uses the least amount of energy is,
thermodynamically, the most efficient. Alternatively, the machine that delivers the highest
amount of useful work from a given quantity of
energy is the most efficient. Thus, it was found
that an internal combustion engine is more
efficient than a steam engine or an electric motor

67

is more efficient than an internal combustion engine in performing specific tasks. Of course there are other economic factors that determine if a particular machine will be actually used in commercial production. Only in recent times have the machines employed in many production processes reached a level of efficiency which cannot be further improved. Also, bigger and better machines capable of using a vast quantity of energy have opened up the possibility of an output per head which is thousands of times greater than that in the days of pre-industrial phase of production. The process that started more than two hundred years ago may be appropriately called the process of mechanization.

The degree of material abundance per head was further enhanced by the introduction of so-called scientific management in the organization of production, introduced by F.W. Taylor in the 1880s. What the underlined phrase indicates can be best described by quoting David Dickson (1974, p.55):

> Taylor's basic approach was to apply to manual operations in the principles that machine designers have learned to apply to the work of a tool during the early part of the nineteenth century. He broke a task down to its component parts, and then rearranged and reintegrated those parts in the most 'efficient' way. This was a major advance on the more straightforward division of labour; it indicated to management not only what each worker should do, but how he should do it.

When this technique was introduced in a steel plant in Pittsburgh, U.S.A., production per head increased almost four times. The introduction of the concept of the 'assembly line' for mass production of commodities is also another organizational innovation based on similar ideas but it overlaps technological innovation at the same time. Taylor's ideas also had a significant influence on the organization and mechanization of office work.[2] The first half of the twentieth century witnessed further improvements in per capita productivity though organizational changes brought about by the introduction of operations research techniques such as linear programming, queuing theory, programme evaluation and review technique (PERT) and critical path analysis (CPM). Similarly, a significant improvement in productivity and efficiency was

achieved in cargo shipping with the container-
ization of cargo which in turn was supported by
computers and telecommunications.

Mechanization has virtually raised man from
the state of the beast of burden to the state of an
intelligent thinking being. However, in a
mechanized society a vast amount of labour is still
needed to operate the machines though they are
powered by nonhuman sources of energy. Human
operators mainly provide information or guiding
intelligence which is mostly monotonous,
repetitive, mindless and uninteresting routine
work. This type of work is unacceptable to anyone
who believes that the true manifestation of
humanity lies in creative thinking and activity,
and in the pursuit of pleasure. Either as a
consequence of this or because of the recognition
of the fact that with plentiful energy and the
machinery to use it under our command the only
constraint to unlimited affluence is the provision
of sufficient guiding intelligence. At last the
limitations of the human brain have started to
show. Therefore, in the last three decades we have
seen the emergence of machines with automatic
feedback mechanisms that operate with a minimal
human interference. Of course, attempts to design
automatic machines, machines that can largely
provide their own guiding intelligence, have been
made over a hundred years with limited success.
Only in recent times, with the development of
digital computers and their use in process control
in industry, has the true automatic machine come of
age.

Those machines that use the principles of
automatic feedback and digital computation are
called cybernetic machines, and these machines are
already revolutionizing the whole production and
distribution system:

> The central fact of the cybernetic revolution
> is that it is introducing machines which
> augment our human capacity for rational data
> processing on a scale analogous to that on
> which steam, electrical and internal
> combustion engines augmented our physical
> powers in a first Industrial Revolution. The
> effects of mechanization proved to be
> tremendous and few would argue that it has
> left the course of human civilization
> unchanged. Yet mechanization multiplied those
> powers which are certainly not the most

important assets of man - his physical strength and energy. But man owes his mastery over the planet mainly to his mental capabilities. Cybernetic machines, since they augment the latter, have, therefore, much greater potential for increasing man's control over his environment (Demczynski, 1969, p.23).

Software developments in parallel with those of hardware are heading towards the creation of machines that are even capable of limited creative thinking. We are already witnessing workerless factories in the industrial world.

Another important phenomenon observed in all industrialized societies is that modern large-scale production and the expansion of markets beyond national boundaries generate a massive amount of information or data the processing of which is a nightmarish task no matter how many human brains are employed to do it. At the same time, all industrial democracies have multiplied the functions of public administration by assuming the role of the welfare state and thereby generating a huge amount of data. The processing and transmission of data again is mostly routine work. But the sheer volume of information to be processed or communicated at a reasonable speed is beyond human capability. The computer is just in time for the rescue.

Let me digress for a moment to quickly trace the development of information technology leading up to digital computers. To be useful, information needs to be processed and/or transmitted. It is important to remember that the main source of information is learning. The process of learning in human society made a great leap forward with the development of spoken languages, which made it easier for interpersonal transmission of information. The next great innovation is the development of writing and printing, which facilitated both processing and transmission of information. Further progress in the technology of information transmission occurred with the inventions of radio, telecommunications and more recently, television. All these revolutionized the technology of information transmission and, thereby, changed the nature of human society. At the same time the global transmission of information is giving rise to a unified culture by making information itself universal. These developments are mainly with respect to the transmission of information. But the processing of information could be done mainly in the human brain for a long period in history. The earliest invention in the field of processing of information is probably the abacus, still widely used in some parts of the world. Since then apart from the minor inventions of the slide rule and calculators, the major inventions were the machines used for sorting of information based on the ideas of Herman Hollerith, which could be considered as the forerunners of modern-day digital computers. In the late nineteenth century Hollerith developed machines to sort and tabulate data and established a company which later became the International Business Machine Corporation (IBM). The significance of computers in the field of processing as well as in the transmission of data could not be overemphasized. The advent of computers truly marks the beginning of the second industrial revolution. Like the first industrial revolution that mechanized the production process by delivering nonhuman energy, the second industrial revolution is automating the production process and mechanizing the processing and transmission of information.

However, my main concern is any change in the means of delivering energy and information or their sources in all production processes including the production of services. The steam engine technology symbolizes '...a working knowledge and capacity for applying the power of steam to perform useful work. At this stage the steam engine represented a potential; it was a power source which could be used to do many possible things: most obviously, it could turn the machinery of a mill or factory or it could propel a vehicle over land or water.' (Rosenberg, 1972, p.62). Appropriately, Matthew Boulton, the first commercial manufacturer of the steam engine and the flag bearer of the Industrial Revolution, is said to have said to Boswell, the biographer of Dr. Samuel Johnson, "I sell what the whole world wants - power." The variety of electrically powered machines and appliances would not have been possible without the electric motor, and the electric motor could not be conceived in the absence of electricity. Essentially, production is nothing but the application of energy and information to raw materials. While it is true that a new technique that optimizes the use of scarce raw materials, or substitutes it by a relatively plentiful resource is vitally important and should be considered as a technological

71

breakthrough, an individual's command over energy and information per unit of time crucially determines his productivity. The importance of the time factor can be demonstrated by an extreme example. Suppose our task is to move a heap of sand weighing 50 tons. An ant that moves one grain at a time could be employed to do the job which will be completed in fifty years, or a diesel-powered earth-moving machine could to the job in a matter of minutes. Of course there could be a number of intermediate alternatives. If the job is urgent we have only the last alternative.

Most of the inventions in the eighteen and nineteenth centuries were sporadic and they often were the results of problem-solving efforts of individuals based on crude empiricism. Though they might be based on some practical knowledge of the existing technology, organized scientific research was virtually unknown because various branches of modern science were hardly established as academic disciplines.

Once the sciences were established as organized bodies of knowledge, industry-oriented scientific research led to the diversity of inventions which is simply spectacular. In the twentieth century, progress in three fields, namely, chemical engineering, genetics and electronics, is going to have far-reaching influence on overall productivity and human welfare.

Until now an important characteristic of technological change has been its capacity to respond to any challenge posed by the shortages of specific raw materials or natural resources. Not only newer minerals but also newer alloys and myriads of synthetic materials have been invented and have come into human use. They have been invented not always as a response to the need for a substitute for scarce resources but also as a result of active search for the right material for the right purpose.

CAUSES OF TECHNOLOGICAL CHANGE

Many would argue that most innovations have taken place because of certain social conditions prevalent at the appropriate time. Thus, while it may be true that increased efficiency and productivity were the main driving forces of technological innovations, it is also true that socio-economic conditions have to be appropriate to take advantage of the opportunities provided by new technological advances. There are numerous historical facts to support this line of argument. To cite only one, it may be known to most scholars that a perfect working model of a steam engine existed in the famous library of Alexandria and the ancient Greeks invented a mechanically sound steam turbine, yet the ancient world could not think of their utilization in productive activities. The reason for this must be that the ancient world did not feel the social necessity for the power of the steam engine. On the other hand, the factory system of production could not have become a reality if trade and commerce had not increased to expand the market, creating the necessity for an increased volume of production. Also the accumulation of mercantile capital and the concomitant development of financial institutions were the necessary prerequisites to finance the factories. It is certainly true that much of the machinery of modern industrial production would only be suitable in a factory system of production.

Let us now review the Marxian explanation of the origin and development of capitalism and industrial technology. Marx and Engels have the following to say on the emergence of the capitalist class and the mode of production which, I presume, is meant to be industrial technology:

> From the serfs of the middle ages sprang the chartered burghers of the earliest towns. From these burgesses the first elements of the bourgeoisie were developed. The discovery of America, the rounding of the Cape, opened up fresh ground for the rising bourgeoisie. The East-Indian and Chinese markets, the colonization of America, trade with the colonies, the increase in the means of exchange and in commodities generally, gave to commerce, to navigation, to industry, an impulse never before known, and thereby, to the revolutionary element in the tottering feudal society, a rapid development.
>
> The feudal system of industry, under which industrial production was monopolized by closed guilds, now no longer sufficed for the growing wants of the new markets. The manufacturing system took its place. The guild-masters were pushed on one side by the manu-

facturing middle class; a division of labour
between the different corporate guilds
vanished in the face of division of labour in
each single workshop.

Meantime the markets kept ever growing,
the demand ever rising. Even manufacture no
longer sufficed. Thereupon, steam and
machinery revolutionized industrial production. The place of manufacture was taken by
the giant, Modern Industry, the place of the
industrial middle class, by industrial
millionaires, the leaders of whole industrial
armies, the modern bourgeoisie (Marx and
Engels, 1970, pp.31–32).

From this it may be safe to conclude that
since bourgeois society or capitalism is the
natural transition from feudalism, capitalist
production technology is also the natural evolution
of feudal production technology. However, one may
not be quite sure if 'steam and machinery' as they
are employed by the bourgeoisie are the results 'of
a long series of revolutions in the modes of
production and exchange' or they were developed by
the bourgeoisie for the purpose of creating
increased <u>surplus value</u> and therefore exploiting
and controlling the working class. In fact it is
not clear even in the writings of Marxist authors
as to which view is upheld. It is quite difficult
to make out what Marx had in mind as to the
interpretation or implication of bourgeois
industrial technology and its change. The
prominent Nobel laureate Simon Kuznets (1965, p.89)
made the following remarks:

> Malthus, Ricardo and Marx, great economists,
> made incorrect prognoses of technological
> changes at the very time that that scientific
> bases of these changes were evolving. On the
> other hand, imaginative tyros like Jules Verne
> and H.G. Wells seemed to sense the
> potentialities of technological change.

However, it is more likely that technological
development is a continuous process where each step
precedes the previous step in a logical fashion
while existing socio-economic conditions can
effectively accelerate or retard its speed. The
support for this view seems to be implicit in **The
Communist Manifesto**, where we get the clear
impression that capitalism has already outlived its

role and is now creating hindrance to technological advances. This is also supported by Lenin (1984, p.49) in his unequivocal acceptance of capitalist industrial technology as the starting point of socialist economic development: "We, the workers, shall organize large scale production on the basis of what capitalism has already created, relying on our own experience as workers, establishing strict iron discipline backed up by the state power of the armed workers." It is also remarkable that while both Marx and Lenin disapprove the situation where workers have to work at the pace of industrial machinery, thus making the workers slaves to the machines, they, nevertheless, accept it along with the iron discipline on the part of the workers, probably in the hope that the situation will change with the further advancement of technology. As a prophet Marx was unable to foresee that though the worker was made a slave to the machine, the introduction of the same machine would liberate him from his toil of approximately 70 hours a week and at the same time increase his real wage substantially. Again, the focus of attention being the industrial working class, Marx was unable to predict the future occupational distribution where the industrial workers would constitute only a minority (approximately 30 percent) of the total working population. What is more, even within most manufacturing industries in the U.S.A., and other industrialized countries workers in the shop floor, i.e., those who are actually involved with the machines, are only around 25 per cent of the workforce employed in the industry.

It is sometimes argued that technology has a will of its own which is independent of all political, social and economic forces. In other words, it is an exogenous force which may influence other forces in the society without being influenced by them in turn. Some scholars go to the length of asserting that technology uniquely determines the nature of the society and its culture. This extreme view is called technological determinism. Moreover, whatever may be the economic and social structure technological change is bound to take place in any country and in the long run the same technology is bound to emerge in all nations of the world.

A number of important qualifications are needed before we can accept this proposition. Consider the steam engine which was introduced virtually everywhere in the world but initially

75

some countries used it mainly for its motive power
while others used it for its tractive power. Thus,
steam as a power source was established as a
scientific truth but whether the steam engine would
be employed to carry out any productive task or
even if it is employed the specific productive task
to which it is employed will certainly depend on
other social and economic conditions. Secondly,
social, political and economic forces certainly
could retard the process of technological change.
It is well known that agriculture developed in
widely dispersed and isolated civilizations; and
all agricultural societies used similar equipment
like the plough or the sickle. Domestication of
animals was also common and all variations in the
type of the beast of burden, e.g., the horse or the
buffalo, can be explained by the differences in
climatic conditions. If technology uniquely
determines the type of society that is most
appropriate then feudal social structure is the
most efficient type for an agricultural society, as
it has always been observed. The evolutionary
character of technology then dictates that at some
stage the feudal system must give way to a
different form of society, in this case capitalism,
for the industrial technology to emerge. It must
be emphasized that once a specific social system is
established certain social forces and institutions
develop that maintain coherence and resist any
disruptive influence. J.D. Bernal (1965, p.918)
cites religion in India and bureaucracy in China as
the two institutions that acted as major deterrents
to technological development.

Scholars often advance various explanations
for specific technological changes. For example,
with reference to England, the pioneer of
industrial technology, Priyatosh Maitra (1980,
1985, see also Chapter 2 of this volume) argues
that all labour-saving technological innovations
took place due to the shortage of labour.
Historical evidence contradicts that. Labour-
saving technology was introduced even when there
was substantial unemployment. Secondly, any labour-
saving technology was never introduced peacefully.
There were always labour discontent and strong
resistance to new technology as exemplified by the
activities of Luddites and other groups. Luddites,
for example, were so active that the government had
to employ an army of 12,000 to curb their
activities. In Holland, the textile workers tried
to prevent the introduction of power looms by

76

throwing their 'sabots', their wooden shoes, into the looms; hence the word 'sabotage'. On the other hand, the introduction of modern technology was more peaceful in northern America, the borrower of European technology in the nineteenth century.

Since the above discussion has been carried out without first defining the phrase 'labour-saving technology', I could legitimately be accused of putting the cart before the horse. Therefore, let me now digress on the definition and meaning of the phrase 'labour-saving technology'. Although the literature on development economics is not quite explicit about it, the most likely meaning of the phrase is that with the new technology a larger volume of production is achieved using proportionately less labour, or the same level of output is achieved with less labour than was used previously, on the implicit assumption of unchanged factor price ratio. More precisely, with the new technology, labour per unit of output is lower than before. The meaning of the phrase 'labour-using technology' seems to be more elusive. It could mean a pure substitution of labour for capital without technological change; or with technological change, labour per unit of output is higher. The latter meaning is more likely but it is hard to find an example of such a technological change. In the light of our discussion of the history of technological progress, such a change will be considered as regress rather than progress. Most, if not all, technological progress led to a diminution in the use of both labour and capital corresponding to the same level of output.

It has often been said that the growing demand necessitated the need for increased production. It is then worthwhile to trace the source of growing demand. In a purely agricultural society, most people produce a bare subsistence and they have nothing left over as surplus to trade. In a predominantly agricultural society, the magnitude of agricultural surplus uniquely determines the extent of non-agricultural economic activities. Judging from the historical perspective, the physiocrats' argument that agriculture is the only source of national wealth, is quite acceptable. In feudal society the only section that had any surplus was the landowning class, the lords. The feudal lords therefore used this surplus to buy the services of craftsmen who had specialized skills for making objects considered to be luxuries by the common people. Consequently, there was an almost

total absence of markets for manufactured articles.
At that stage, nonfood items necessary for survival
were made by the user of the good himself.
Historians call this practice usufacture. Improved
agricultural techniques such as the use of animals
in farming probably were the origins of the
generation of surplus that enabled man to think in
terms of trade and culture. This must be the stage
at which craftsmanship as a profession developed
and the cities as trading centres started emerging.
In the absence of a modern-day transport system,
water transport was the only major network known to
man and as a consequence all cities were located on
waterways. When trading expanded beyond local
boundaries and eventually beyond the national
boundary, the size of the effective demand became
large enough to necessitate the factory system of
production. It should also be mentioned that
banking and finance developed due to the needs of
trading and commerce. The question may arise as to
why all trading nations did not develop the same
production technology. Apart from different factor
price ratios, other factors influenced the course
of history. Probably the most important factor was
the uneven development of military technology in
different parts of the world. One trading partner
because of its superior military might could
dictate the terms of trade to another or even
politically dominate others as has happened through
the ages. Therefore, all trading partners may not
have the same magnitude of capital accumulation or
it may not be in the best interest of the dominant
partner to let the other develop similar
technology.
    Trading is essentially exchange of
commodities. To exchange each partner must have
some commodities that others want. It so happened
that in the early days of European trading with
Asia, Europe did not have much to offer except gold
and silver bullion, which is not quite
inexhaustible. Hence, the need for technological
development was more urgent for Europe. On the
other hand Spain, being the earliest trading
nation, did not feel the need for technological
change as she discovered rich sources of gold and
silver in the New World, virtually free.
    The question may arise as to why the
relatively rich agrarian civilizations of Asia,
e.g., China and India, failed to develop industrial
technology. History shows that in those regions,
as in many other societies, almost all agricultural

surplus used to be expropriated by the ruling classes which used it for their personal consumption or on unproductive enterprises like building spectacular edifices, like the Great Wall of China or the Taj Mahal of India, to immortalize their own glorious achievements.

GLOBAL DIFFUSION OF TECHNOLOGY

That scientific laws are invariant with respect to time and space is of course a platitude. The discovery of scientific laws is a continuous process that has been going on for thousands of years. The transmission and diffusion of scientific knowledge around the face of the earth have taken place throughout history. All technological developments are nothing but applications of scientific laws to productive enterprises. With the modern transport and communications network, scientific knowledge and information of technological advances spread at a lightning speed around the globe. In this situation, whether some specific technological innovations will be adopted in any part of the world will depend on external constraints. In the absence of any constraint, it is hard to conceive of anything but technological uniformity around the world. What then are the constraints? For the successful adoption of a new technology the first requirement is the appropriate infrastructure, e.g., electric locomotion is an impossibility without adequate electricity generation. Again, we need skilled personnel to operate and manage the technology. The creation of appropriate training facilities and education could also be considered as part of the infrastructure. No less important is a technological culture which creates a positive attitude and psychological discipline for the successful adoption of a new technology. The importance of these factors is aptly demonstrated in the following observation which is equally valid for many Third World countries today:

In Europe the war had destroyed factories, power plants, railroads and other facilities, but the knowledge required to run an industrial economy remained intact. This knowledge, accumulated over a century or more, was drawn on to make good use of the new machines as soon as they were installed. In

79

> most of the Third World there was no such pool
> of experience, and as a result many of the
> imported machines were installed only after
> considerable delay; frequently they were
> operated far below capacity, and they were
> poorly maintained. (Ginzberg, 1982, p.41)

There could also be bureaucratic constraints, as
they are prevalent in many Third World countries,
which could effectively arrest the growth of
technology. On the other hand, one of the main
reasons for Singapore's rapid technological
transition is believed to be its bureaucratic
efficiency.

Of course, the main requirement for
industrialization of a country is the availability
of capital. Given that a sufficient investible
fund is available, the criterion for choice of
technology is always predetermined in a free
enterprise system. An entrepreneur always chooses
the most cost-effective technology, and the most
cost-effective technology mostly happens to be the
latest technology. An exception to this could be
the situation where the specific resource endowment
of a country does not make the latest technology
the most cost-effective. In such a case, there
would not be any entrepreneurial incentive to adopt
such a technology. Again, the absence of the
appropriate infrastructure could stand in the way
of the adoption of the most cost-effective
technology.

Therefore, even if the country is kept in
technological isolation the course of scientific
knowledge and technological advances cannot be
prevented although they may be retarded for a
period. What I mean specifically is that the urge
for the command over power is basic to human nature
and man will find a way of increasing this demand.
Of course, the specific purposes for which this
power will be utilized are likely to vary between
countries. For example, whether the electric motor
would be used inside a washing machine or a
toothbrush might depend on external circumstances
but the electric motor as a social phenomenon is
bound to occur in any society.

It is probably high time that economists, and
development economists in particular, abandon the
classical and the neoclassical world of static
technology and the almost infinite, continuous
variability of labour and capital along the
isoproduct curve at least for industrial produc-

tion.   It is more realistic to think that at any
point in time an entrepreneur faces a set of
technologies with physically different means of
production and qualitatively different labour, and
within each technology there is only a small and
discrete variability of labour and capital.   The
choice then is more among technologies rather than
among specific combinations of labour and capital
within a given technology.   Within the given
constraints the entrepreneur chooses the most cost-
effective technology.   It is always possible that
the optimum choice bypasses the most advanced
technology due to relative factor prices or some
other constraints.   The wisdom of entrepreneurial
choice is something to be followed even by public
enterprises engaged in manufacturing activities.

Development economists often lose sight of the
main purpose of developmental planning.   They talk
about the generation of employment, capital-
labour ratios or capital-output ratios, while the
rate of economic growth remains only in the
background.   For any less developed economy, it is
only rational that its primary aim should be the
maximum possible rate of growth from given rates of
investment.   If that is to be achieved, often the
only resort is the adoption of the most advanced
technology.   Historical data for the United States
and European countries clearly demonstrate that all
through their technological advances not only the
output-labour ratio but also the output-capital
ratio increased significantly.   Any technological
advancement leads to a lower level of both capital
and labour corresponding to the same level of
output or, a higher level of output corresponding
to the same level of capital and labour.   There is
hardly any disagreement about the desirability of
increasing the output-capital ratio, which
singularly determines the general standard of
living in any society.   However, we must keep in
mind that technological change is not the only
means of increasing output-capital ratio.   If the
amount of capital per head is increased, labour
productivity will increase even in the absence of
any technological change.   Again, education and
skill have direct effects on labour productivity.
History shows that the general affluence enjoyed in
the Western world is largely due to increased
labour productivity achieved through technological
progress.   Thus, in the face of a conflict between
output and employment the rational choice is the
maximization of output.

Technology and its Transfer to LDCs

The main preoccupation of development economists with the capital-labour ratio must be due to
their concern about the distribution of income. No
doubt the question of distribution is of vital
importance in any economy, but its priority before
anything else means that in a typical less
developed country equitable distribution of a cake
of a fixed size will push everyone under the
poverty line. Instead of putting the cart before
the horse, the priority should go to efforts in
making the size of the cake bigger in the minimum
possible time. Once the size of the cake is
bigger, we can ponder on how it should be shared.
Otherwise, all that will be achieved is the
distribution of poverty.

There could be several reasons for choosing
the generation of employment, hence, labour-
intensive technology, as the primary objective of
development planning. One of them is that work
gives one dignity and self-esteem, and therefore
unemployment is socially undesirable. This idea is
implicit in the writings of many economists because
they grew up in an industrial society where the
work ethic was paramount. It is doubtful if a work
ethic in the sense used in the European context
exists in the less developed world, and even if it
does it is never nearly as strong. As Frances
Stewart and Paul Streeten (1971,p.150) point out:

> The feeling of worthlessness arising from
> unemployment is likely to be more closely tied
> to long-term urban unemployment than to labour
> underutilization in the rural areas, which has
> a long and respectable history. More rapid
> expansion of urban employment opportunities
> may have little impact on the number of urban
> employed in so far as the expansion of
> employment opportunities adds to the flow of
> migrants from the rural areas seeking
> employment.

The only valid proposition in the debate on
the generation of employment is that employment is
often the only means of generating and distributing
income, especially in the Third World countries.
In the absence of any kind of social security
benefits the situation could be quite appalling.
However, as we all know, the saving grace in those
societies are the social values and extended family
structure which make an employed person gladly
share his income with his peers. An advanced

82

technology always increases the real income of those who are employed and in the process, shared income also increases. An adequate social security system can develop only when the level of aggregate output is high enough to make it possible. Also, it is elementary economics that the level of employment increases with technological advance only when the overall rate of growth exceeds the rate of growth brought about by technological growth. Therefore, it is clear that the main focus of any development planning should be the rate of growth of output.

It is also true that work is desirable mainly because work brings income. Hardly anyone will be willing to work if there is no money in it. Also, people will not be prepared to work if the wages are below a certain level. Sometimes there is government legislation even in the less developed countries on minimum wages. A student of economics will tell us that a majority of unemployed have marginal productivity which is below this legislated minimum wage. Even in the absence of institutional barriers, low productivity is the reason for unemployment of unskilled labour. The solution of this problem is obviously training and education of the unskilled.

It is the common experience of all growing economies that the service sector grows very rapidly. Therefore, it stands to reason that if the rate of growth can be accelerated, additional employment can be found in the service sector. I shall also argue that any development policy should look closely into the alternatives of employment as the means of distributing income. Although it is not the objective of this chapter to prescribe policies for generating employment or distributing income, I would like to emphasize that much of the confusion in setting development objectives arises because it is implicitly assumed that employment is the only means of distributing income. Alternative means of achieving a desirable income distribution in the Third World countries should be the subject matter of an independent debate in its own right.

PRIYATOSH MAITRA ON INDUSTRIALIZATION

Priyatosh Maitra (1980) maintains that industrialization can take place through an industrial revolution or in the absence of an industrial revolution. He describes industrial revolution by way of the example of Britain:

> The profound changes in the system of
> agricultural production that preceded the
> technological revolution reduced the risk of
> famine, and thus provoked the consequent
> changes in socio-economic and political
> organization, the sum total of which may be
> termed the industrial revolution. (Maitra,
> 1980, p.22)

He elaborates the concept further in connection
with the industrialization of Japan, which
according to him took place without an industrial
revolution:

> ...for the successful completion of an
> industrial revolution the following conditions
> must be met. First the agricultural structure
> and organization must be made more productive
> so that more resources can be released for
> technological development and industrial-
> ization. Second, the manufacturing and
> industrial sector must be the product of the
> needs of the primary sector, the largest
> sector, and be based essentially on indigenous
> resources. Borrowed .technology and capital
> will result in dualism and monopolistic
> economic organization in a prematurely
> capitalist economy, thus retarding the best
> possible utilization of resources. Thirdly,
> the fulfillment of the above criteria requires
> fundamental social and economic change.
> (Maitra, 1980, p.54)

Elsewhere in the same treatise Maitra concludes:

> In the mid-twentieth century, underdeveloped
> countries are attempting to bring agrarian
> change through land reform, but instead of
> developing indigenous technology of their own
> with resources released through such changes,
> they are depending on imported technology from
> labour-short, high income countries which have
> different histories and factor endowments.
> Consequently, indigenous resources are lying
> idle and unproductive thereby perpetuating the
> problems of underdevelopment and of so-called
> overpopulation. (Maitra, 1980, p.152)

Accordingly, Maitra maintains that the general

welfare of the whole population could be increased only with an indigenous technology that evolves on the basis of specific factor endowments of the country. For that to take place not only should the country be placed in complete technological isolation but also all the modern technology of foreign technology should be completely uprooted and banished from the country. Moreover, since an industrial revolution must embrace the majority of the working population, it is implied that the indigenous technology must be labour-intensive.

Whereas in this chapter I have stressed the importance of technological determinism, Maitra believes just in the opposite. Innovations in agriculture prior to the Industrial Revolution in England took place due to population pressure. But Maitra does not tell us what caused this population pressure. The industrial sector initially developed to meet the needs of agriculture. According to him all modern technology is the result of the capitalist profit motive. The process is somewhat like this: In the beginning of capitalism, division of labour was the only means of increasing per capita output, which led to a higher rate of capital accumulation. The higher rate of accumulation leading to increased investment, in the absence of any technological change, raised the demand for labour which was somewhat in fixed supply. Therefore wages rose which led to a lower rate of profit. This is what led to the search for a technology where capital could be substituted for labour, hence the emergence of modern technology.

The above thesis could be subjected to several criticisms. To start with, Maitra's model of the British Industrial Revolution is based on faulty observations. It is generally accepted that an agricultural surplus is a necessary precondition for any industrial development. It is true that the agrarian revolution in Britain increased agricultural production enormously in absolute terms. But the statistic cited in Maitra's book shows that per capita agricultural output hardly increased. Estimates made by Paul Bairoch (1969) show that the rate of growth of agricultural production in Britain during the agrarian revolution was less than 1 percent. Compared to that, the rate of increase of agricultural output in most present-day developing countries is significantly higher. There is ample historical evidence that before and during the period of

Technology and its Transfer to LDCs

industrial revolution Britain continuously imported agricultural products from its colonies in America, Asia and even from Eastern Europe. In 1815, the Corn Law was introduced to restrict the importation of food grain due to its falling price. Even then it could be imported on payment of a duty that varied according to its current price (Heaton, 1948, pp.416-418 and 640-41). But then only the importation of foodgrain was restricted. From the very beginning pressure mounted to repeal those laws. Later Malthus was noted to have said that England should leave the growing of corn to America and concentrate in manufactures and commerce. Therefore, it stands to reason that even agricultural surplus may not be a necessary precondition of industrialization. It is doubtful if it is the pressure of population that increased agricultural production in England. It could well be that growing trade and manufacturing opened up the possibility of profitable farming, i.e., of the commercialization of agriculture. However, it seems that this controversy is similar to that of the chicken and the egg. We have seen that what matters most is the rate of accumulation of capital. Contrary to Maitra's belief, British industrialization in the eighteenth or nineteenth century was not based on full utilization of indigenous resources. The growth of the cotton textile industry, which probably was the main focus of the British Industrial Revolution, entirely depended on imported cotton, and most of the finished product had to be sold in overseas markets, which was accomplished even by using force. Similar examples of other British industrial products are plentiful. The 'socio-economic and political' changes, as described by Maitra, occurred due to the pressure of the rising bourgeois class, and not due to the pressure of the agricultural sector. About the full utilization of the labour force, during the early days of industrial revolution in England, I can only quote Leo Huberman (1946, p.146):

> They (the capitalists) paid as little in wages as they had to. They were in the market for as much labour-power as they could use at as little cost as was necessary to buy it. Since women and children could tend the machines and would be paid less than men, women and children were given work while the man in the house was often idle.

Technology and its Transfer to LDCs

As for the state of general welfare of the
population at large, we only have to visualize the
bleak picture so vividly painted by Charles
Dickens. It is then clear that Maitra's thesis is
hardly based on much historical evidence. I have
already discussed at length the question of labour-
intensive technology in this chapter and have shown
that rational choice would normally lead to the
most up-to-date technology in the absence of non-
economic restrictions. The rate of employment
generation will then depend on the speed at which
the economy is expanding. Nevertheless, there may
be strong adherents to his thesis since it promotes
development of indigenous technology. The question
then is: should a country keep itself in technological isolation? From our discussion on the development of technology it should be clear that an
affirmative answer to the above question would mean
that we have to rediscover the wheel, to use a
metaphor. In the process vast resources will be
wasted and the economy will remain in a low income
trap much longer than is necessary. The main
purpose of development planning, namely rapid
growth of the economy, will then be severely
undermined.

The last point I would like to make is that
there is nothing sacrilegious about importation of
foreign technology. History abounds with successful adoption and adaptation of technology of non-
indigenous origin. Wherever that happened the rate
of industrialization accelerated. As Caldwell
(1972,p.5) said,

If Europeans were imitative and adoptive in
the early middle ages, the English were, in
the seventeenth and early eighteenth
centuries, commonly regarded by their European
neighbours as unoriginal imitators of
continental inventions; and this was just
before the efflorescence of English inventive
genius that accompanied the industrial
revolution. More recently the Japanese have
had the same reputation as copiers; this time
of the Europeans, English and Americans. But
it is clear enough now that the Japanese have
acquired their own technological momentum. In
brief it seems probable that imitation,
adoption and adaptation are essential steps
whereby the art of invention is transmitted
from one culture to another. But willingness

to submit to instruction, as it were must be there in the first place.

Maitra (1985) would still argue that in the past successful technology transfer was possible in those countries only because the state of technology at that stage was far less advanced than it is today. The invalidity of this argument would be quite obvious in the light of the elaborate discussion in the earlier sections of this chapter. Moreover, it is not difficult to find cases of successful technology transfer in recent years.

CONCLUSION

Development efforts of the so-called Third World have been criticized on the ground that they have followed the Western model. Since the East is not the West these efforts are doomed to failure. What then are the alternatives? One could think of a model of socialist development in the twentieth century. There could be some model common to all less developed countries, or each country could find a model unique to itself. To me the whole controversy is confusing and misleading. While it is true that most of the development efforts of the Third World have been unsuccessful or, at least unsatisfactory we should not summarily put the blame on the Western model. If the model has been found worth following, it must be because the model was successful in the West. First, we must spell out what is exactly meant by the Western model. If by the Western model we mean modern productive technology, we are talking of something concrete. The reality is that the same technology has been found useful and successful by some latecomers in the scene of industrialization. If it failed in other countries, it is then worth researching the causes of this failure. If an experimental scientist finds that the result of the same experiment is different in two different places, he will immediately look for the causes of the difference in the conditions surrounding the experiment. If we follow this method, it will immediately become obvious that the institutional framework, in which the new technology is transplanted, is the cause. A country can import the technology, and thereby the command over energy but they have to be combined with social, political and cultural factors for their proper use so that the standard of living could be raised, which cannot be readily imported. In this context the remark made by Arnost Tauber (1974,p.103) is worth quoting:

> The situation which we are facing now, is, of course, not a failure of modern science and technology but of the methods of its transfer and introduction, and last but not the least of the existing social structure of the developing countries.

There are always two types of diametrically opposite forces in any cultural milieu. One type always resists and vigorously fights the introduction or invasion of any hitherto unknown or unused mode of operation: the old adage being, "We do things differently." At the same time the other type welcomes the change from the tradition. The success of any technology transfer would then depend on which force happens to be dominant. The question then is: Should we reject an efficient productive technology or should we try and change the institutional framework so that the technology becomes useful? The answer should be obvious. The way to proceed is to try and create an environment and infrastructure that is suitable for the adoption of the technology. The task is by no means easy as the Third World countries are mostly ruled by plutocracies or military juntas who have their own biases and vested interests.

Here I have tried to establish that knowhow, which is the very basis of production, represents the embodiment of scientific knowledge, whether in human beings, machine or physical medium, and has a universal character. Like truth, scientific knowledge and its applications cannot be nationalized. Moreover, man's repertoire of scientific knowledge is one of the few things that is, in general, not subject to the law of entropy. In fact, it is anti-entropic in the sense that it is always growing due to the insatiable human thirst for further knowledge. In the long run, this scientific knowledge is going to spread across national boundaries, although its applications may depend on specific circumstances.

In recent years, literature on economic development distinguishes between 'growth' and 'development'. Development is supposed to mean a mixed basket of equitable distribution of income, generation of employment for all in the range of

89

working age, provision of health and medical services for the masses, provision of clean water for all, universal education and training, transport and communications, etc., whereas growth is supposed to refer to either the growth of gross national product or the rate of industrialization. No doubt, all those things mentioned under development sound grand and are highly desirable. At the same time we have to ask the simple question: Can a less developed economy afford any of those desirable things without rapid growth of GNP?[3]

NOTES

1. Efficiency can be measured both in terms of the first law and the second law of thermo-dynamics. Total efficiency then is the product of the first law efficiency and the second law efficiency. Thus, if first law efficiency is .8 or 80% and the second law efficiency is .2, total efficiency then is .16 or 16%. Here we are concerned with the total efficiency.

2. For a detailed discussion see Giulisno (1982, pp.124-135).

3. I am indebted to Professor Priyatosh Maitra of the University of Otago, New Zealand, who initially suggested I write the paper on which this chapter is based and encouraged me during its completion. I also had a number of fruitful discussions with Mr. Richard Nolan of the University of New South Wales which helped me to clarify some conceptual problems. However, I am solely responsible for all the errors and omissions.

REFERENCES

Bairoch, Paul (1969) **Agriculture and the Industrial Revolution**, Fontana, London

Bernal, J.D. (1965) **Science in History**, C.A. Watts & Co. Ltd, London

Caldwell, D.S.L. (1972) **Technology, Science and History**, Heineman, London

Demczynski, S. (1969) 'The Tools of Cybernetic Revolution' pp. 10-28 in J. Rose (ed.) **Surveys of Cybernetics**, Gordon and Breach Science Publishers, New York

Dickson, David (1974) **Alternative Technology and the Politics of Technological Change**, Fontana/Collins, Glasgow

Ginzberg, Eli (1982) 'The Mechanization of Work', **Scientific American**, 247, 3, September, pp. 38-47

Giulisno, Vincent E. (1982) 'The Mechanization of Office Work' **Scientific American**, 247, 3, September, pp. 124-135

Heaton, Herbert (1948) **Economic History of Europe**, Harper and Row, New York

Huberman, Leo (1946) **Man's Worldly Goods**, People's Publishing House, New Delhi

Kuznets, Simon (1965) **Economic Growth and Structure**, W.W. Norton, New York

Lenin, V.I. (1984) **The State and Revolution**, Progress Publishers, Moscow

Maitra, Priyatosh (1980) **The Mainspring of Economic Development**, Croom Helm, London

Maitra, Priyatosh (1985) 'Population, Technology and Economic Development', paper presented to **The 14th Conference of Economists**, Australian Economics Society, 1985

Marx, Karl and Engels, Frederick (1970) **Manifesto of the Communist Party**, Foreign Languages Press, Peking

Rosenberg, Nathan (1972) **Technology and American Economic Growth**, Harper Torchbooks, New York

Stewart, Frances and Paul Streeten (1971) 'Conflicts Between Output and Employment Objectives in Developing Countries', **Oxford Economic Papers**, 23, 2, pp. 145-168

Tauber, Arnost (1974) 'Some Remarks on the Transfer of Technique and Technology in the Developing Countries', pp. 100-109 in Julian West (ed.), **Alternatives in Development**, Pergamon Press, Oxford

Chapter Five

PARTNERSHIP IN RESEARCH: A NEW MODEL FOR
DEVELOPMENT ASSISTANCE

Joseph V. Remenyi

INTRODUCTION

Technology transfer has always been at centre stage
of development theory and practice. However, it is
only very recently, within the last generation,
that due emphasis has been given to 'appropriate'
technology, and the dearth of same for ready
transfer to less developed countries. The reasons
for this late perception are many, but relate
fundamentally to the models of development that
have guided thinking and action in foreign aid.
      This chapter examines the link between
development models and the perception they provide
of the technology transfer and technology
generation problems. The thesis of it is that the
technical assistance model is no longer the optimal
model for technology transfer and development.
Only where the indigenous capacity to do research
remains weak and limited is the foreign expert,
technical assistance model still an efficient means
of delivering development assistance in the
research for development arena. With growth in
research capacity, especially in Asia and South
America, a new model is needed. This new model
must respond to locally perceived priorities and
needs in research, and must maximize the capacity
for complementarity in research collaboration. In
the long term, this implies that donor countries
and agencies will have to re-examine their mode of
operating, with a view to reducing dependence on
aid delivery through technical assistance.
      There are many options available to replace
the technical assistance model, but in the final
analysis strategies will be needed that complement
and develop the skills and capacities of developing
countries rather than substituting for these. This

92

will require a thorough-going assessment of each donor's comparative advantages in foreign aid, with an eye to the mutual benefit available to both donor and recipient country from an appropriate shift towards specialization. This shift will tend to occur naturally the more that donor countries rely on developing country collaboration in the identification, design, and implementation of research for development projects. Moreover, the shift will tend to integrate bilateral aid-trade relations along lines of national self-interest.

FROM DEVELOPMENT MODELS TO PRACTICE

In the contemporary lexicon of development assistance, development is portrayed as a process by which less advanced economies 'catch up' to the more advanced. In classical economics this was not so; the issue was far simpler. The classical economists believed development to be a natural progression from a lower to a higher state of material and social well-being (Smith, 1776, pp. 69-83; Winch, 1965; and Spengler, 1975, p.392 f. espec.). Even when different economies have attained the maturity of the stationary state, there is no hint in Adam Smith's **Wealth of Nations** that they will have achieved 'equality' in material wealth. Obvious and well-recognized initial differences in resource endowments precluded even the thought of such a result arising (Smith, 1776, Book II, Chs. 1, 5 and Book III, Ch.1). In classical economics, therefore, the question of 'appropriate' technology transfer could not arise. Appropriateness depended entirely on the stage of development attained. No special intervention was necessary to ensure that technology transfer would be consistent with the socio-cultural and economic needs of the technology-importing country. Technology would not transfer unless it was appropriate, and selection could be left to the descriminating power of the invisible hand of the market.
A subtle but important change accompanied the neoclassical revision of classical economics. In place of the rigid stages process, neoclassical economics spoke of an appropriate international 'division of labour'. Individual economies fitted into this pattern of 'mutual cooperation and benefit' depending upon the bountifulness they enjoy in the distribution of their factors of

93

production - land, labour, capital and 'state of
the art'. The latter was a rich rag-bag of
elements designed to capture the importance of
entrepreneurship, institutional complexity,
intellectual heritage and capacity to exploit the
channels of international trade. Contrast Davis
(1930), Rosenstein-Rodan (1943), Lewis (1954), and
Higgins (1956). Here too, however, the viability
of technology transfer continued to be seen as
neutral vis-a-vis the socio-cultural milieu and
entirely dependent upon market forces. Indeed, the
success of modern 'enclaves' in the midst of
backwardness seemed to confirm the transferability
of even the most sophisticated technologies, given
the political will to carry it through.

Until well into the 1950s the direct
transferability of technology from the advanced
temperate economies of Europe to the humid tropics
was an article of faith. It seemed to be confirmed
by the early success of nascent manufacturing
ventures, especially textiles in South Asia. This
gave rise to a fear that the primitive, typically
labour-abundant economies might adopt strategies of
development that would undermine global prosperity.
These economies were seen as having the ability to
eschew their designated place in the international
division of labour in favour of industries directly
competitive, rather than complementary, with those
of Britain and Europe. Writing on the eve of World
War II, Dennis Robertson (1938) lamented the loss
in global 'gains from trade' that the collapse of
free trade in the 1920s and 1930s had occasioned.
His prescription for regaining lost ground was to
'do our best to widen and exploit gaps in
comparative advantage'. He wrote:

> In manufacture there is still room for
> specialisation between the simple and the
> complex, the low grade and the high, the goods
> for consumption and the machine that makes the
> goods. If...manufacturing industries abroad
> are assisted to grow on sound lines...the
> inevitable decline in the export of directly
> competitive goods should be accompanied by
> increasing exports of capital and other
> specialised goods. (Robertson, 1938, p.13)

The fear of global destabilization that could
result from 'unwarranted' competition from the
newly industrializing countries of the developing
world was a phenomenon largely brushed aside by the

onset of World War II. Nonetheless, it did provide an impetus for innovative thinking of some importance. It provided the intellectual climate for a rapid rise in popularity of the 'balanced growth' and 'big-push' theories of the Rosenstein-Rodan (1943) variety. It also created renewed awareness of the long-term dependence of successful national development on domestic rather than global factors. In 1943, Frankel, writing at the Oxford Institute of Statistics, summarized contemporary thought in the following warning: "The industrialization of a country...holds some dangers for other countries, if the production of manufactured goods is undertaken mainly for foreign and not for home consumption, or if the bulk of the population does not benefit from...industrialization' (p.196). He drew from this insight the further conclusion that foreign aid "...should be linked up with...social improvements to be undertaken simultaneously with industrialization, creating this larger market for foreign goods and lessening the tendency to export abroad the produce of new industries" (Frankel, 1943, p.196).

There is much that we could draw from these quotations. Suffice to say, it is to be lamented that the prescription that industrialization (here used in its broadest sense to include the modernization of agriculture and the rural sector generally) ought to benefit the bulk of the population did not receive the attention it deserved. In part this is attributable to the myopia that surrounded the topic of technical progress, capital accumulation and international technology transfer. Distributional issues were simply not recognized as significant. Consequently, appropriate technology generation or transfer were not prominent in the problem set recognized by development economists. It was to take more than a decade before the problem of development was to be perceived as involving an intimate link between capital accumulation, capital transfer and the flow of 'appropriate' technology.

The received wisdom in the 1950s on development assistance reflected a simplistic perception of the development problem. In many respects, it was a perception that was a retrogression on the rich insights of the classical economists and pre-Keynesian neoclassical economists of earlier generations. Recovery from the disruptions of the 1930s depression and the success of industrialization efforts of 'backward' economies during the war years of the 40s and 50s, seemed to confirm the widespread belief that there is an advantage in being a late starter in the development stakes. All the hard work of technology generation and scientific discovery on which the industrialized countries had had to wait were now available for the choosing. All that remained was to generate the flow of savings for investment, disseminate the necessary knowledge as to the technology available and to enlighten a few community leaders who could act as 'models' for others to imitate. All this could be achieved using techniques of modern macro-economic planning, pioneered by the Soviets, exploited by the free-market economies during World War II, and legitimized by Keynesian macro-economic practice in the late 1940s and throughout the 1950s. A new era of development as 'stages' in the inevitable path of economic growth quickly took hold, led by W.W. Rostow's **The Stages of Economic Growth** (1960). The propositions in this book seemed to mesh easily with the formula approach to development planning that was embodied in the plethora of five-year development plans generated in the late 1950s and 1960s. They embraced, in an indiscriminate way, the precriptions of those who argued for import-substitution strategies, the key variables being apparent high-potential foreign exchange savings and an adequately high domestic savings rate, however achieved. The cause of development thinking was derailed; the critical issues of appropriate technology and comparative advantage were virtually lost to the inherited wisdom until almost the 1970s.

REDISCOVERING AGRICULTURE AND THE RATIONAL FARMER

A seminal volume that helped return development thinking and practice from the errors of the simplistic formulae approach of Rostow, the ECLA (Economic Commission for Latin America) import-substitution thesis, two-sector surplus labour models of development and Soviet-style five-year plans, was **Transforming Traditional Agriculture** by T.W. Schultz (1964). In hindsight it seems almost incredible that this work had to be written. The development specialists had become so preoccupied with development as 'industrial revolution' that they lost sight of the importance of agriculture in the whole of the developing world. This bias also contributed to the belief that the technology necessary for modernization was available, waiting to be taken off the shelf. Hence the global currency given in the 1940s and 1950s to extension, community development, and other technology diffusion strategies of development. It never occurred to the proponents of these strategies that the source of their failure was the absence of 'appropriate' technologies for transfer. Rather, the explanation for failure was sought in emotive and unsubstantiated references to irrational action by the peasants of these backward or primitive societies. Schultz challenged this explanation. Moreover, he rejected the 'exploit' agriculture to 'fund' development in other sectors strategy that the surplus labour models of development promoted.

Schultz hypothesized a 'poor but efficient' subsistence agriculture sector, which was in long-run equilibrium consistent with available technology. The Schultz thesis rejected the assumption that apparently underemployed resources in the agricultural sector could be more efficiently employed in other sectors of the economy without loss. He argued instead that since agricultural growth is essential to economic growth, development demands investment in rural infrastructure and financial markets, plus support for research and human capital improvement to develop new technologies to raise the production possibility frontier. Schultz summarized his views as follows:

> The economic basis of the slow growth of a penny economy is not to be found generally in observable inefficiencies in the way the traditional agricultural factors of production are allocated; nor is it to be explained by sub-optimum rates of savings and investment in such traditional factors, because the rate of return at the margins is generally too low to warrant additional savings and investment, given anything like normal preferences and motives. The economic basis for rapid growth under these circumstances does not lie in exhortations pertaining to work and thrift. The key to growth is in acquiring and using effectively some modern...factors of production...rapid sustained growth rests heavily on particular investments in farm people related to the new skills and new

97

knowledge that farm people must acquire to succeed at the game of growth from agriculture. (Schultz, 1964, pp. 176-7)

Theorists of agricultural development have been quick to expand on the Schultz thesis. Prominent among these are Yujiro Hayami and Vernon Ruttan (1971) in their book **Agricultural Development in International Perspectives**. Their 'induced innovation' hypothesis provided new insights into explaining the development experience, while also suggesting a way in which to assess technology's appropriateness. It was an important contributor to the necessary intellectual base needed to popularize on-farm research and ultimately, the rationale for design and use of farmer-managed trials in farmers' fields. (A more detailed and systematic account of the evolution of thinking in the agricultural development literature can be found in Coxhead and Remenyi, 1985; and Eicher and Staatz, 1984.)

At the practical level, however, Schultz's work, which began in the mid-1950s and culminated in the book published in 1964, was instrumental in guiding the actions of the USA-based philanthropies, especially the Rockefeller and Ford Foundations. He interacted with Rockefeller's program in Mexico and was a frequent consultant to the nascent international agriculture program at Ford, headed by the newly appointed vice-president Dr. Forrest F. Hill. Ford and Rockefeller looked to Schultz to critically examine what was recognized as a radical new approach to agricultural development in the tropics. This approach began with the assumption that low agricultural yields in the tropics are the result of a dearth of technology. Moreover, by concentrating effort so as to specialize on commodities important to the bulk of farmers and consumers in many countries, new and improved technology transferable across political boundaries could be generated. It is now a matter of history that the effort began with wheat and rice and resulted in the so-called 'green revolution'. No comprehensive account yet exists of the green revolution, however, some useful insights can be found in Breth (1985), Critchfield (1982), Dalrymple (1978), Leaf (1983), Lipton and Longhurst (1985), Ruttan (1982), Scobie and Posada (1977) and Wortman and Cummings (1981).

Few issues in development in the past thirty

years have generated as much debate as the green
revolution. Critics have attacked the new
technology it has generated as excessively
disruptive to traditional peasant societies, biased
in favour of wealthy farmers and larger land-
owners, the cause of disturbing increases in rural
landlessness, growth in rural unemployment, and
many other social ills (Pearse, 1980). As it
happens, few of these charges have been sustained
and the early judgement of the green revolution's
supporters has been vindicated by experience. As
Lester Brown (1970) put it: "It (the green
revolution) is literally helping to fill hundreds
of millions of rice bowls once only half full. For
those for whom hunger is a way of life, technology
can offer no greater reward" (p.4).

It is not intended here, however, to review
the voluminous literature that has sprouted on the
pros and cons of the green revolution. Rather, I
wish to use the model on which the research for
development of high-yielding varieties was based to
argue for a new model. Moreover, the new model
follows from the very same principles on which the
old was based, yet, if change is not forthcoming we
can expect the flow of 'appropriate' technologies
to decline more than is optimal.

Once the dearth of available technology
relevant to tropical agriculture was recognized, a
critical choice faced development planners and
donor agencies. This choice was between support
for research programs within existing national
agricultural research systems and support to new
efforts in completely separate research
institutions. The United Nations, through UNDP and
the FAO, favoured building up the capacity of
national programs, as did most development
professionals including a majority of those
employed by the major US philanthropies, the Ford,
Rockefeller and Kellogg Foundations. Indeed,
Rockefeller had begun its support for tropical
agricultural research within national programs in
Mexico, Peru, India, Pakistan and Taiwan. By the
late 1950s, however, the experience had prompted a
rethink that strongly reflected the influence of
the new vice-president at the Ford Foundation, an
economist from Cornell, Dr. Forest F. Hill.

Both the Ford and Rockefeller Foundations had
been active in agricultural development in the
tropics throughout the 1950s. The Ford Foundation,
in particular, had major commitments to traditional
community development style programs in South Asia

and the Middle East. Rockefeller, on the other hand, worked more directly with national agricultural research programs. Neither had achieved a major breakthrough. Dr. J. George Harrar, an agronomist and head of the Rockefeller global effort, and 'Frosty' Hill, his counterpart at Ford, were conscious of this and discussed it at length in their many meetings. It is a happy coincidence that Hill and Harrar worked so well together. The ability to relate well to biological scientists is one of Frosty Hill's unique characteristics that soon cemented a long and lasting partnership between these two men, and subsequently the two Foundations. Through its country programs, especially in Mexico, Taiwan and India, Rockefeller had the research experience on which to build, while Ford had the money to fund a major international experiment in research for development. That experiment was IRRI (International Rice Research Institute) and CIMMYT (International Centre for the Improvement of Maize and Wheat), the rice and wheat/maize research centres from which the green revolution and the present-day International Agricultural Research Centre (IACR) system of the Consultative Group for International Agricultural Research (CGIAR) derive. It is not intended to review the history of the IARC system or the CGIAR; that must be left to another place. However, brief accounts can be found in Anderson, et al, (1986), Pinstrup-Andersen (1982), Ruttan (1982), Wortman (1973) and the World Bank's **World Development Report** (1982).

IRRI and CIMMYT did not come into being without opposition. Even within the Foundations there were those who felt that the objectives sought could' be achieved within the context of existing national agriculture research systems/ programs in the developing world. The funding that IRRI and CIMMYT would require was seen as competing directly for funds that could be used to strengthen national systems of agricultural research. However, Harrar and Hill had become convinced that to work through existing national systems would excessively delay the achievement of results. The immediate task of raising rice, wheat and maize yields was too urgent in the face of chronic famine and starvation, especially in Asia, to justify taking what was believed to be the slow road. Today, with more than two decades of success behind us, we are apt to miss the genuine sense of crisis that prevailed in the late 1950s and early 1960s. We do well to

100

remind ourselves by referring back to Segal's 1965 classic **The Crisis of India.** Today India is a food exporter and not the famine-plagued focus of the global food problem of twenty years ago.

It serves our purpose, however, to review some of the obstacles perceived as justifying the creation of commodity-specific research centres, rather than working through existing institutions. Primary amongst these was the philosophy behind the new strategy. It was missionary and revolutionary in its conception. It eschewed the purist pursuit-of-knowledge approach to scientific endeavour in favour of a research program that would discover ways of raising yields on farmers' fields, irrespective of whether the causes were well understood or not. The search was on for 'what works' rather than 'why it works', though the latter was not to be ignored: it simply took second priority to the primary goal of increasing yields on farmers' fields. Vernon Ruttan (1982) described this new approach "as audacious in the extreme", but concluded: "I am now convinced that the articulation of the IRRI objective in terms of impact on rice yield rather than in terms of contribution to scientific knowledge about rice was a key factor ..."(Ruttan, 1982, p.8). But why was this a key factor?

The answer lies in how agricultural research was conducted in the inherited institutions of the day. Typically it was discipline-bound rather than commodity or problem oriented; it was laboratory-based, with the difficult and less glamorous work in farmers' fields left to lesser mortals employed in the extension services; and it was not free to work across political boundaries, able to draw from experiences common to other cereal producers in similar agroecological zones. Biggs (1985) offers a modern litany of these problems. Moreover, there was a recognized shortage in a critical input – the supply of well-trained and experienced plant breeders. These factors combined to convince the Ford and Rockefeller Foundations that a concentrated effort within a commodity-based, problem-oriented 'international' agriculture research centre was the best alternative. Looking back on where they had been and what had been achieved, Frosty Hill summarized the consensus in the following way: "Experience suggests that... efforts to increase yields rapidly and substantially...in a country currently following traditional agricultural practices are likely to be

101

disappointing and often wasteful of resources"
(Hill and Hardin, 1971, p.23).

Four years later, Frosty wrote to Lowell
Hardin:

> International centers were created to focus on
> food production research problems because of
> the belief...that specialised institutions
> could help accelerate the rate at which
> improved high-yield production technology
> suitable for use in LDCs is developed.
> International centers were not viewed as
> possible substitutes for research services in
> LDCs or for the efforts of bilateral,
> international or private agencies assisting
> them in their efforts. (Hill and Hardin,
> 1975, para. 4, p. 2)

The model on which the IARC system was
developed made sense and fitted the circumstances
of a world where human capital was one of the
scarcest resources. While the number of scientists
indigenous to tropical economies remained small,
the need to rely on modes of operation that
economize on expertise was a rational reaction to a
limiting resource constraint. The **Second Review
Report of CGIAR** described the evolution of the
model as follows:

> The initial model of the International Centre
> involved a "critical mass" of scientists
> concentrating their effort on a single
> commodity...
> At first, most of the Centres concentrated
> their research effort at their headquarters.
> Links were built with national programmes
> through testing networks, training courses and
> information services. Progressively, some
> core research was established at other
> locations in order to expand the ecological
> basis for breeding programmes and for wider
> validation of the results obtained at the
> Centres. In recent years the System has seen
> major increases in outposted staff working
> closely with staff of national programmes, in
> core programmes and in technical assistance
> projects. Although concentration of physical
> plant and staff at each headquarters remains
> the basis of the Centre model, the operation
> of the research programmes has moved signi-
> ficantly in the direction of regional activi-

ties and closer association with national programmes. (CGIAR Secretariat, 1981, p.60)

BEYOND SIMPLE COOPERATION WITH IARCs AND FOREIGN EXPERTS

The IARC model has borrowed from the success of others and reflects the dominant role that 'technical assistance' programs have come to play in international development assistance generally. However, the climate is now ripe, especially in research for development, for a significant move away from the technical assistance mould. The cadre of research scientists ready, willing and able to work as equal partners with their counterparts in the advanced economies has increased from a handful at the start of the first UN Development Decade to many thousands today. Anderson, et al. (1986) report that "only three African agricultural scientists were working in all the experiment stations in Kenya, Uganda and Tanzania in 1964" (p.82). By 1982, Kenya alone had more than 300.

This increase is a rich legacy and a testament to the successful efforts made in the last thirty years to build up the stock of available human capital in the Third World. Simultaneously, considerable success has also been achieved in nurturing and strengthening indigenous research-oriented institutions in both the public and the private sector. Today, there are, therefore, substantially increased numbers of colleagues in the humid and semi-arid tropics with whom developed country scientists can collaborate and share the task of technology generation. Moreover, these colleagues have a depth of local knowledge, language skills and socio-cultural perceptions that alter the comparative advantage of the foreign expert in development assistance.

In decades gone by, the foreign expert largely had a monopoly of the science leadership involved in research for development. The developing country input was often limited to following instructions regarding field experiments, management of experimental plots, or work normally assigned in Western research centres to laboratory technicians or research assistants. In many cases the developing country partner worked to the requirements of a foreign adviser rather than with a colleague. This worked quite well and fostered

alumni-style relations between the 'teacher and the
student'. It also exploited the critical scarce
resource (i.e., the skills of the foreign adviser)
to the full while maximizing the opportunity for
both formal and on-the-job training. It provided a
means by which continuity in contact and some
research kudos could be dispensed through
involvement of developing country people in plant
yield, nursery activity, insect screening, disease
testing and other plant-breeding-related networks.
The exchange of seed and results gave participants
a sense of belonging to a global fraternity,
serviced and cared for by the senior scientists who
regularly visited 'co-operators'.
     As successful as these cooperative networks
were, however, they too are subject to diminishing
returns and diminishing relevance to the
increasingly situation-specific problems of Third
World agriculture. The early gains from the 'plant
breeding' strategy of cereals research of the green
revolution, especially at the IARCs but also in the
stronger national programs in Asia and South
America, appear to have been made. Change in the
architecture of the cereal plant to exploit the
benefits of the dwarfing gene has essentially been
achieved, as has day-length insensitivity. These
were fundamental breakthroughs of relevance over
many agroecological zones, but especially where the
environment could be controlled through the use of
irrigation and inorganic fertilizers. Massive
spillover benefits were achieved, with consumers
being the major gainers through lower staple food
prices. In the future, however, the challenge will
be to do the same for non-cereal crops, especially
legumes, pulses, root crops and horticulture and
increase yields and rural productivity in less
favourable and less manipulable environments. Here
local knowledge and understanding will be critical,
with the comparative advantage of the foreign
expert confined in many instances to complementary
disciplinary skills. However, if the benefits of
this complementarity are to be harvested, research
will increasingly need to rely not on teacher-
student-style cooperation but on collaboration as
colleagues and equal partners in research.

THE PROOF OF THE PUDDING IS IN THE EATING

The shift toward collaboration and partnership in
research for development is in its infancy, but

evident in several areas of official development
assistance. The USAID (United States Agency for
International Development) funded Small Ruminant
Collaborative Research Support Program (CRSP),
begun in 1979, is one of the earliest examples
(Blond, 1984). Another is Canada's International
Development Research Centre (IDRC), formed in 1970,
which has increasingly eschewed projects relying
primarily on technical assistance in favour of
co-operation and, in more recent years, genuine
collaboration. Similarly, the international
centres of the CGIAR system are moving away from
the technical assistance model, especially in their
outreach and farming systems research activities.
This is especially so in their relations with
countries that have built up their human capital
base in their national agricultural research and
extension systems.

An institutional innovation that has taken the
philosophy of equal partnership in development
assistance further than any other organization in
international agricultural research for development
is the Australian Centre for International
Agricultural Research (ACIAR). ACIAR is an
innovation. It is a statutory body created by an
Act of the Australian Parliament in June 1982,
commissioned to facilitate partnership in research
as a new initiative within Australia's bilateral
foreign aid program. It is an experiment also in
that the enabling legislation includes a sunset
clause requiring the Centre to show cause to a
ministerial review in its tenth year why the Centre
should continue to exist.

It is not the intention here to provide a
justification for the existence of ACIAR nor to
present an apologia for its style and activities.
Rather, as an innovation ACIAR relies on full
collaboration in the identification, design,
implementation, monitoring and review of its
projects, and this bears attention. The lessons of
ACIAR'S experience, even at this early stage, are
of relevance not only to development assistance
professionals and agencies generally, but also to
the clients of international development assistance
- our partners in the global war on want and
poverty.

The functions of ACIAR, as described in its
Act are:
>(a) to formulate programs and policies with
>respect to agricultural research for either or
>both of the following purposes:

(i) identifying agricultural problems of developing countries;
(ii) finding solutions to agricultural problems of developing countries
(b) to commission agricultural research by persons or institutions in Australia (whether the research is to be conducted in Australia or overseas) in accordance with such programs and policies; and
(c) to communicate to persons and institutions the results of such agricultural research.

In the consultations with the Australian and international scientific and aid communities prior to the decision to establish ACIAR, it was considered that Australia had a special contribution to make to development in the field of agricultural research. This was because of the existence of its extensive and highly successful network of research establishments and their comparative advantage derived from working in physical environments similar to those in much of the developing world.

Although ACIAR formally came into existence in May 1982, it has (to June, 1986) actively engaged in collaborative research for development activities for only three years. In that time 95 research projects have been put in place, covering the eleven program areas shown in Table 5.1. These projects involve more than two hundred partners, at least half of which are overseas institutions. Their contribution to projects in terms of personnel, facilities, logistics and direct funding, typically at least matches that from ACIAR. In other words, ACIAR projects have had a multiplier effect of at least 3 on aid and associated investments in research for agricultural development. In a real sense, therefore, support for collaborative research 'drives the aid dollar further'.

As of June 1986, ACIAR's accumulated commitment to research projects totalled some $Aust.45 million. The largest proportion of this amount is committed to projects in Southeast Asia and the South Pacific, where Australia's principal political and economic interests are concentrated. ACIAR's largest single project, however, is in Africa. It seeks to capitalize on the agroecological analogue that exists between parts of northern Australia and East Africa as a base for examining technologies that may form a basis for

Table 5.1: The Per Cent Distribution of ACIAR (Australian Centre for International Agricultural Research) Research Expenditures to June 1986 by Region and Program

Programs	South Asia	S.East Asia	S.Pacif. & PNG	Africa/ W.Asia	China	Total
1. Plant improvement	3.89	7.90	2.87	0.00	2.45	17.10
2. Plant protection	0.85	2.76	1.56	0.09	0.69	5.95
3. Soil & water mngt	0.00	2.29	0.00	0.00	0.00	2.29
4. Plant nutrition	0.52	11.87	0.06	0.21	0.00	12.65
5. Postharvest techn.	0.14	15.69	1.29	0.14	0.00	17.25
6. Farming systems	0.63	1.64	1.77	8.77	0.00	12.82
7. Socio-economics	0.00	1.79	3.56	0.00	0.00	5.36
8. Livestock	5.62	8.79	0.51	0.49	2.62	18.04
9. Fisheries	0.59	0.95	2.43	0.00	0.00	3.97
10. Forestry	0.00	0.27	0.00	2.38	0.72	3.36
11. Communications	0.00	1.14	0.06	0.00	0.00	1.20
Total	12.23	55.10	14.11	12.08	6.48	100.00

Source: Based on ACIAR unpublished data.

environmentally acceptable, productively viable, sustainable dryland farming systems.

SOME PRELIMINARY LESSONS

Lesson 1 - Developing Countries Want Collaborative Projects
The rapidity with which ACIAR's research portfolio has been assembled is indicative of the excess demand that exists in the developing world for genuine collaboration in research for development. It also attests to the wide range of research problems in which developed country researchers have a common interest and concern with their developing country counterparts. Developing countries want projects that respond directly to their needs and priorities, and are prepared to put their resources behind collaborative efforts of this sort.

Partnership in Research for Development

Lesson 2 - What Makes ACIAR Unique is an Important Factor Shaping its Impact

The principal unique features of ACIR are:

(i) In the Australian context, ACIAR is an experiment with a sunset clause attached. ACIAR will be subject to ministerial review and evaluation in 1992, the primary aim of the retrospective being to assess whether ACIAR ought to continue to exist.

(ii) ACIAR is small. The Australian Development Assistance Bureau (ADAB), the principal arm of Australia's official development assistance effort, has an annual budget of almost $Aust.1 billion. In 1986-87 ACIAR has a recurrent budget of only $Aust.12.5 million.

(iii) In keeping with its small budget, ACIAR's main contribution to research for development is not money, but the development and transfer of human capital. ACIAR facilitates collaboration in research by scientists employed in Australian institutions with colleagues in institutions overseas.

(iv) ACIAR is directed by its charter to focus its activities in areas of research where Australia has a claim to 'comparative advantage'. There is a tendency to presume that this implies a bias toward dryland agriculture, but practice has shown disciplinary skills and experience in developing a sound approach to the solution of research problems are equally important aspects of Australia's strengths in agricultural research.

(v) The Centre does not pay its project partners to undertake research. It facilitates a partnership between groups already committed to research. It does this by helping to bring together groups/individuals with complementary research interests. Partnership strengthens both sides.

Lesson 3 - Collaboration is More than Cooperation

It implies shared responsibility for all aspects of the project cycle and the research to be undertaken, plus a mutual interest and commitment to a successful conclusion. The collaborative approach needs, therefore, to be problem-oriented, the successful solution of which is beneficial to both the Australian and overseas partners. Without this mutuality of interest and benefit, the commitment needed for true partnership for the whole of the research period is unlikely to be as firm as it needs to be.

Lesson 4 – Rewards for Collaboration Flow from Successful Paralleling of Interests

Collaboration is entirely different from the usual model of consultancies and 'have skills will travel' format of contemporary technical assistance. Rewards in collaborative projects, especially for project leaders, do not depend on a consulting fee or retainer received at the end of the day. In ACIAR's case these do not exist since the research leaders are already employed by their home institutions. The rewards depend fundamentally upon the contribution that collaboration in a foreign context, often involving access to genetic materials and environments not available at the 'home institution', will make to the on-going research commitments of the research leaders themselves.

Collaboration involves coming alongside activities already being supported to complement/ strengthen existing efforts in both partner countries. Some examples may be helpful:

(i) ACIAR supports research on foot-and-mouth disease between Australian researchers and colleagues in Malaysia and Indonesia. Through this research Australian scientists have access to live foot-and-mouth virus and are able to work on the disease without having to introduce it into Australia. At the present time Australia is free of foot-and-mouth disease, but should it ever break out, the involvement of Australian scientists in this research will contribute to the readiness and ability of Australia to respond quickly and professionally.

(ii) Australia is a major exporter of cereals, and bulk handling methods characterize the Australian industry. Substantial support has been forthcoming from Australian industry to model the postharvest system in an effort to economize on infrastructure, handling costs, losses due to pests, pathogens, quality deterioration, and transport. ACIAR has sought to tap into this on-going work by supporting the adaptation of existing models to bulk handling, transport and storage of rice in Malaysia, and the further development of these models to incorporate certain externalities, market-determined price-quality relationships, and farmers' reactions to price signals. These developments will strengthen Australia's own postharvest activities, while collaboration with Malaysia is proving an effective way of establishing that Malaysia can make substantial savings by rationalising current handling and storage facilities, altering delivery schedules, and changing pricing systems.

(iii) Biological nitrogen fixation is a characteristic not all plants share. It is common to legumes and could save millions in fertilizer cost if this ability could be incorporated into staple cereals and other food crops. ACIAR's plant nutrition program has entered into several projects that are examining a number of aspects of this area of research. In so doing, it strengthens on-going research at Australia's Commonwealth Scientific and Industrial Research Organisations's Division of Plant Industry, and at the Australian National University in Canberra. This is difficult research and the probability of success may be less than even, but the potential benefits of success are enormous.

(iv) Research priority assessment is a difficult process that all research leaders must address. Australian researchers have been at the forefront of the effort to develop operational models for assessing ex-ante research priorities in agriculture. ACIAR is using some of these models as a component in the process by which it sets its own research priorities. It is also supporting work in partnership with overseas researchers to further develop these models and test their application in country case studies. Success will not only increase Australia's capacity in this area, but also contribute here and overseas to generating credible data on the opportunity cost of research resource allocation decisions. In time, we expect that such data will strengthen the case of those who must defend research budgets and present a convincing case against the chronic problem of international agricultural development - excessive underinvestment.

Lesson 5 - Mutuality of Benefit is a Sine qua non of Genuine and Successful Collaboration

If one is to ensure that research supported will improve welfare as well as the stability, productivity, and sustainability of agricultural output in developing countries, it is essential that the donor agency ascertain the developing

110

country's priorities. This requires the donor
agency to work with potential partners in the
process of project and program development. Both a
professional and an entrepreneurial role is
involved, relying on the partnership during
investigation of joint research opportunities,
planning and development of research programs,
organization and contracting for technical
resources, and receipt and management of supporting
funds from third parties. There is no substitute
in this process for a brokering role by the donor
agency, the goal being to ensure that the interests
of the scientists of the donor and the developing
country are brought together.

During this brokering process it is critical
that the donor agency not substitute for the
potential partners in the detailed preparation and
drafting of the final research proposal. It is the
donor agency's role to ensure adequate peer review
of the draft proposals. This document will be the
centerpiece of collegial 'to-ing' and 'fro-ing'.
It ought to benefit from professional input by
relevant experts retained by the donor agency, but
it must be the work of the research leaders from
whom the collaborative commitment is to be sought.
Moreover, this document must not only contain
details of the research proposed, but also agreed
indicators of performance against which progress
and anticipated impact can be monitored and
assessed.

CONCLUDING COMMENT

Collaboration in development assistance implies a
commitment to complementing the skills and
capacities of the developing country partner rather
than substituting for local resources. In
collaborative research for development this tends
to preclude projects that are worthy but do not
depend on specialized inputs from the donor
country. For example, in ACIAR's socio-economics
and farming systems programs there are requests
aplenty for projects that are little more than data
collection exercises designed to fill an
information vacuum or establish a data base. Data
collection, however, especially in foreign
socio-cultural and institutional environments, is
not an activity in which Australian researchers
have a comparative advantage. They do, however,
have considerable expertise in the design of survey

questionnaires, computer-aided data processing, and survey data analysis. Hence, while ACIAR is reluctant to substitute for local resources in data collection, the Centre has been willing to assist in identifying more efficient data collection methods, data analysis and data interpretation. The philosophy has been that if the collaborating developing country is not prepared to take responsibility for data to be collected or needed for the project, then the problem is unlikely to be important enough to warrant getting involved. This is a useful measuring stick to use in distinguishing high-priority and appropriate collaborative projects from those that are less urgent or offer less potential benefit.

There are substantial reasons for public support for research for development. Not least of these is the spillover of benefits back to donor countries. The green revolution has benefited not only developing countries but traditional cereal-producing countries in the First and Second Worlds also. Although it is too early to judge the success or otherwise of ACIAR, there is reason to believe that the increasing relevance of genuine collaboration in development assistance projects will tend to increase this spillover to donor countries.

The trend to greater recognition of the spillover benefits to donor countries of foreign aid is to be welcomed. Not only does it reflect the success that has been achieved in Third World development, but it must, in time, reinforce the shift in foreign aid from programs of charity to programs of genuine development. It can also provide a base on which to strengthen the popular mandate donor countries have for long-term commitments to foreign aid. In these respects both aid donors and recipients have reinforcing interests. If we are clever enough these complementary interests can be harnessed to improve the process of technology transfer by ensuring greater effort is devoted to the generation of appropriate rather than inappropriate technology.

REFERENCES

Agarwala, A.N. and Singh, S.P. (1963) eds., **The Economics of Underdevelopment**, Oxford U.P., London

Anderson, J.R., Herdt, R.W. and Scobie, G.M., (1986) **Science and Food: The CGIAR and its**

Partners, Parts I and II, CGIAR Secretariat, Washington, D.C.

Biggs, S. (1985) 'A Farming Systems Approach: Some Unanswered Questions', **Agricultural Adminis-tration,** 18, pp. 1–12

Blond, R.D. (1984) ed., **Partners in Research,** University of California, Davis

Breth, L. (1985) **Summary of International Agricultural Research Centers: A Study of Achievements and Potential,** CGIAR Secretariat, Washington, D.C.

Brown, L.R. (1970) **Seeds of Change,** Praeger, New York

CGIAR Secretariat (1981) **Second Review Report of the CGIAR,** Washington, D.C.

Coxhead, I. and Remenyi J. (1985) **Agriculture: Development Experience in the Third World,** Deakin U.P., Geelong

Critchfield, Richard (1982) 'Science and the Villager: The Last Sleeper Wakes', **Foreign Affairs,** Fall, pp. 14–41

Dalrymple, D.G. (1978) **Development and Spread of High Yielding Varieties of Wheat and Rice in Less Developed Nations,** USDA, Foreign Agriculture Economic Report, No. 95, Washington, D.C.

Davis, J.J. (1930) 'Economic Factors in Mexico', **American Economic Review, Papers and Proceedings,** 20, pp. 40–48

Eicher, C.K., and Staatz, J.M. (1984) eds., **Agriculture Development in the Third World,** Johns Hopkins, Baltimore

Frankel, H. (1943) 'Industrialization of Agricultural Countries and the Possibilities of a New International Division of Labour', **Economic Journal,** 53, pp. 188–201

Hayami, Y. and Ruttan V. (1971) **Agricultural Development in International Perspectives,** Johns Hopkins, Baltimore

Higgins, B. (1956) 'The Dualistic Theory of Underdeveloped Areas', **Economic Development and Cultural Change,** 4, pp. 194–205

Hill, F.F. and Hardin L.S. (1971) 'Crop Production Successes and Emerging Problems in Developing Countries', pp. 3–29, in Turk, K.L., **Some Issues Emerging from Recent Breakthoughs in Food Production,** Cornell University Press

Hill, F.F. to Hardin L.S. (1975) Memo: 'Helping LDCs Improve the Effectiveness of their Agri-cultural Research Services', Food Foundation, 25 April, New York

113

IDRC (1986) **With Our Own Hands: Research for Third World Development; Canada's Contribution through IDRC 1970-85,** International Development Research Centre, Ottawa

Leaf, M. (1983) 'The Green Revolution and Cultural Change in a Punjab Village, 1965-78', **Economic Development and Cultural Change,** 31, pp. 27-70

Lewis, W.A. (1954) 'Economic Development with Unlimited Supplies of Labour', **The Manchester School,** 22, pp. 139-191

Lipton, M. and Longhurst, R. (1985) **Modern Varieties, International Agricultural Research, and the Poor,** CGIAR Study Paper No.2, The World Bank, Washington D.C.

Pearse, A. (1980) **Seeds of Plenty, Seeds of Want,** Clarendon Press, Oxford

Pinstrup-Andersen, P. (1982) **Agricultural Research and Technology in Economic Development,** Longmans, London

Robertson, D.H. (1938) 'The Future of International Trade', **Economic Journal,** 48, pp. 1-14

Rosenstein-Rodan, P.N. (1943) 'Problems of Industrialization of Eastern and South-Eastern Europe', **Economic Journal,** 53, pp. 202-211

Rostow, W.W. (1960) **The Stages of Economic Growth,** Cambridge University Press, Cambridge

Ruttan, V.W. (1982) **Agricultural Research Policy,** Minnesota University Press, Minneapolis

Schultz, T.W. (1964) **Transforming Traditional Agriculture,** Yale University Press, New Haven

Scobie, G.N. and Posada, R.T. (1977) **The Impact of High Yielding Rice Varieties in Latin America,** CIAT, Series JE-01, Cali, Colombia

Segal, R. (1965) **The Crisis of India,** Penguin, Ringwood.

Skinner, A.S. and Wilson, T. (1975) eds., **Essays on Adam Smith,** Clarendon Press, Oxford

Smith, Adam (1776) **The Wealth of Nations,** (ed., E. Cannon), Modern Library edition, 1937, New York

Spengler, Joseph J. (1975) 'Adam Smith and Society's Decision Makers', pp. 390-414, in Skinner, A.S. and Wilson, T., eds., **Essays on Adam Smith,** Clarendon Press, Oxford

Turk, K.L. (1971) ed., **Some Issues Emerging from Recent Breakthroughs in Food Production,** Cornell University Press, Ithaca

Winch, D. (1965) **Classical Political Economy and Colonies,** Harvard University Press, Cambridge, Mass.

World Bank (1982) **World Development Report,** Oxford University Press, New York

Wortman, S. (1973) 'Extending the Green Revolution', **World Development, 1,** pp. 45–51

Wortman, S. and Cummings R.W. Jr. (1981) **To Feed This World,** Johns Hopkins University Press, Baltimore

Chapter Six

APPLICABILITY OF ECONOMIC EVALUATION TO CHINA'S
URBAN TRANSPORTATION PROJECTS IN A CHANGING SOCIETY

Hsu O'Keefe

INTRODUCTION

This chapter explores the applicability of economic
evaluation methods developed and applied in
countries with market economies to alternative
urban transportation development projects in China.
China is a centrally planned developing economy
which now appears to be evolving into a mixed
economy and which has adopted modernization goals.
The changing nature of the society has implications
for new transport projects and systems.

The presentation is organized into five
sections. The first describes China's overall
economic development since initiation of its
"opening to the rest of the world" policies. This
is followed by an analysis of the dimensions of
China's urban transportation systems. An overview
of formal economic evaluation methods for urban
transportation projects is the subject of the
following section. Applicability of those methods
to China's needs, given the unique characteristics
of that country, is then explored paying attention
to social and environmental impacts and methods for
taking account of the economic efficiency of
alternative transport systems.

BACKGROUND

China began the decade of the 80s with a new
post-Mao leadership, headed by Deng Xiaoping. He
established the basic objective of generating a
growth rate which would sustain attainment of the
Four Modernizations: the targets set by a ten-year
economic program (1976-1985) to modernize
agriculture, industry, science and technology, and

116

defence. The underlying goal is for China to be considered as a developed nation by the year 2000.

Implementation of the decision to modernize China has not been without obstacles and problems. Wang (1982) pointed out that China's new leaders soon recognized that the plan exceeded the country's resources and capabilities. The key factors identified as obstacles for the country's modernization and development were energy, raw materials and transportation, where the supply fell far behind the demand: "...by the end of 1978, the central leadership had concluded that a new three-year period of economic reform (1979-1981) was necessary. A rolling policy of readjustment, consolidation, restructuring, and improvement of the economy was introduced" (Wang, 1982, p.2).

The decade of the 80s was defined as the period of transition necessary to introduce the process of adjustment and reform required to attain the final goals of the Four Modernizations.

Under these new policies of economic adjustment and reform, emphasis was given to light industry and agriculture. Chen and Lee (1984) estimated that the gross value of agricultural and industrial output increased by 10.2% between 1982 and 1983. Progress was also observed in construction, domestic commerce and foreign trade, and living standards improved (Chen and Lee, 1984, p.vii).

Reforms were initiated in the areas of foreign trade and international exchange. Perkins (1986, p.44) noted that "...if China was going to modernize its economy quickly, it could not afford to waste the scientific and engineering talent it did have, and it could not turn its back on the rapid gains to be made through the adaptation of foreign technology." Results of these efforts to promote foreign trade could be measured by monitoring the amount of foreign investment realized, the number of joint ventures formed and the rate of expansion of exports. Results of the efforts to promote international exchange could be measured by monitoring the number of students and scholars sent to the Western countries.[1]

Agricultural reforms, which concentrated on replacing the commune system with the "responsibility system", permitted the peasants to keep their surplus production and sell it at the market if they wished. This generated a positive economic impact in the rural areas. The rural sector statistical indicators presented by Perkins

117

(1986, p.50) show that both income and consumption of the rural population have increased. These data also indicate that, in real terms, the 102 percent increase in income observed between 1978 and 1983 was higher than that of consumption, which only increased by 80 percent. Analysis performed by Chow (1985) concluded that economic efficiency in the rural areas "...could be further improved by the appropriate pricing of the services of land and labor and of other inputs" (Chow, 1985, p.116).

Reforms in urban areas started in late 1984. They involve changes in two major aspects of the urban scenario: operation of the state-owned enterprises and the pricing systems. The majority of the state-owned enterprises in China (around 6,000 units) are located in the urban areas. In the past, these enterprises acted as follows:

> ...for the enterprise, the key objective is to guarantee the supply of inputs it needs to meet its output targets. The first step is to bargain with the planners to get as large an allocation as possible. The next step is to establish formal and informal contacts with other enterprises, not only to guarantee delivery of the goods provided in the plan but also to trade unneeded inputs of one's own for key inputs over and above those in the plan. If an enterprise is allocated inputs that it does not need, it puts them in its warehouse rather than returning [them]....Inventories in China, as a result, are typically very large. (Perkins, 1986, p.53)

This process is changing. The scope for flexibility by these enterprises has increased and they are becoming profit-oriented as well. Some are being allowed to hire people directly, to a certain extent. One of the objectives of the urban reforms is to reduce the role played by the central government in order to allow urban enterprises to function with more discretionary power and in response to market signals.[2]

From the theory of microeconomics, it is known that an enterprise which maximizes its profit produces the amount of output at the point where marginal cost equals marginal revenue. Such concepts are new to enterprises of a centrally planned economy such as China's. Prices in a centrally planned economy "can affect consumption but cannot encourage or discourage production if

the enterprises do not operate to make profit"
(Chow, 1985, p.42). The need for price reform was
evident and recognized early by Chinese economists.
For example, He (1982) stated that

> ... in the prevailing price system, there are
> a number of inconsistencies in the relative
> prices between industry and agriculture, as
> well as among industrial products. Prices of
> processed industrial goods tend to be high,
> and prices of intermediate goods and raw
> materials are low. In fact, the latter are so
> low that there is little margin for profit.

He continued by saying that this price system

> ... can hardly regulate production according
> to social needs... there is no incentive to
> curtail production of the goods that are in
> excess of demand, nor is there incentive to
> raise production of the goods that fall short
> of supply... Under the existing over-
> centralized price system, an enterprise is
> deprived of the power to set prices of its
> products, and the prices are subject to
> frequent consultation and approval by the
> higher state authorities. As a result, the
> delays and interruptions leave many remaining
> price problems unsolved. (He, 1982, pp.
> 75-76)[3]

Prices of inputs in China were fixed by
central planning authorities in the 50s. Prices
established in this way do not necessarily reflect
the relative scarcities of the goods and services
offered in an economy. These prices remained
largely unchanged until price reform was initiated
in 1984. The objective of reforms is to let the
prices of the goods and services be influenced and
eventually determined by the market system of
demand and supply (Chow, 1985, p.131). These types
of reforms are quite difficult to institute. Most
Chinese-studies scholars agree that it is still
premature to attempt an assessment of the outcome
of the price reform effort.[4]

URBAN TRANSPORTATION SYSTEMS IN CHINA

The transportation sector has been identified as
one of the bottlenecks to China's economic

development. Demand in this sector far exceeds supply of required infra- and super-structures of the country.[5] The World Bank Country Study (1983) describes China's transportation as a "dual economy" with respect to its technological aspect. It consists of a traditional system (for example, animal - or human-drawn carts, pack animals) and a modern transportation system (World Bank Country Study, 1983, p.280).

China's urban transportation systems are undergoing change. The current urban transportation situation can be considered and described in terms of (i) passenger transport (ii) freight[6] transport and (iii) transport infrastructure.[6]

(i) <u>Passenger transport</u>: The basic means of passenger transportation used is the bicycle. Beijing with its population of around 10 million people had some 5 million bicycles in 1985. Shanghai, with around 12 million people, had some 7.5 million bicycles in the same year. According to the World Bank Country Study (1983, p.307), China produces more than 10 million bicycles per year and the total number of bicycles in that country is over 100 million. The next major mode of passenger transportation within the urban areas is public transport, which consists of diesel, articulated and trolley buses. The bus fleet consists of vehicles developed in the 50s. These vehicles present problems such as low capacity and high operating cost and are fuel inefficient.[7] Mass transportation by metro system is part of the urban setting of Beijing and Tianjing. Shanghai is presently constructing its own system. To meet the increasing demand of foreign tourists and business visitors, the number of foreign-made taxis and minibuses imported has increased greatly in recent years.[8]

(ii) <u>Freight transport</u>: Goods are transported into the cities primarily by motorized trucks. According to the World Bank Country Study (1983), few vehicles in China's truck fleet exceed 8 tons in capacity. Light trucks up to 1 ton capacity are uncommon. The majority of the fleet consumes gasoline as opposed to diesel (World Bank Country Study, 1983, p.268). Distribution within cities is done basically by carts drawn by bicycles.

(iii) <u>Transport infrastructure</u>: This consists of narrow and congested multiple-use streets. Except for the central areas of large cities, urban streets are rarely paved. It is understandable how congested these streets become when they are shared by the traffic mix described above plus pedestrians.

Given the above overview of China's current urban transportation systems and given all the changes that the country desires to make, the urban transportation system needs to be modernized to facilitate economic growth in China and not hamper it. In general, urban transportation equipment modernization involves vehicles with expanded capacity and improved overall technical quality for buses and trucks; and motorization of carts at present drawn by bicycles to improve efficiency.

Improvements in the urban transportation infrastructure involve upgrading of the existing transport network or building new roads to relieve hazardous and congested traffic locations. Beijing, for example, is building "ring roads" around the city to reduce the traffic bottlenecks (Burns, 1986). Alternative transit systems to increase the supply of road space to meet the increasing demand for its use may include limiting further growth of the bicycle fleet[9] and encouraging greater use of public bus transport. The present shortage of buses to meet current demand within major urban areas may be solved in different phases. In the short run, for example, a likely solution is to acquire buses from abroad either to replace worn-out vehicles or to add to the existing fleet. In the long run, it may be possible to produce vehicles domestically and become self-sufficient.

In addition, due to over-crowding of urban road spaces and due to lack of flexibility in reallocating people and businesses, underground metro systems seem to be a highly attractive alternative to most Chinese urban transportation planners as a way of dealing with urban congestion.[10]

Alternative ways to improve the urban transportation systems need to be carefully assessed so that scarce resources are allocated efficiently. In other words, for a project to be considered desirable, the social benefits should surpass the social costs of the project under consideration. Economic evaluation serves a purpose here along with technical and financial analyses of the projects.

Evaluation of China's Urban Projects

ECONOMIC EVALUATION OF URBAN TRANSPORTATION PROJECTS

This section reviews what are generally considered to be the practical aspects of an economic analysis of an urban transportation project.[11] Economic evaluation is viewed as a tool to assist decision-makers and analysts when selecting between alternatives. The essence of economic evaluation involves forecasting and comparing the economic effects of the alternatives formulated.[12]

Urban transportation projects, either alternate investment programs or alternate operational strategies, present effects that can be measured in economic terms as well as those that are difficult to quantify in economic terms. These effects (the ones that are difficult to measure economically) can be subdivided into two groups. The first includes effects that can be calculated in physical terms, such as air pollution and noise pollution.[13] The second includes those effects that are difficult to quantify, such as impact on visual and aesthetic aspects or community disruption caused by a particular urban transportation alternative.

The sum of the economically quantifiable costs and benefits gives a measure of economic efficiency. A project is economically desirable, in principle, when the result is a positive economic efficiency, that is, the measurable benefits exceed the measurable costs. Since urban transportation projects involve assessment of costs and benefits to the public, economic evaluation is designed to assess the social desirability of the alternatives. Socio-economic data required for project elaboration differ from private project evaluation. Also, examination of the distribution of the costs and benefits generated by the alternatives among different user and non-user groups and by income levels is usually suggested.[14]

The economic data required for economic efficiency calculations include estimates of investment costs, operating costs and maintenance costs of the alternatives considered. Proportions of taxes, subsidies and transfers of these costs have to be identified. Shadow prices of foreign exchange and labour and appropriate social discount rates have to be investigated in certain cases. The net present value technique is used to calculate the flows of the costs and benefits that are quantifiable in monetary terms.

Although economic evaluation within the structure of an urban transportation study usually follows demand and supply analyses, "...it is not a one-shot affair at the appraisal stage" as pointed out by Ray (1984, p.6) Ray continues that "if...it is limited to the appraisal stage, then, it can serve only as a final check on the overall soundness of the project proposal..." (Ray, 1984, p.6) Economic evaluation is very useful, both before and after the appraisal stage. In project development, it can be of great use in formulation of the project. After analysis, economic evaluation can be useful in final design and costing to define and resolve critical issues as they are met throughout the elaboration of the project (Ray, 1984, p.6).

Economic evaluation of an urban transportation project is usually performed along with analyses of land use, traffic demand and transport supply. The supply analysis involves transport network simulation, where networks modelling the existing transportation system are built, and technical assessment is made of the transport technology available. The supply analysis is interrelated with the demand analysis during the traffic assignment phase, when data on distributed values of trips by mode are collected and assigned to each network link. The demand studies involve land use and traffic demand analyses. Land use refers to the analysis of spatial distribution of population, employment and economic and social activities for the existing and proposed urban systems. Traffic demand analysis focuses basically on three steps of the demand modelling process: trip generation, trip distribution and modal split.[14]

Consequences of different transportation alternatives are formulated on the basis of the above analyses. Economic evaluation is utilized to verify the economic desirability of each alternative.[15] Economic evaluation apart from being used to evaluate the urban transportation system as a whole, can be used to evaluate segments of the system.

THE ROLE OF ECONOMIC EVALUATION IN CHINA'S URBAN TRANSPORTATION PROJECTS

This section explores basic elements required for economic evaluation of China's urban transportation system. It is divided into two parts: analysis of social and environmental impacts and analysis of economic efficiency.[16]

Analysis of Social and Environmental Impacts

Due to the socialistic nature of the Chinese economy, there is a high degree of concern among the transportation planners about negative social impacts on individuals. Since there is no private ownership of land in China, to my knowledge, social assessment of factors such as impact on land values seems to be irrelevant. This aspect leads to a difficult issue of reallocating people and businesses for the purpose of widening road space in the congested urban areas. The question of how to encourage people and businesses to move elsewhere or compensate them for the disruption of moving remains a challenge.

Despite this, analysis of social impact focuses on location of housing, working and shopping facilities, and availability of public transportation.[17]

Concerns about the environment in China seem to be reasonably recent issues. Impact studies appear to be done in qualitative terms and focus on the air pollution generated by the diesel bus system. Noise pollution does not appear to be a major concern as yet.[18]

Analysis of Economic Efficiency

Demand Studies. The economic reform policies of China have introduced new elements into the urban scenario. Increased living standards of the population are leading to more leisure and widening shopping options. Control of the movements of rural population into cities is being relaxed. Decentralization of decision-making is allowing state-owned enterprises to hire some people directly. Salaries and wages once set by the central government are increasingly being decided at the enterprise level. The enterprises are being given autonomy to set prices according to demand and supply of the inputs and outputs. Privately owned small businesses and services are being allowed to develop.

The above scenario plus natural increases in urban population lead to the expectation that the low use of transport and relative immobility of the

124

Chinese people observed in the past (World Bank Country Study, 1983, II, p.324) are likely to reverse in coming years. If growth of Chinese urban boundaries follows[19] the same trend as in other developing nations due either to population growth or due to increasing level of economic and service activities, both passenger and freight demands will increase. An efficient urban transportation system is, then, more than ever, important to avoid wastes in the urban socio-economic structure.

Data on income levels and on the origin-and-destination of passenger and freight plus the projection techniques usually used in the transportation modelling process were irrelevant to the transportation planning process in China until recently.[20] Inclusion of these issues as pertinent factors in the urban transportation planning process is a fairly new experience for Chinese urban transportation planners.

Adding to the changing urban scene, the increasing flow of foreign and domestic tourists has made prediction of future traffic demand more difficult. This trend of increasing uncertainty and complexity will persist and even accelerate, especially if the reform policies cited above stay on course.

Supply Studies. As described in the section on China's urban transportation systems, China's drive towards modernization will require a number of modifications within that system. The growth of urban transport demand, both passenger and freight, puts more pressure on the already unbalanced supply of urban transport, infrastructure, equipment and vehicles.

China wishes to improve the existing urban transportation system by diminishing its reliance on bicycles. Expansion of mass transportation by bus or metro, with minimal impact on air pollution, is being seriously considered as a means to this end. But these alternative transit systems will increase consumption of energy. Energy avail-ability is considered to be one of the constraints on the country's development during the 80s.[21]

Heavy reliance on the bus system, whether trolley, articulated or diesel, requires replacement of vehicles built on truck chassis with vehicles incorporating modern technology. China needs to analyze the technological innovations in the area of mass transportation, freight transportation and traffic engineering developed in other countries and to adapt the most appropriate technology to its particular needs. The Chinese urban transportation planners have adopted the trial-and-error process to ensure successful implementation of a full-scale project.

China has available a tremendous amount of data on the existing supply system. This includes data on items such as the bus and trolley bus fleets by type, year and operating condition, bus routes, load factors, passengers carried, peak/off peak schedules, and so on. Appropriate analysis of these data will be a great benefit to China when assessing its current supply capabilities as well as projecting its future needs.

Technical feasibility of urban transportation projects however does not imply economic feasibility. Economic possibility is more important than technical efficiency for selection of projects.

Economic Evaluation.[22] Economic evaluation of urban transportation projects seems to be a recently introduced requirement for project approval in China. Although profitability of a project appears to be a familiar concept to Chinese urban transportation planners, the concept of discounted cash flows for the different alternatives considered seems to be relatively new to them. The technique of present value, concepts of social discount rate and shadow prices are part of the newly acquired evaluation tools.

As pointed out in a previous section (Background), China is undergoing price system reform. The outcome of this reform will have a great impact on the reliability and usefulness of economic evaluations performed on urban transportation projects. Until recently, prices have been fixed by the central planning group and have not reflected the scarcity of the inputs and outputs.[23] Therefore, adopting such prices for the economic evaluation of urban transportation projects will contribute to erroneous interpretation of the results and misallocation of scarce resources.[24]

Another practice which makes the pricing of urban transportation projects more difficult is the way operating costs are calculated. Chinese urban transportation accounting practices only calculate fixed costs. Variable costs are not normally calculated at present. Absence of a composition of fixed and variable costs, as well as inclusion of items such as capital interest, make it difficult to determine the correct or less distorted prices for different transport modes. Thus, optimum fare levels for the various urban transport services cannot be defined. Accurate assessment of output maximization level is also complicated because marginal costs are not estimated.

The valuation of land is an important concept in calculating the investment cost of urban transportation projects. Urban property values in market economy countries tend to increase over time. This phenomenon encourages quick action in implementation of urban transportation projects. When expansion of right-of-way is needed in the urban centres, delays are avoided in order to minimize probable increases in acquisition costs. The Chinese situation is unique since all land is owned by the government. The lack of a market for land makes it difficult to put a monetary value on the land. Calculation of property values does not appear to be a component of investment cost estimation in China.

A key aspect in social evaluation of alternative urban transportation projects is to assess their impact on users/non-users of the urban transportation system by income group as well as on operators and government. In a market economy, this is usually done to ensure a more equitable distribution of resources. That is, to ensure that the lower income groups of the society benefit from the project. This feature of social evaluation is irrelevant to China's urban areas since income distribution is approximately equal. However, it seems that China wishes to achieve a new situation with respect to income in the future. In this case, income differentials within urban areas will increase. Examination of distributional effects of urban transportation projects will become a relevant feature.

The process of adapting economic evaluation techniques to China's urban transportation projects requires economists, or transportation planners with skills in economic analysis. China's long period of isolation from the rest of the world and its reliance on a centrally planned economy have inhibited the development of expertise in this field. Therefore, a cadre of specialists conversant with urban transportation project economic appraisal methods is not readily available.

CONCLUSIONS

The Chinese economy is undergoing a process of great change. The gradual modernization of all sectors of the economy, as well as the gradual relaxation of control on many aspects of the economy and the society, are creating entirely new prospects for the country.

The urban transportation system is also undergoing a great change. The new demands on the system will require increases in the amount of road mileage. They will also require improvements in the various aspects of the system. These improvements include: upgrading the pavement of the road surface, expanding and synchronizing the signalling system, and modernizing and expanding mass transportation by bus, trolley and metro. Economic evaluation can be a useful and relevant tool for assessing the economic desirability of these projects.

The degree of applicability of economic evaluation methods to China's situation will depend, to a certain extent, on the following factors: first, price reform; secondly, availability of data; and thirdly, availability of specialists with economic evaluation training.

One way to improve the degree of applicability is to learn about it and apply it to urban transportation projects. Application of the methods will facilitate the development of a cadre of specialists in urban transportation project appraisal and evaluation.

Perhaps the most useful short-run application of this knowledge will be in the appraisal of foreign technology for use in urban transportation systems. In the intermediate term, better understanding of the concepts and techniques of economic evaluation and greater awareness of the types of data required for elaborating a sound urban transportation project will help create the momentum necessary to start building the appropriate data base required for effective evaluation analysis. Finally, in the longer term Chinese urban transporation planners and Chinese economists can be expected to develop ideas for applying economic evaluation of urban transportation projects in a mixed economy situation. Thus, by becoming familiar with the concepts and need for adequate application of economic evaluation methods (originally developed in market economies) to China's urban transport- ation projects, Chinese economists may contribute a new focus and approach applicable to a mixed economy by$_{25}$ drawing on their own accumulated experience.

NOTES

1. Perkins (1986, p.47) states that China realized US$1.66 billion in foreign investment in the first nine months of 1984, which was double that of the same period in 1983. A total of 239 new joint ventures were approved in 1984 and total exports increased by 14.6 per cent in real terms compared to the previous year. The total value of China's foreign trade was less than 12 per cent of the national income in 1978. By 1984, this ratio has increased to 22 per cent (p.48). Perkins (1986, p.45) also states that in 1984 there were 12,000 students and visiting scholars from China in the U.S. alone.
2. Chow (1985) describes how a centrally planned economy works as a means to better understanding how the Chinese economy functions. Decisions concerning consumption, production, income distribution and investment are made by the central authorities (Chow, 1985, pp. 41-42). In 1984, the Chinese economy functioned basically as a centrally planned economy. However, with elements of a market economy, it "now can be considered as a mixed economy with emphasis on central planning" (Chow, 1985, p. 59).
3. A collection of papers presented by China's renowned economists can be found in Wang (1982). It reflects their views of China's economic system's strengths and weaknesses and what can be done to change and improve the system. Also see Mao (1986) for a discussion of price adjustment within micro-economic and macro-economic frameworks in China.
4. See Barnett and Clough (1986) for the analyses and interpretations performed by senior specialists on the changes that have occurred in different sectors of the country since Mao's death.
5. See, for example, Chen and Lee (1984, p.7), The World Bank Country Study (1983, Vol.II, p.279) and Mao (1986, pp.7-8) for the problems faced by China's railway system that burdened the

economy with high transportation costs.

6. Published data on China's urban transportation systems is inadequate. See, for example, The World Bank Country Study (1983, Vol.II, pp. 273-405) and China Handbook Series (1984, pp. 262-303) for descriptions of China's transportation sector. Both publications analyse the transportation system and related issues of the country as a whole. This section has benefited from Mao Yushi's comments.

7. It was interesting to visit the bus maintenance stations in Beijing. Operation and maintenance of the buses are combined at the same facility.

8. China does not have private ownership of automobiles. According to the World Bank Country Study (1983, p.368), the number of cars averaged one per 10,000 people then. Thus, despite the concentration of cars in the major urban areas, the total number of automobiles in China is low compared to those in developed or some developing nations.

9. This transport mode is a low-cost alternative, privately and socially speaking. Both Roy Rotheim and Jacobus Doeleman are advocates of bicycles as the principal mode of locomotion. I believe that automobiles will not replace this transport mode in China as has been the case in most technologically advanced economies as well as of some developing nations. However, due to the sizeable fleet of bicycles, I understand the concerns of the urban transport planners in terms of establishing some kind of restriction on the increasing bicycle fleet.

10. Armstrong-Wright (1986b, p.48) points out that "...underground rail systems may appear attractive, but the justification for building such systems, and their full cost implications - in particular their massive construction costs- are rarely properly appraised".

11. See Harberger (1976) and Mishan (1971) for discussions of the traditional approach to cost-benefit analysis. See Dasgupta, Marglin and Sen (1972) and Little and Mirrlees (1974) for operational guidelines for cost-benefit analysis focused on development issues. See Ray (1984) for discussion of controversial issues of cost-benefit analysis.

12. Jacobus Doeleman raised his concern about cost-benefit assessment. Doeleman points out that "fault can be found when examining dollar

efficiency. Cost/benefit assessment, whether private or public, suffers from being pragmatic and accommodative in nature... The same cost/benefit assessment carried out in a different country, or, in the same country, but in a different decade, will define different levels of optimality in congestion, in pollution, in public/private transport mix..." (Doeleman , 1985, pp. 50-51). This indeed has been a concern among economists including myself. The controversial aspect of this type of assessment does not, however, invalidate its usefulness, especially in LDCs where efficiency considerations are important parameters for project elaboration. I agree with Doeleman that goals, standards, norms or targets have to be well defined and set first. Cost-benefit assessment has to be viewed as part of those macro guidelines and should not be considered as the single decision-making parameter. See Stopher and Meyburg (1975, p.21), for example, for a description of systems analysis procedure for urban transportation planning where the macro guidelines are shown as part of the planning process.

13. See, for example, Tisdell (1983) for a review of policies suggested by economists to control pollution. Note that the paper does not focus specifically on pollution emitted from motor vehicles.

14. See, for example, Ray (1984) for a discussion on Issues of Distribution Weights (chapter 2) and Social Valuation (Chapter 3). Roy Rotheim pointed out in commenting on an earlier draft of this Chapter that in the U.S., for example, less weight is given to the economic efficiency aspect. This is especially the case for transport projects, including urban transportation investments, where Environmental Impact Studies are considered to be more crucial for decision-making.

15. See, for example, Stopher and Meyburg (1975) for a presentation of the urban transportation modelling process.

16. See, for example, Armstrong-Wright (1986a, pp.29-38) for a screening of options for urban transit systems. Also, see Bertucci, O'Keefe, Lago and Soubhia (1980) for an application of the conventional economic evaluation structure to assess the rapid train system between two major cities in Brazil.

17. This section has also benefited from helpful comments by Mao Yushi.

18. Shanghai's Planning Bureau, for example,

has shown a great deal of concern about the need to coordinate land use and transportation planning. The location of future residential units is being carefully studied by taking into account the availability of a proper public transportation system and community services.

19. Although there are concerns about environmental aspects generated by urban transportation systems, I think that, currently, emphasis is given more to economic efficiency analysis of the projects.

20. See Armstrong-Wright (1986b), for example, for a presentation of the growth of Sao Paulo urban area between 1930 and 1980.

21. The World Bank Country Study (1983, p.292) points out that forecasts of future traffic growth were not available in China.

22. See ibid., for an analysis of transport and energy, p.292.

23. See Wood (1984) for an analysis of the possibilities and problems of applying Western economic evaluation methods to China's overall investment projects.

24. See Zhang (1985) for an analysis of the role of prices in China.

25. Mao (1986) points out problems caused by the distorted price system in China including a uniform railway tariff for the entire country. This had led to mis-allocation of different investment projects (Mao, 1986, p.7). He also points out how important the price structure is in economic appraisals of alternative schemes in economic planning (Mao, 1986, p.15).

26. I, Hsu O'Keefe, wish to express my gratitude to the United Nation's Development Program (UNDP) for the financial support of my 1985 assignment to China to present a series of lectures on issues related to urban transportation development. I also wish to express my great appreciation to the Ministry of Urban and Rural Construction and Environmental Protection of China and the Public Utilities Bureau of Shanghai for hosting my presentations. I am grateful to Professor Clem A. Tisdell, from University of Newcastle, Australia, who encouraged me to prepare a paper (on which this chapter is based) for the IV World Congress of Social Economics. His continuous support has been greatly appreciated. I wish to thank each of the following scholars for their comments which I have utilized when revising this paper. They are: Professor Roy Rotheim, from

Skidmore College, U.S.A.; Professor Mao Yushi, from the Chinese Academy of Social Science, China; and Professor Jacobus Doeleman, from University of Newcastle, Australia. The paper benefited, in particular, from Professor Mao's comments on China's socio-economic and transportation aspects. My thanks also go to my husband Dr. William M. O'Keefe for preliminary discussions and for his enthusiastic support.

REFERENCES

Armstrong-Wright, A. (1986a) **Urban Transit Systems-Guidelines for Examining Options,** The World Bank Technical Paper No. 52, The World Bank, Washington D.C.

Armstrong-Wright, A. (1986b) "Urban Transport in LDC's", **Finance and Development,** 23, 3, pp. 45-48

Balassa, B. (1982) **Economic Reform in China,** World Bank Reprint Series, No. 235, The World Bank, Washington, D.C.

Barnett, A.D. and Clough, R.N. (1986) **Modernizing China, Post-Mao Reform and Development,** Westview Press, Boulder

Bertucci, V., O'Keefe, H., Lago, P. and Soubhia, W. (1980) "Study of the Transportation Corridor Between Rio de Janeiro, Sao Paulo and Campinas", **Transportation Research Record,** No. 775, Transportation Research Board, Washington, D.C., pp. 1-7

Burns, J. (1986) "Peking Mayor's Motto: Pay Heed to Mop and Pail", **The New York Times,** New York, April 24, p.Y-4

Chen, N.R. and Lee, J. (1984) **China's Economy and Foreign Trade 1981-1985,** U.S. Dept. of Commerce, Washington

China Handbook Series (1984) **Economy,** Foreign Language Press, Beijing

Chow, G.C. (1985) **The Chinese Economy,** Harper & Row, New York.

Dasgupta, P., Marglin, S., and Sen, A. (1972) **Guidelines for Project Evaluation,** UNIDO, New York

Doeleman, J.A. (1985) "Public Reflections on Private Motorcars in the Urban Environment", **Research Report,** No.115, Department of Economics, University of Newcastle, Australia

Harberger, A. (1976) **Project Evaluation, Collected Papers,** University of Chicago Press, Chicago

Evaluation of China's Urban Projects

He, J. (1982) "The Current Economic Policies of China", pp. 69-77 in George C. Wang (ed. and translator), **Economic Reform in the PRC**, Westview Press, Boulder

Little, I. and Mirrlees, J. (1974) **Project Appraisal and Planning for Developing Countries**, Basic Books, New York

Mao, Y. (1986) "The Chinese Experience in the Introduction of Market Mechanism into a Planned Economy: The Role of Pricing". Paper presented at the IV World Congress of Social Economics, Toronto, August 1986

Mishan, E.J. (1981) **Economic Efficiency and Social Welfare**, Allen and Unwin, London

Mishan, E.J. (1971) **Cost-Benefit Analysis**, Allen and Unwin, London

Perkins, D.H. (1986) "The Prospects of China's Economic Reforms", pp. 39-62. A. Doak Barnett and Ralph N. Clough, eds., **Modernizing China, Post-Mao Reform and Development**, Westview Press, Boulder

Ray, A. (1984) **Cost-Benefit Analysis, Issues and Methodologies**, John Hopkins University Press, Baltimore

Stopher, P.R. and Meyburg, A. (1975) **Urban Transportation Modelling and Planning**, Lexington Books, Lexington

Tisdell, C. (1983) "Pollution Control: Policies Proposed by Economists", **Journal of Environmental Systems**, 12, pp. 363-380

Wang, G.C. (1982) **Economic Reform in the PRC**, Westview Press, Boulder

Wood, A. (1984) **Economic Evaluation of Investment Projects: Possibilities and Problems of Applying Western Methods in China**, World Bank Staff Working Papers, No. 631, World Bank, Washington, D.C.

World Bank Country Study (1983) **China Socialist Economic Development**, Vol II, World Bank, Washington, D.C.

Zhang, W. (1985) "On the Role of Prices" in **Social Sciences in China**, 6, No.4, China Social Science Publishing House, Beijing

134

Chapter Seven

STRUCTURAL CHANGE AND ADJUSTMENT IN THE AUSTRALIAN
RURAL SECTOR: THE SOCIO-ECONOMIC CONSEQUENCES OF
BEING A LOW-COST RESIDUAL SUPPLIER

Warren Musgrave

INTRODUCTION

Since European settlement in 1788, agriculture has
been of pivotal importance to the Australian
economy, initially as a source of sustenance, then
as a source of export income and as a basis for
development. Until very recently the sector has
been the dominant earner of foreign exchange. For
the last 20 years, however, the significance of the
sector both in terms of its contribution to exports
and to national income has diminished. For
instance, in 1949-50 the agriculture, fishing and
forestry sector contributed 24 per cent of
Australian Gross Domestic Product (GDP) but in
1984-85 this percentage was 5 per cent. Again in
1966-67 this sector contributed 49 per cent of the
value of Australian reports but by 1984-85 this had
declined to 37 per cent.
  Of course, Australia is not alone in
experiencing such structural change in its economy.
In fact, the ubiquitous nature of the declining
importance of agriculture makes the experience of
individual countries of interest to many. Most
developed countries are confronted by analogous,
though not identical, problems which bring with
them significant policy issues related to
efficiency, equity and welfare. In developing
their responses to these problems individual
countries stand to benefit from studying the
experience of other countries. The purpose of this
chapter is to contribute to such an exchange of
ideas. The chapter relates to a number of broad
issues such as: the integration of social justice
with the pursuit of economic efficiency; the
provision of income support to small businessmen;
the provision of income support in parallel with

the promotion of structural change; the role of psychological status in determining the behaviour of potential recipients of income support.

The chapter consists, first, of a discussion of the forces underlying the changing position of agriculture in the Australian economy. This is followed by a review of the changing structure of the sector, both farm and non-farm, by a discussion of the adjustment associated with this structural change, and by a review of some consequential policy responses. The key issue is that of providing income support to poor farmers in an efficient and equitable way that does not destroy the competitiveness of a sector of the economy that must be competitive in the distorted and depressed agricultural commodity markets of today.

REASONS FOR THE CHANGING POSITION OF THE SECTOR

One important reason for the decline in the importance of the Australian agricultural sector has been the overall growth of the national economy. That is, what is being witnessed is not a sector in absolute decline but one in relative decline as the total economy expands and diversifies. There are, however, a number of forces at work that have produced a secular decline in the terms of trade confronting the sector, particularly in recent years (Bureau of Agricultural Economics, 1986b). This downward trend has exerted a significant and chronic braking effect on the overall performance of the sector. Indeed, persistent, positive productivity growth has been necessary for farmers to achieve growth in incomes and for the export sector not to retard grossly the performance of the whole economy. As it is, there are those (Gruen 1985) who argue that a decline in the national terms of trade is one of the root causes of the relatively poor performance of the Australian economy over the last quarter of a century.

Stoeckel (1986) identifies three areas of policy action that could improve Australian export competitiveness. These are to reduce world protectionism, to remove domestic impediments on the traded goods sector, and to remove domestic impediments within the traded goods sector.

The protection of agriculture provided by many of the developed countries is particularly significant and has contributed significantly to

the inadequate growth in the prices received by
Australian farmers. Along with many other low-cost
agricultural exporters, Australia stands to benefit
considerably from any reduction in the protection
afforded agriculture in those countries. The
Bureau of Agricultural Economics (1985) has
estimated that the Common Agricultural Policy of
the European Community costs the Australian economy
(mainly, in the first instance, the Australian
farmer) about $Aust 1 billion per year in 1984-85
dollars. Protectionism in developed countries is
not, of course, the only reason for the relatively
poor performance of international agricultural
commodity prices. Other influences have included
the growth of agricultural output in a wide range
of countries. Not least of these have been the
countries benefiting from the success of the green
revolution. In recent years, good production
performances by centrally planned economies have
depressed markets, as too have the improved export
performance of a number of the debtor nations of
the world. The net consequence of these various
developments has been erosion of the markets of
"traditional" exporters who are the residual
suppliers referred to in the title of this chapter.
    Stoeckel's two other areas for policy action
are domestic in nature and, presumably, are more
amenable to such action than is the first.
Policies included under these two headings relate
to macro-economic strategy, the labour market,
tariffs, the efficiency of rural markets, and
on-farm and off-farm productivity growth. The
general thrust is that regulation in the past has
acted to disadvantage the sector and that some move
toward deregulation and flexibility of the economy
should benefit it. This view is held, not only by
government policy advisors and academics, but by
farmer organizations as well.
    These impediments to sector performance all
raise complex policy challenges. The government
has taken action on many fronts (Australian
Government, 1986) but a number of realities, mainly
political in nature, mean that policy action can do
little other than ameliorate the overall decline in
terms of trade. In particular, Australia is
unlikely to be able to change the protectionist
stance of the developed countries. Thus the
challenge for the Australian agricultural sector is
to maintain its viability in the face of a
continued decline in its terms of trade and so,
while some progress may occur at home (e.g., the

recent devaluation), the intransigence of these countries means that the terms of trade are likely to continue to decline.

THE SECTORAL RESPONSE TO DECLINING TERMS OF TRADE

The sector has responded to its declining terms of trade by restructuring. This restructuring, encouraged by changing factor price ratios, has taken the form of an increase in the ratio of capital to labour and an increase in the use of purchased inputs such as chemicals and machinery.

These changes in factor proportions, along with the new technologies associated with them, have enabled an increase in labour productivity which appears to have been high enough to enable maintenance of parity between farm and non-farm incomes. Figure 7.1 suggests that average farm incomes, though much more unstable, have more or less kept pace with relevant non-farm incomes over the last three decades. Australian farmers would

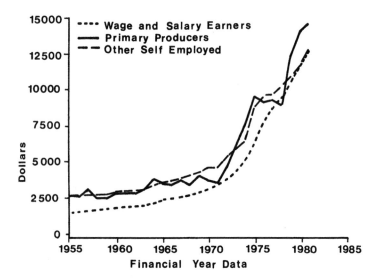

Figure 7.1: Net income: Comparisons between different groups of Australian taxpayers 1954-55 to 1980-81. Based on Stoeckel (1983)

seem to have been on a treadmill but, at least, by running hard on it, they appear to have managed to keep up. The point could be made, however, that

138

there has been a relative decline from a more remote historical position of farm incomes being greater than comparable non-farm incomes (Kuznets, 1959).

Figure 7.2 shows the trend in the volume of output of Australian agriculture and of the volume of inputs over the 25 year period ending 1979-80.

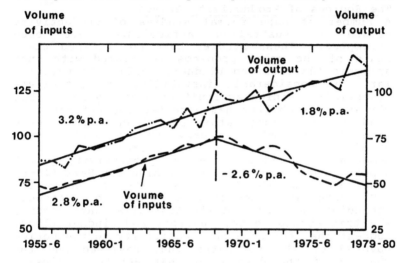

Figure 7.2: Indexes of volume of agricultural outputs and inputs, Australia. Base: 1968-69 = 100. Based on Stoeckel and Miller (1982)

There is no reason to think that these trends, particularly that with regard to inputs, will have changed in recent years. These trends must be interpreted with caution (Stoeckel and Miller, 1982) but they suggest that the impact of the relatively faster rate of decline in terms of trade since the late sixties has been met by some economizing in input use and a decline in the rate of increase of output. If the decline in the rate of input use (or the rate of substitution of cheaper for dearer inputs) has been great enough, there could well have been a dramatic rise in productivity over the last fifteen years. On the face of it, Australian farmers would seem to have reacted to the economic pressures they have been facing by lifting their productivity. The negative trend of the index of the volume of inputs does, however, raise the question as to whether the economizing of input use merely reflects farmers disinvesting in order to maintain incomes. If this question were to be answered in the affirmative then the productivity gains of the last decade or so could be quite ephemeral. Current wisdom has it that this is not the case.

The Sources of Productivity Growth

A number of more formal studies of productivity growth in Australian agriculture have been attempted. These studies have not escaped their share of the usual problems associated with such analysis (Jarrett and Lindner, 1982). In particular, the considerable instability of Australia's essentially rainfed agriculture probably means that climatic variability has affected the estimates of productivity trends rather more than would be case with similar studies in many other countries (Beck et al., 1985). As has been the experience in most temperate countries, rates of productivity growth appear to have been reasonably high but Herr (1966) concluded that the Australian rate was below the U.S. rate and suggested a number of reasons, including the nature of the Australian environment, why this should be so. Jarrett and Lindner (1982) suggest that the apparent sensitivity to the period covered of the estimates they reviewed and the quality of the data mean that Herr's conclusion should be discounted.

A number of estimates of the annual rate of productivity change of Australian agriculture using the residual method of Solow (1957) have yielded widely varying results. Thus, Young (1971) has reported an average rate of 1.7 per cent for the period 1949-68 and Powell (1974) 0.8 per cent for the period 1921-70. Within each of these periods both these authors reported rates varying from -2.7 to 4.0 per cent. A number of studies, using the Tornqvist index method (Tornqvist, 1936) to estimate productivity change in the important sheep industry, have given estimates, for a number of periods between 1950 ad 1983, ranging from 1.1 to 3.0 per cent with rates at the higher end of the range predominating (Beck et al., 1985; Laurence and McKay, 1980; Paul, 1984; Paul et al., 1984). Knopke and Jervois (1985), and, using the Tornqvist index approach modified for the uncompetitive nature of the industry, provided estimates of productivity growth in the Australian dairy industry over the period 1967-68 to 1982-83 of 0.72 per cent.

Not surprisingly, arriving at conclusions as
to the rate of productivity growth of Australian
agriculture is difficult. The feeling is, however,
that the rate, though very variable, has been high
enough to counteract the depressing effects of
declining terms of trade in farm incomes. The
ability of the sector to compete in the residual
international markets open to it would seem to have
been preserved.

Not all of the increase in rural productivity
has been due to technological change (shifts of the
production function). Between 1960-61 and 1975-76,
the average farm became bigger over the period in
question with land, capital and purchased inputs
substituting for labour (McKay et al., 1983).
Similar results were produced (Beck et al., 1985)
for the sheep industry between 1952-53 and 1982-83.

More or less similar patterns of change to
those in the sheep industry and the resulting
change in the structure of the industry aggregate
is shown in Table 7.1 where the total rural
workforce can be seen to have declined by almost a
quarter (22.6 per cent) between the early sixties
and the mid-eighties. This change has been
concentrated in the employed labour force and
unpaid family labour. According to Table 7.1 the
number of employers and self-employed in the rural
work force, while fluctuating, has stayed virtually
constant from the late sixties to the mid-eighties.
The total number of farms appears to have fallen to
a lesser extent (14.8 per cent) than has the total
labour force. The discrepancy between this decline
and the apparent stability of the number of
employers and self-employed is probably explained
to a large extent by the increase in partnership
and company formation on family farms as a device
to reduce income tax. The average size of farms
increased from an estimated 2214 hectares in
1955-56 to 3499 hectares in 1977-78 (Stoeckel and
Miller, 1982).

Raising productivity by means of changes in
factor proportions implies a movement of resources
both into, and out of, the industry. Labour, in
particular, is one of the resources moving out of
the industry. In comparison with most other developed countries this out-migration of labour would
seem to have been at a relatively low rate. Pandey
et al. (1982), in reporting estimates of increases
in the elasticity of aggregate agricultural supply,
argue that the importance of resources moving out

Structural Change in Rural Australia

Table 7.1: The Number of Rural Establishments and Total Rural Labour Force, Australia

Average of 3 years ended	Rural establish- ments	Rural Labour Force			
		Employers and self- employed	Wage and salary earners	Unpaid family labour	Total
1953–54	204350	na.	na.	na.	485500
1963–64	201600	na.	na.	na.	445400
1966–67	199500	248200	141800	25200	415300
1971–72	187650	242600	143600	21000	407200
1972–73	185900	235000	140600	20700	396300
1973–74	184150	236700	134700	18000	389400
1974–75	182250	238500	128500	18800	385600
1975–76	180400	242400	121600	20000	384000
1976–77	173650	248300	107100	17600	373000
1977–78	176150	237700	107200	19900	364800
1978–79	177220	234700	114200	14000	362900
1979–80	179080	240500	124200	14700	379400
1980–81	175760	244300	124200	13400	381900
1981–82	174470	235800	131500	11900	379200
1982–83	175730	252400	120100	16800	389300
1983–84	174030	248700	121400	12200	382300
1984–85	na.	248100	116700	11200	376000

Source: Bureau of Agricultural Economics (1986c).

of the industry in order to combat declining terms of trade could increase in the future.

The Adjustment Process

The out-migration of labour from agriculture is probably desirable for the nation as a whole, as well as for those staying in the industry. The resulting more efficient industry is better equipped to face the continuing decline in the terms of trade, while those leaving the industry presumably decide to do so on rational grounds and feel better off for having done so. As can be imagined, however, the process is not frictionless and so is not without its costs to the individuals involved and to the nation. Important among these costs are chronic and ephemeral poverty among rural people. This poverty represents a welfare problem for society as a whole. There may, however, be other costs to society due to inefficient resource use springing from lags in the adjustment process. Australia is unusual in that it has a specific program, called the Rural Adjustment Scheme (RAS), intended to tackle the social costs of the process of rural adjustment. This program will be described but, first, the nature of some costs associated with adjustment will be discussed further.

Actually the costs of concern are associated with a lack of adjustment; that is, of adjustment that occurs at too slow a rate. In particular, the argument could be advanced that the extent of poverty on farms is a function of the rate of adjustment and that, if it was accelerated, the extent of farm poverty would decline.

An empirical problem associated with this argument is that the extent of farm poverty is difficult to measure. This is because poor farmers (i.e., those with low cash incomes) are often asset rich; because farmers receive perquisites peculiar to their calling; because farm incomes are not reported on a family basis; because the farming way of life confers important non-cash benefits; and because farm income is extremely variable, particularly in Australia (Vincent, 1976). These difficulties are now discussed.

People with equity in assets, upon receiving low cash income, may, in principle, liquidate some of those assets or borrow using them as security. The observed cash income of such people should be augmented by some notional component related to their net worth. When such a notional allowance is made, people classified as poor on the basis of their cash income may no longer be so regarded. The problem is, how should this notional allowance be determined. In this respect, a relevant consideration is that, because agriculture is an unstable business, some assets are held to ensure the security of the farm business and this may actually be done at some cost to the farm family. A further consideration is that farmers tend to accumulate wealth for intergenerational transfers in the form of tangible investments, such as education, to do so. Further considerations are that the capacity of farmers to sell or borrow on their assets may be limited in difficult times, and that farmers tend to save and invest at the expense of consumption to the extent that they may 'live poor and die rich'. Despite these complexities the observation remains valid that cash incomes may

143

understate real incomes and farm poverty may not be as widespread as observation of cash income alone might suggest.

The perquisites of farming range from the consumption of farm produce, through certain tax benefits to the rent-free occupation of the farm dwelling (Davidson, 1969). Taking these into account could once again lower the number of farmers categorized as poor. Any adjustment which is made to income estimates in order to allow for these benefits should, however, be done with care, not only because they may be difficult to measure, but also because other income groups in society with whom farmers are compared would probably enjoy perquisites as well. The question then becomes one of determining whether farmers enjoy net positive perquisites. Davidson (1986) estimates the value of items of expenditure paid by non-farm households which are deducted as farm costs in Bureau of Agricultural Economics surveys of farm income, as being on average $A7549 per annum in 1984. This amounted to about 28 per cent of the average income of all Australian married couples in that year. What should be made of this in the absence of consideration of the possible perquisites of such married couples is not clear.

As well as these perquisites there are the various non-cash benefits that farmers may gain from their way of life. That is, to many farmers, their work is also a consumption activity, though theirs is not the only occupation with this feature. To the extent that this is true, cash incomes, whether or not adjusted for perquisites, would understate the total utility gained from farming. These non-cash benefits would appear to be significant if the number of farmers who stay in the industry, despite every indication that they would be better off out of it, is any guide. Presumably, for many such people the higher cash benefits to be gained outside agriculture would not compensate for the loss of life-style involved in moving. An important point is that, for most city dwellers, drastic changes in either place of residence or life-style do not necessarily accompany changes in occupation. This can be particularly important in Australia where many farmers live in sparsely settled, remote areas.

Agriculture is an inherently unstable occupation, particularly in Australia. This makes generalization about farm poverty difficult. A farmer may be poor one year and not poor the next.

For this reason, distinction between chronic and temporary farm poverty is sensible. Because farming is risky, and because periods of low farm income are to be expected, most farmers would manage their assets so as to survive such periods. In an analysis of taxation data from the early seventies, Vincent (1976) concluded that, despite the existence of a sizeable group of aged and sub-commercial farmers in chronic poverty, Australian farm poverty is more a product of the instability of agriculture than of a chronic small farm problem. Despite the continued decline in the terms of trade, structural change of the industry has probably been sufficient to ensure that the situation, a decade later, is much the same.

If the relative incidence of poverty among Australian farmers is not clear the same cannot be said of the rural sector as a whole. A Commission of Inquiry into Poverty reported in the mid-seventies that the relative incidence of poverty was highest in rural areas (Commission of Inquiry into Poverty, 1975a, b). One reason for this higher incidence of poverty in rural areas was the large number of people and families with characteristics that put them at risk of poverty. There was a marginally higher proportion of aged people and a markedly higher incidence of large families in rural areas. In addition, there was a higher incidence of unemployment, a higher proportion of which was of long duration, than in urban areas. Perhaps even more important were the low incomes among rural employees with the incidence of poverty being higher among rural labourers and their families than among other occupation groups.

Employment opportunities in rural areas are relatively lower than elsewhere, the range of job vacancies is limited while structural change in agriculture feeds more unskilled people onto the rural labour market. The rural labour force tends to be less educated, trained and skilled. Its mobility is restricted, in Australia particularly, by distance and the low value of its real estate. The picture painted by the Poverty Commission was a dismal one and suggested a chronically disadvantaged group in society which is largely ignored because it is 'physically invisible to the mass of society' (Commission of Inquiry into Poverty, 1974).

Ten years later the situation in rural Australia is probably much the same. In fact, the precipitous fall in farm terms of trade over the

last few years probably means that the situation is
currently worse than it was in the mid-seventies.
Tables 7.2, 7.3 and 7.4 show that, in 1981-82:
  - there was a higher incidence of poverty in
rural Australia than in the major cities;
  - within rural areas the highest numbers in
poverty were in income units where the head was not
working and among non-farm workers; but
  - the groups in rural Australia with the
highest percentages of poor were farm owners and
farm workers (Policy Coordination Unit 1986).

Table 7.2: Percentage of Family Farms with Zero or Negative
Farm Incomes in Selected Agricultural Industries, Australia,
1978-79 to 1984-85

Industry	1978-79	79-80	80-81	81-82	82-83	83-84	84-85
Sheep-only	19.7	13.6	21.9	37.5	50.8	39.4	41.9
Beef-only	20.6	15.4	30.2	35.0	45.8	39.2	35.5
Sheep-Beef	15.0	17.8	21.2	24.5	56.3	24.5	32.5
Wheat	7.8	11.4	18.9	14.1	63.3	22.9	30.8
Dairy	9.2	9.7	6.6	12.0	22.7	10.4	28.1
Horticulture	-	-	25.0	31.0	32.0	35.0	40.0

Source: Economic Planning and Advisory Council (1986).

Table 7.3: Proportion of Income Units by Urban Centre
Population Level Receiving Less than a Poverty Line of
$7,000, 1980-81

INCOME UNIT TYPE	
Population of Urban Centre	All Income Units
100,000 and over	24.97
50,000 to 100,000	32.18
Less than 50,000	28.16

Source: Policy Coordination Unit (1986).

This analysis does not take into account such factors as farmer asset ownership and farm perquisites. Table 7.2, which shows the proportion of family farms with zero or negative farm incomes in selected industries, provides an illustration of the volatile income situation in Australian agriculture and the potentially devastating effects of such adverse occurrences as drought (1982-83) and market depression (1984-85). Table 7.3 provides evidence of the higher incidence of poverty in smaller (and so rural) urban centres, while Table 7.4 shows the distribution of poverty between occupational groups in non-metropolitan areas.

Table 7.4: On-Farm and Off-Farm Poverty[a] in Non-Metropolitan Areas[b] Australia, 1981-82

	Total Income Units		
	All	Poor	
	No.	No.	%
Occupation			
All income units	2,418,975	334,541	14
Head not working	662,283	148,476	22
Farmers & Farm Managers	182,904	47,734	26
Farm Workers Incl Farm Foreman	89,427	20,686	23
Other			
Non-metropolitan Workers	1,484,361	117,645	8
Industry			
All income units	2,418,975	334,541	14
Head not working	662,283	148,476	22
Agriculture, forestry, fishing			
and hunting	289,655	69,142	24
Other industries	1,467,037	116,923	8

Notes: (a) Detailed Henderson (before housing) equivalent disposable income below $6,652. (b) Excludes mainland State capital statistics districts and ACT and NT. All Tasmania is included.
Source: Policy Coordination Unit (1986).

Farmers counteract downward pressures on their incomes in a number of ways, apart from raising productivity. One of these ways is to gain additional income by working or investing off-farm.

147

Structural Change in Rural Australia

The evidence suggests, however, that while many farmers receive off-farm income, the bulk of them earn less than $5,000 in this way while, of those earning more than $5,000, the great majority earned comparatively low farm incomes (Bureau of Agricultural Economics, 1986a).

Another way in which farmers cope with pressures on their income is to maintain high equity levels. This is important in coping with income-instability but is a stratagem which results in equity levels that seem ludicrously high by most standards. For example, equity levels on Australian farms with more than 200 sheep were 96 per cent in June 1953, 86 per cent in June 1971, and 89 per cent in June 1986 (Rae, 1986). That such conservatism is not excessive is illustrated by analysis which shows that farmers with equity levels below 70 per cent are 'at risk' and would likely have difficulty meeting debt and other commitments in the short term if their 'farm cash margin' (farm cash operating surplus minus a living allowance and estimated principal repayments) fell below zero. Table 7.5 shows the proportion of Australian farmers at risk in 1984-85 and 1985-86. While, in some industries, this proportion is unpalatably high it indicates that relatively fewer farmers are threatened with ruin than is indicated by the data on farm incomes already discussed.

Table 7.5: Proportion of Farmers at Risk by Industry, Australia, 1984-85 and 1985-86

Year	Wheat & other crops	Mixed live-stock	Sheep	Beef	Sheep-beef	Dairy	Horti-culture	All indust-ries
1984-85	6	2	9	0	3	9	8	5
1985-86	10	3	9	3	3	11	13	7

Source: Bureau of Agricultural Economics (1986a).

Adjustment Lags and the Efficiency Gap
The process of adjustment of Australian agriculture is essentially autonomous. Resources are recombined, people leave the industry, firms go out of existence and new firms are created with little or no government involvement. Saying that there is an

adjustment problem amounts to saying that this autonomous rate of adjustment is not high enough. This implies, in turn, that there are farmers staying in the industry who would be better off out of it and that there are farm resources that could be employed more efficiently if adjustment was occurring more quickly.

The most plausible explanation of immobility of many poor farmers and the persistence of low returns in the industry is the fact that farmers become 'trapped' in farming. That is, despite their poverty, the returns from liquidating their assets and their prospective earnings in off-farm employment would not be sufficient to compensate for the associated loss of on-farm earnings and the costs of relocation. In effect, the price for which such farmers are prepared to move is above the price at which buyers will buy. Kingma and Samuel (1977) discuss this issue in greater detail.

The possibility exists, then, that the need to adjust, as perceived by an outsider, and as suggested by low returns to capital or low farm incomes may, in many cases, be more apparent than real because the resources involved would not earn enough elsewhere to justify relocation. To the extent that this is true the adjustment problem becomes less a question of inefficient resource use and more a matter of welfare. This conclusion has important implications for policy advice for, if the objective of policy is to improve the efficiency of resource use, then it should, desirably, operate on those resources and their markets. If, however, the objective of policy is to pursue an equitable income distribution, or to compensate those disadvantaged by the adjustment process, then it should preferably operate directly on incomes and not on resource markets. Often, however, this latter objective is difficult to achieve and some efficiency eggs have to be broken in order to make the welfare omelette.

Parallelling the changes in the farm sector and, as indicated, possibly more than rivalling it in terms of the associated incidence of poverty, is a process of structural change in the rural urban sector. As in the farm sector, this rural urban process of change is characterized by a struggle on the part of small towns to survive and by the growth of the larger towns, particularly of certain natural provincial centres. An analogy with what is happening in the farm sector seems appropriate but, if so, should not be taken as implying that

Structural Change in Rural Australia

the urban change is being driven by the farm
sector. In fact, the structural change in the
country towns is probably occurring to a
considerable degree independently of that in the
farm sector.
The overall tendency is for the urban needs of
rural Australia to be met increasingly by the
larger regional centres, with the result that a
number of small towns are either stagnating or
declining. Towns losing population have been those
of fewer than 10,000 persons, though not all such
towns are stagnating, let alone declining. In this
respect Sorensen and Weinand (1981) have advanced
the notion of a 'fulcrum population size' for
service settlements about which population growth
and decline are balanced. They hypothesize that
the size will vary depending on the geo-economic
characteristics of the region so that the size that
may be associated with decline in one region could
be associated with growth, as a vital regional
centre, in another. Probably for this reason,
there is no clear relationship, for towns under
5000, between size and trend in population
(Gregory, 1980). There is, however, a trend in
rural Australia for regional centres to grow and
for smaller towns in the hinterland, perhaps beyond
a 'dormitory' perimeter, to stagnate or decline.
As suggested, this trend reflects an autonomous
process of structural change which, in turn,
reflects changes in communication and transport
technology along with rising incomes.
If, as has been indicated, certain classes of
welfare problems are disproportionately represented
in country towns, then presumably they are even
more strongly represented in these small, declining
communities. Following the Australian Rural
Adjustment Unit (1981), the groups which probably
contain the bulk of the casualties of decline would
include:
a) children, because of declining educational, social and recreational opportunities;
b) job-seekers who are faced with a small
number of vacancies near their place of residence
and with the probable need to leave their community
and buy into a higher-value real-estate market;
c) the owners and operators of small
businesses who are disadvantaged by falling
turnover and asset values;
d) the aged, who are rather immobile and are
seriously affected by the erosion of retail public
and social services;

150

     e) ratepayers who are likely to find local
government becoming either more expensive or of
lesser quality; and
     f) those not included among the above who for
a variety of reasons, would be among the disadvantaged in most communities.
     A comprehensive assessment of the welfare
service network in the Australian rural community
would probably reveal a situation which is judged
to be less satisfactory than that in metropolitan
areas. In the sparsely settled rural Australian
hinterland, services such as health, welfare,
education, communication and transport are thinly
spread. Roads and cars are vital, particularly in
the smaller (and therefore probably declining)
rural communities which rely on remote regional
centres for all but the most common of everyday
services. Often the roads are poor while, for many
of the disadvantaged, car ownership is a burden and
their use may be a hazard. The personnel providing
services are insufficient and sometimes not
adequately trained. Services are insufficiently
diverse and poorly co-ordinated. Local government
should be central to the provision of services but,
in many areas, there is no interest among the politically potent to assume a greater role or the
economic base is incapable of supporting such new
initiatives. Finally, while the network of voluntary helping services in rural areas is often well
developed and cohesive it may be poorly supported
by professional back-up from official agencies.

THE FARM POLICY RESPONSE

The central thrust of agricultural policy in
Australia over the last ten years or so has been to
increase its exposure to market forces. This is
particularly true of beef, sugar, wheat, and wool,
which are major export industries. These
industries receive low, and sometimes negative
effective rates of protection (Industries
Assistance Commission, 1985). Some industries
(dairy, eggs, tobacco for example) receive quite
high effective rates of protection. In effect the
export industries, in the long run, have to be
viable at world market prices. This is the sense
in which Australia is a residual supplier of
agricultural commodities to world markets. As has
already been indicated, along with a number of
other traditional exporters of agricultural

products, Australia supplies markets which are severely eroded by, and at prices that are markedly depressed by, a number of influences, important among which are the protectionist policies of a number of major industrialized countries.

This is not to say that price-distorting policies are not to be seen in Australian agriculture. Indeed, of all the major industries, only beef could be said to be free of policies that distort the price of the product that is perceived by farmers and, even in that industry, along with all others, a variety of policies exist that distort input prices. The structure of assistance to Australian agriculture is reviewed by the Industries Assistance Commission (1983).

Since the mid-seventies there has been a de-regulationist trend in Australian agricultural price policies which has seen a diminution of the importance of 'stabilization' policies that chronically distort price signals, typically by paying farmers a price that is a weighted average of the world price and a higher domestic price, and the progressive introduction of price 'underwriting' at times of depressed world prices. Underwriting is, in fact, a form of deficiency payment scheme but one where the trigger price is closely aligned with the world price and can be below it. Such policies are now in place for the wheat and a number of other industries. As already indicated the beef industry remains the only industry not subject to some degree of regulation of its product price (other than levies to fund the activities of the Australian Meat and Livestock Corporation) while the wool industry operates a self-financing buffer stock scheme.

Australians would seem, therefore, to have resisted blandishments for the provision of all-round protection (Harris et al., 1974) which would surely lock the economy into a scenario of stagnation and decline. The currently preferred policy, which appears to be striving for all-round reductions in protection, while not leaving agriculture totally unprotected, does expose the sector to substantial downward pressure on its income. While this pressure has been resisted by a mixture of technological and structural change, it is not without its costs in terms of poverty and deprivation. Governments have reacted to these costs by the provision of policies ostensibly aimed at mitigating their adverse effects. In addition, a number of initiatives have been proposed for the improvement of the effectiveness of this area of policy.

Lloyd (1986) groups policies to address farm poverty under four broad headings. They are:
1) income smoothing measures;
2) provisions of the Rural Adjustment Scheme (RAS);
3) income support arrangements; and
4) financial counselling services.

Income Smoothing Measures
Such measures are intended to diminish the severity of fluctuations in farm income. Included under this heading are income averaging arrangements for income tax purposes, crop and rainfall insurance, and loan repayment rescheduling. The last of these does not appear to be a matter of public policy so much as an arrangement to be negotiated between farmers and those lending to them for deferment of interest and capital repayments, the capitalization of interest, or debt insurance. Public policy is, however, important in this respect because of the importance of government institutions as lenders to farmers (in 1984, farmers owed 30 per cent of their debt to government institutions), and also because of the influence government exerts on the general banking scene. In this respect, recent extensive liberalization of the Australian capital market appears to be creating an environment in which banks are more prepared to negotiate arrangements such as those listed above than was previously the case. At the same time, this less restrained situation adds to the instability of the farm business environment.

Australia has a scheme for the averaging of farm incomes for income tax purposes which, while beneficial when nominal incomes are rising, can actually increase the tax burden and exaggerate the effect of lowered incomes in bad times. Alternative and superior arrangements have been proposed (Davis, 1981) but will not be discussed here because taxation measures are actually of little relevance to farmers who are subject to genuine financial distress.

While it is provided by the private sector to a limited extent, crop and rainfall insurance has not, to date, been a matter for public policy in Australia. The generally held belief is that comprehensive crop or rainfall insurance is not economic and that there is no efficiency argument

153

for government intervention to promote the provision of such insurance. The correctness of this
view is indicated by recent work by the Bureau of
Agricultural Economics (1986b). Despite this the
Bureau suggests that a subsidized regional rainfall
insurance scheme would meet the objectives of
drought relief more effectively than do existing
measures. Such a possibility is to be welcomed as
the existing arrangements tend to be inefficient
and inequitable (Freebairn, 1983). The question
remains, however, as to whether intervention to
mitigate the effects of such a specific cause of
income stability is desirable as it will tend to
encourage the retention in farming of those who
would not otherwise be able to cope with this
natural feature of the instability of their
business environment. This outcome would not be in
the national interest and represents a danger that
is present in any welfare policy targeted at a
specific sector. That is, provision of the welfare
assistance may retain resources in the sector which
would be better employed elsewhere in the economy.
In the case of Australian agriculture, a desirable
feature of welfare programs currently targeted at
the rural sector is that they are intended to
provide a net inducement for such resources to
ultimately leave the industry.

The Rural Adjustment Scheme
The current rural adjustment scheme, which was
introduced in 1977, was preceded, from the early
seventies on, by a number of similar, but more
industry-specific schemes that were significant not
only for what they did, but also because they
represented a move away from the dominance of rural
industry assistance measures by interference with
the price mechanism. A further significant feature
of the present RAS and its predecessors is that
their rationale is the facilitation of adjustment
of farm firms and hence of structural change in the
industry. Specifically the policy contains provisions intended to assist farmers to leave the
industry.
    The current version of the RAS was introduced
in 1985 and provides assistance for debt reconstruction   (consolidation),   farm   build-up
(enlargement), farm improvement (investment without
enlargement), carry-on finance (which is made
available for from four to seven years to
industries that are agreed to be suffering severe

154

market downturn), household support (a form of income support), and rehabilitation grants. The scheme has concessional elements in its lending packages. The administering authority can also offer an interest subsidy on loans obtained through normal commercial channels.

The scheme is administered by individual state authorities employing funds provided by the Federal government, some of which are supplemented by state funds. Allocations to the scheme fluctuated through time varying inversely with the fortunes of the sector. This flexibility is an attractive feature of the scheme.

Of the various forms of assistance provided by the RAS, debt reconstruction, farm build-up, farm improvement and carry-on finance are only made available to farmers judged to be 'viable', that is, to farmers who appear to have a reasonable prospect of being able to survive if they were to remain on their farms. The other two measures, household support and rehabilitation, are intended to assist non-viable farmers who are judged to have poor prospects in the industry. These are the measures that are particularly relevant to this chapter.

The purpose of household support is to provide assistance to farmers who have insufficient resources to meet living expenses and who are in need of assistance to alleviate conditions of personal and family hardship while the farmer considers whether to adjust out of farming. The assistance is given for three years and brings household income to the level the family would receive were the farmer receiving unemployment benefits. Extension to the second year is only possible if the farmer can demonstrate that a reasonable effort is being made to cease farming. If the farmer leaves his farm within three years of receiving support then the support becomes a grant; if he does not it is repayable with interest (that is, it becomes a loan).

Neither of these forms of assistance constitutes a significant part of RAS expenditure. Thus, in 1983/84, they absorbed only 1.3 per cent of total expenditure and 3.5 per cent in 1984/85 (Bureau of Agricultural Economics, 1986c). Why these provisions are so little utilized is not clear. Probable causes include lack of promotion of them by authority staff who see themselves more as bankers than welfare workers, and a reluctance on the part of potential users to take the decision to leave their farms at a time when they are likely to be suffering considerable stress. The second point is developed further below.

From a pragmatic point of view the RAS has a number of very desirable features. In particular, it provides a relatively flexible way of channelling assistance to financially distressed industries over finite periods. Significant in this aspect is the provision for carry-on assistance. For example, in 1983/84 over $20m were provided in the form of carry-on assistance to the sugar industry at a time of severely depressed prices. In 1984/85, there was no expenditure under this heading.

From a more analytical point of view the RAS has a number of undesirable features and, despite the important evolution it represents in Australian agricultural policy, it has not escaped criticism. This criticism covers the concessional features of the scheme, the lack of monitoring of its performance, neglect of farmers classified as non-viable, lack of integration with welfare services in general, poor targeting of lending operations, a tendency for the lending operations (which represent the bulk of RAS activity) to become an adjunct to the normal commercial banking system, confusion over objectives, and distortion of resource use. Finally, concern has been expressed over the neglect of regional economies in adjustment policy (Musgrave, 1982; Industries Assistance Commission, 1984). The Industries Assistance Commission (1984) has recommended discontinuation of the scheme but retention of its measures and their provision, following appropriate public inquiry, to "...farmers in a specified industry, region or such other appropriate grouping as may be determined". This recommendation was not accepted by the Commonwealth government and, as noted, a new version which is very much the same as the old scheme was introduced in 1985.

Income Support
Accompanying the shift in policy emphasis away from the provision of support through the price mechanism has been an increase in the attention to the problems of poor farmers and the provision of income support targeted at them specifically. Direct income support to farmers is a vexed question because it involves the provision of such support to a particular group of small business

156

proprietors who may be experiencing low incomes but who may have positive equity in their assets, whose income is difficult to measure and who may be encouraged to remain in an industry they should be leaving on grounds of economic efficiency. On the other hand, farmers' assets are often of little value or are significantly reduced in value at a time of financial crisis, while alternative employment can be difficult to find and may involve severe problems of relocation or domestic disruption.

Creation of farmer-specific direct income assistance is undesirable because of the problems of equity, abuse and selectivity it would introduce and the retardation of adjustment it would cause (Australian Rural Adjustment Unit, 1980). On the other hand, according to the Departments of Primary Industry and of Social Security (1986; henceforth referred to as the Departments), existing measures probably leave a 'gap' which according to conventional welfare criteria should be filled (the Departments, 1986). The nature of this gap will now be discussed.

The Welfare Gap

Apart from disaster relief, income support for impoverished farmers is provided through the RAS on the one hand and the universal system of social security payments on the other. The former has already been reviewed. The social security system provides support under a number of headings in order to guarantee a 'minimum level of income to those who are not expected to work, have some restriction on their ability to work or are unable to find employment' (the Departments, 1986, p.11). The forms of payment are mainly flat-rate, income-tested and cover old age, invalidity, sole parenthood, sickness and unemployment. A discretionary payment, special benefit, can be made to those who are in need but do not qualify under any of the other headings. Family allowance payments are paid to all families with children without regard to income or workforce status while a family income supplement is paid 'to low income families with children where the claimant is not in receipt of a pension or benefit' (the Departments, 1986, p.11).

Farmers, along with all other members of the community, are eligible to apply for the above payments, and to receive them if they satisfy the appropriate criteria. Despite this, farmers usually find themselves ineligible actually to receive payment in the event that they do apply. The reasons for their ineligibility is typically that their 'disability' is an inadequate return from a business venture which they might not be able to 'moth ball' in order to seek work elsewhere (the Departments, 1986). These considerations can disbar them from the two forms of benefit they are most likely to seek, unemployment benefits and special benefit. On the other hand, if a farmer who is otherwise eligible can demonstrate he 'has virtually ceased his normal activities' and is willing to undertake alternative work he is eligible for assistance (the Departments, 1986). Finally, spouses of farmers can receive benefit if they are not active partners in the farm (financial partnership is permitted), are willing and able to accept off-farm work, and are taking reasonable steps to obtain such work. This does provide a back-door way of obtaining benefit for many families but discriminates against single farmers while the problem of the work test remains.

On the face of it, the special benefit provision would appear to offer a way of meeting the needs of farmers who are financially distressed but cannot satisfy the work test for unemployment benefit. The problem is that there are limits to the discretion that can be exercised in providing special benefit. In particular, according to the Departments (1986) '... low or negative return to a primary producer does not of itself constitute the intended basis for the exercise of that discretion' (p.20). Despite this, instances have arisen where circumstances are such that the discretion has been exercised in certain farmers' favour.

In summary, the income support provided by social security payments, while covering a wide range of disabilities, including some of those experienced by financially distressed farmers, would appear to leave uncovered the needs of those who cannot satisfy the work test, or whose spouses cannot do so, and who do not fall within the discretionary scope provided for under the heading of special benefit.

Income support is provided by the RAS through its debt reconstruction and household support provisions. The first of these is not meant to be available to farmers falling in the 'welfare spectrum' but would provide income support to those who benefit from it. If the measure is correctly targeted then these beneficiaries should be

marginal farmers with good prospects of remaining
viable following the provision of assistance.
Inadequate monitoring does not permit determination
of the success or otherwise of the targeting, while
the welfare benefits of the income support provided
need to be balanced against the costs resulting
from the distortion it causes of the credit and
other input markets, and from the retention of such
marginal farmers in the industry which results.
While debt reconstruction may be preparing welfare
candidates for the future, it is not intended to
plug any welfare gap that may exist in the present.
Household support, on the other hand, is
directed at farmers who are classified as unviable,
most of whom would fall into the welfare spectrum.
Being specifically targeted at such a group, the
possibility of it plugging the welfare gap is
suggested. Not all distressed farmers would
qualify for household support, however, because
some of them would not be prepared to commit
themselves to placing their farm on the market, as
is necessary in order to receive benefits in the
first year, nor to actually do so, as is necessary
for the continuation of support into the second and
third years. The possibility of a gap therefore
remains. Whether this gap should be filled is
another matter given the non-discriminatory basis
of social security and the objective of adjustment.
A pragmatist's response to this could be that the
provision of limited support to clearly identified
farmers in need could be defended as part of the
RAS. A tentative outline of a way in which this
might be done is outlined below.

Financial Counselling

At a time of acute financial distress farmers are,
like most people in such a situation, stressed,
confused and demoralized. Their business affairs
are probably disorganized while their domestic and
social life can be under strain. The trauma
associated with acute financial distress has been
described by Salmon et al., (1977) and by Cary and
Weston (1978). Commonly, stressed farmers
experience difficulty in comprehending the true
nature of their dilemma and they instinctively
retreat to the farm which is their home, the key to
their life-style, and their sources of income.
Even if they are capable of comprehending the
reality of their situation, the stress they are
experiencing may so disorient them that they cannot

159

do so. Such people can benefit greatly from consultation with trained counsellors who can help them cope with their stress and confront their problems. Such counselling would deal with both personal and financial matters.

Some limited experience with the provision of counselling services to distressed farmers has been obtained in Australia, particularly in the Sunraysia area of Victoria which has been suffering from the consequences of a collapse of dried vine fruit prices. Evaluations of this experience (Lees, 1986) suggest that the counsellor should be primarily a financial expert but should have personal counselling skills, that he should be employed by a community organization that has few visible links with bureaucracy, and that the community should, at least in part, fund the counselling service.

Whether the provision of community-based counselling services should be made a component of the rural welfare service package and, if so, how, is the subject of current discussion in Australia. The matter is complex and space prevents further discussion of it in this chapter. Suffice to say that the operation of such services in rural areas suffering from acute market collapse (and there appears to be always one such area in Australia at any time) offers a way of providing, not only effective financial advice and personal help, but also a mechanism for boosting community morale, valuable links between the distressed and the various helping services, and co-ordination of service delivery.

The Rural Development Centre has proposed a way in which the Commonwealth and state governments might promote and participate in such activity, as follows:

a) A mechanism should be created for the declaration of selected rural areas as 'special adjustment zones' following agreement between the Commonwealth and state governments that this should be done. To qualify, such areas should be suffering from a serious and acute income decline in the economic base.

b) Once an area was declared a special adjustment zone it would be eligible for the provision of welfare assistance from the Commonwealth:

    - to fund partially the establishment of local action groups (LAGs)(other funds should come

from state government, industry and the local community);
       - to provide short-term training for financial counsellors;
       - to provide financially distressed farm families with cash grants, for 12 months only, which are equivalent in value to unemployment benefits and which are conditional on an appropriate report and subsequent supervision by a LAG counsellor: and
       - to fund the preparation, by Commonwealth, state and local authorities, of a social impact statement relating to the zone, which should include investigation of the adequacy of social and welfare services in the zone (McKay et al., 1985, pp.47-48)[2].

To many, the provision of cash grants to one group of small businessmen in the way suggested, would be unacceptable. If this is so, then the support could come from the household support component of the RAS. Such support should take the form of a loan but not require an undertaking to leave the farm. If, however, the support was to continue, for a further period of up to two years, such an undertaking should be required, and the farm must be placed on the market, and in the event of the farmer leaving his farm the loan could become a grant. While such an arrangement would no doubt contribute to closing the welfare gap it would not be without its critics.

CONCLUSION

The persistent decline in Australia's terms of trade, due in no small part to agricultural protectionism in the Northern Hemisphere, has retarded Australian economic performance for several decades. As the single biggest export sector, agriculture has been on the front line of the Australian battle to remain competitive in such a deteriorating environment. While the sector has, by and large, successfully met this challenge, the accompanying process of structural change and adjustment has contributed to a rural poverty problem that has posed problems for welfare service delivery, particularly income support. The policy response to these problems which has involved avoidance of the traditional method of providing support through the price mechanism, and which has attempted to adhere to principles demanding

consistency and equity of practice across the
welfare spectrum, should be of interest to
agricultural policy makers in a number of
countries.[3]

NOTES

1. This section draws on Musgrave (1982).
2. At the time of writing the Australian
government was in the process of initiating a
program with most of the features of this proposal.
3. The helpful comments of J. Remenyi, H.
Suchard and R. Stayner are acknowledged without
implications.

REFERENCES

Australian Government (1986) **Economic and Rural
Policy: A Government Statement**, Canberra,
Australian Government Publishing Service
Australian Rural Adjustment Unit (1980) **Rural
Income Support**, Armidale, University of New
England, Australian Rural Adjustment Unit,
Miscellaneous Publication No.3
Australian Rural Adjustment Unit (1981) Submission
to the Working Group Preparing a Policy
Discussion Paper on Agriculture, University of
New England, Armidale
Beck, T. Moir, B., Fraser, L. and Paul, P. (1985)
'Productivity Change in the Australian Sheep
Industry; A Zonal Analysis: 1952-53 to
1982-83', paper presented to the 55th
Australia and New Zealand Association for the
Advancement of Science Congress, Melbourne
Bureau of Agricultural Economics (1985) **Agri-
cultural Policies in the European Community:
The Origins, Nature and Effects on Production
and Trade**, Policy Monograph No.2, Australian
Government Publishing Service, Canberra
Bureau of Agricultural Economics (1986a) **Farm
Survey Reports: Financial Performance of
Australian Farms**, Australian Government Pub-
lishing Service, Canberra
Bureau of Agricultural Economics (1986b) **Crop and
Rainfall Insurance**, Australian Government
Publishing Service, Canberra
Bureau of Agricultural Economics (1986c) **Quarterly
Review of the Rural Economy**, 8, 2, May
Cary, J.W. and Weston, R.E. (1978) **Social Stress in
Agriculture**, University of Melbourne, School
of Agriculture and Forestry, Melbourne

162

Commission of Inquiry into Poverty (1974) **Rural Poverty in Northern New South Wales**, Australian Government Publishing Service, Canberra

Commission of Inquiry into Poverty (1975a) **Financial Aspects of Rural Poverty**, Australian Government Publishing Service, Canberra

Commission of Inquiry into Poverty (1975b) **Poverty in Australia**, 1, Australian Government Publishing Service, Canberra

Davidson, B.R. (1969) 'Welfare and Economic Aspects of Farm Size Adjustment in Australian Agriculture', in Makeham, J.P. and Bird, J.G. (eds) **Problems of Change in Australian Agriculture**, University of New England, Armidale, pp. 140-152

Davidson, B.R. (1986) 'Policies and Events Leading to the Present Alleged Agricultural Crisis', unpublished manuscript

Davis, D. (ed.) (1981) **Taxation and the Farm Sector**, Australian Rural Adjustment Unit, Bulletin No.3, University of New England, Armidale

de Maria, W. (1977) 'From Sulkies to Suburbia: Some Negative Social Consequences of Rural Living', in **KRAU Bulletin No.1**, Kellogg Rural Adjustment Unit, University of New England, Armidale, pp. 42-52

Department of Primary Industry and Department of Social Security (1986) **Review of Assistance Measures for Primary Producers in Financial Difficulty**, Canberra

Economic Planning and Advisory Council (1986) **The Medium Term Outlook for the Rural Sector**, Economic Planning and Advisory Council Paper No. 11, Commonwealth of Australia Council, Canberra

Freebairn, J.W. (1983) 'Drought Assistance Policy', **Australian Journal of Agricultural Economics**, 27, 3, pp. 185-199

Gregory, G. (ed.) (1980) **The ACID Workshop**, Kellogg Rural Adjustment Unit Bulletin No.2, University of New England, Armidale

Gruen, F.H. (1985) **How Bad is Australia's Economic Performance and Why?** Centre for Economic Policy Research, Discussion Paper No.127, Australian National University, Canberra

Harris, S.F., Gruen, F.H., Crawford, J.G. and Honan, N. (1974) **The Principles of Rural Policy in Australia: A Discussion Paper**, Australian Government Publishing Service, Canberra

Structural Change in Rural Australia

Herr, W. McD. (1966) 'Technological Change in Agriculture of the U.S. and Australia', **Journal of Farm Economics, 48,** 2, pp. 264-71

Industries Assistance Commission (1983) **Assistance to Australian Agriculture,** Australian Government Publishing Service, Canberra

Industries Assistance Commission (1984) **Annual Report for 1983-84,** Australian Government Publishing Service, Canberra

Jarrett, F.G. and Lindner, R.K. (1982) 'Rural Research in Australia', in Williams, D.B. (ed.) **Agriculture in the Australian Economy,** Sydney University Press, Sydney, Second Edition, pp. 83-105

Kingma, O.T. and Samuel, S.N. (1977) 'An Economic Perspective of Structural Adjustment in the Rural Sector', **Quarterly Review of Agricultural Economics, 30,** 3, pp. 201-215

Knopke, P. and Jervois, K. (1985) 'Productivity Change in the Australian Dairy Industry', paper presented to the 55th Congress Australian and New Zealand Association for the Advancement of Science, Melbourne

Kuznets, S. (1959) **Six Lectures on Economic Growth,** The Free Press, Glencoe

Laurence, D. and McKay, L. (1980) 'Inputs, Outputs and Productivity Change in the Australian Sheep Industry', **Australian Journal of Agricultural Economics, 24,** 1, pp. 46-59

Lees, J.W. (1986) Personal communication

Lloyd, A.G. (1986) Personal communication

McKay, D.H., Dimeck, N.F., Hanckel, N.P., and Musgrave, W.F. (1985) **Report of the Inquiry into the Grape and Wine Industries,** Australian Government Publishing Service, Canberra

McKay, L., Lawrence, D. and Vlastuen, C. (1983) 'Profit, Output Supply, and Input Demand Functions for Multiproduct Firms: the Case of Australian Agriculture', **International Economic Review, 24,** 2, June, pp. 323-339

Musgrave, W. (1982) 'Rural Adjustment', in Williams, D.B. (ed.) **Agriculture in the Australian Economy,** Sydney University Press, Sydney, Second Edition, pp. 292-308

Paul, P.B. (1984) 'The Measurement of Productivity Change in Australian Agriculture', paper presented to Bureau of Labour Market Research Workshop on Measures and Experiences of Productivity Change, Canberra

Paul, P.B., Abey, A. and Ockwell, A. (1984) 'An Analysis of Income and Productivity Change in the Australian Pastoral Zone', paper presented to Second International Rangelands Conference, Adelaide

Pandey, S., Piggott, R.R. and MacAulay, T.G. (1982) 'The Elasticity of Aggregate Australian Agricultural Supply: Estimates and Policy Implications', **Australian Journal of Agricultural Economics**, 26, 3, pp. 202-219

Policy Coordination Unit (1986) 'Low Incomes and Social Issues in Rural and Provincial Australia', Department of Community Services, Canberra, unpublished document

Powell, R.A. (1974) 'Technological Change in Australian Agriculture, 1920-21 to 1969-70', University of New England, Armidale, N.S.W. Unpublished Ph.D. thesis

Rae, J. (1986) 'Performance of the Farm Sector', paper presented to National Agricultural Outlook Conference, Canberra

Salmon, P.W., Back, I.M., Turnbull, E.D. and Trethowie, R.J. (1977) **The Human Crisis of Change in Agriculture**, School of Agriculture and Forestry, Melbourne

Solow, R.M. (1957) 'Technical Change and the Aggregate Production Function', **Review of Economics and Statistics**, 39, 3, pp. 312-320

Sorensen, A.D. and Weinand, H. (1981) 'Recent Changes in Employment Structures of Non-metropolitan Queensland', in Glass, R.E. and O'Connor, K.B. (eds), **Papers of the Australian and New Zealand Section Regional Science Association, Sixth Meeting**, Surfers Paradise, pp. 71-101

Stoeckel, A. (1983) Personal communication

Stoeckel, A. (1986) 'Australian Agriculture. What is the Future'? **Quarterly Review of the Rural Economy**, 8, 2, pp. 153-166

Stoeckel, A. and Miller, G. (1982) 'Agriculture in the Economy' in Williams, D.B. (ed.) **Agriculture in the Australian Economy**, Sydney University Press, Sydney Second Edition, pp. 166-185

Tornqvist, L. (1936) 'The Bank of Finland Consumption Price Index', **Bank of Finland Monthly Bulletin**, 10, pp. 1-8

Young, R. (1971) 'Productivity Growth in Australian Rural Industries', **Quarterly Review of Agricultural Economics**, 24, 4, pp. 185-205

Vincent, D.P. (1976) 'Economic Aspects of Farm Poverty', **Australian Journal of Agricultural Economics**, 23, 2, pp. 103-115

Chapter Eight

RELATIONSHIPS BETWEEN TECHNOLOGICAL CHANGE AND
SOCIAL DEVELOPMENT: A COMPARATIVE STUDY

Habibullah Khan and John Zerby

INTRODUCTION

In this chapter, technological progress is measured
with the use of five indices: one of which conveys
capital per worker, another of which reflects
scientific manpower and the remainder of which
consist of various combinations of indicators
related to scientific and technical knowledge. A
total of 126 countries are then classified on the
basis of these indices and the resulting rankings
are compared. Social development is measured by
constructing several other indices such as housing
and infrastructure, health, nutrition and culture.
The selected countries are ranked and grouped on
the basis of these disaggregated indices of social
change and results are correlated with those of
technological progress. The countries are further
grouped according to three levels of socioeconomic
development and the intra-group correlations are
compared. Data for 1970 as well as for 1980 are
used to study the changes over the past decade and
a number of taxonomic routines are used for
analyzing the data.
     The results indicate that the adoption of new
technical knowledge varies considerably with
different levels of development and that technological change both affects and is affected by the
level of socioeconomic development. The analysis
also suggests that several measures of technological progress are more informative than any
single measure.
     Bell and Hill (1978, p.225) noted, in 1974,
that while technology has been the subject of
ordered study in the social sciences for long
enough to suggest that a preamble on definitions
must be redundant, the rapid rate of diversifi-

166

cation in the interpretations given to the term makes clarification desirable. Since then, neither the explicit definition nor the implication through the use of the relevant terms has become standardized. While efforts to define words or concepts are tedious, their omission often leads to misunderstandings.

We follow the basic definition of Mansfield (1968, pp.10-11) which suggests that technology is words or knowledge concerning or relating to the practical, productive arts. Thus, a computer, in itself, is not technology but may be said to reflect a particular type of technology if reference is given to the knowledge embodied in its production and use. The term "high tech" refers to the accumulated information associated with a product and not to the product itself. Furthermore, the notion of high or low levels of technology implies a qualitative or quantitative comparison (or both) in the knowledge associated with two or more productive activities.

A similar distinction can be made between technological change and technical change. In conformity with the definition above, technological change refers to a change in knowledge, and, since the process is presumed to be evolutionary, any change is viewed as an addition of previously unknown or unavailable information. Technical change, on the other hand, concerns a change in the used methods of production, and can be defined in terms of a shift in the unit isoquant of the neoclassical production function. Such changes may be either innovative (the first use of a technique) or replicative (the subsequent use of an innovative technique). The latter generally involves a certain amount of research and modification, so that pure replication may not be easily identified. As noted by Bell and Hill (1978, p.228), it is generally more fruitful to visualize technical change on a more or less continuous scale ranging from a very high percentage of innovational components to a very low percentage. In the vast majority of cases, therefore, technical change requires a transfer technology (that is, knowledge) and not simply a transfer of technique.

The foregoing discussion suggests that a change in the total stock of knowledge may be regarded as the "cause", and a change in the productive technique may be the "effect". Not all such changes, however, are easily unravelled into unique causes and specific effects. For example,

the development of an insecticide for use in a
particular region may require a knowledge of
chemistry for the basic ingredients, of chemical
engineering for the most efficient method of
combining the ingredients, and of the environment
of the region for effective use of the product.
Each of these, in turn, may be greatly influenced
by knowledge gained from the development of other
products and techniques, some of which may be
seemingly unrelated to the processes in question.
Nevertheless, an increase in knowledge is a prerequisite for all but the most trivial technical
changes, and an eventual improvement in a
productive technique is, for the purpose here, a
necessary manifestation of an increase in
technology.

MEASUREMENT OF TECHNOLOGICAL CHANGE

An improvement in productive techniques is generally associated with a reduction in real costs and
a net gain in welfare. This notion was conveyed in
the suggestion by Brown and Usui (1974, p.73) that
"by availing oneself of a series of logistic curves
expressing the evolving technical efficiency of
each sector, one may attempt to build a framework
of appraisal of each country's status of scientific
and technological development for given types of
needs". Problems nevertheless arise from the
definition of sectors and from the specification of
types of needs.
    The ultimate sectoral disaggregation rests
with the individual industrial firm, and the
measurement of technological development then
becomes an attempt to assess, in a manner similar
to Hawthorne's (1971), the firm's aptitude in
assimilating technology. The results of that
study, however, indicated that while assessments
differed among firms, each received uniform ratings
among the six elements of technology. Hawthorne
therefore concluded that technology should be
treated as a system (rather than decomposed into
elements), and that progress must occur on a"broad
front" in order for a "worthwhile total result to
be achieved".
    A second approach to the measurement problem
utilizing industry classifications is described by
Brown and Usui (1974, pp.77-78) from a study by
Mitsui Information Development Inc. of Japan. It
involves the construction of an index of relative

168

knowledge-intensity by aggregating scores from five criteria: income elasticity of demand, historic rate of increase in productivity, environmental density, skill content of labour, and source of resource saving. The resulting index differed substantially from the conventional measure of capital intensity.

A third approach, which is closer to the one adopted here, originated with the UNESCO (1970) exploration of scientific and technical development for purposes of long-term planning. The procedure consists of the selection and grouping of a large number of indicators which can be placed into four broad categories. The first consists of indicators of the level of socioeconomic development and includes data on both production systems and social systems. The second comprises anthropological, organizational and capacity indicators which are related to the nation's scientific and technological development. The third category of indicators contains measures of sectoral perform-ance (such as chemical fertilizers used per hectare) and infrastructure characteristics (such as the proportion of single-line railway in use). The final group consists of indicators of scientific and technological potential. The ultimate objective of the approach is to correlate the major categories of indicators.

Several questions have been raised concerning the UNESCO approach, indicating that while the search for a broad strategy for scientific and technological development from an international standpoint has merit, it appears that a number of issues should be settled before proceeding too deeply into the search. First, the approach treats technology in terms of the performance characteris-tics of a nation's outputs delivered into economic life, but the intensive utilization of a complete set of goods and services seems to be a character-istic of economic development generally and not technological development specifically.

Second, the large number of socioeconomic indicators (125), when aggregated, may not reveal the linkages associated with the typically conceived transfer process. For example, it will not show which performance indicators are more closely related to new technological adaptation and may not shed light on the sources of comparative failure to adopt new technology.

Third, more attention must be given to the way in which the indicators are combined (i.e., the aggregation weights). It is extremely difficult to defend any specific method as the best one available. Rather than attempting to do so, it would be more useful to compare and analyze the results of several methods of combining the information. Judgements about the selected method can therefore be based upon the amount of information the method produces. Such ex post evaluations are generally more convincing than ex ante arguments.

TOWARDS A MORE RESTRICTED APPROACH

We begin with the assertion that the important question concerning technological change and development is the disparity (distance) between a nation's available technology and its practical applications of that technology in productive activities. Ideally, then, we require two measurements, one of which conveys numerically the nation's stock of relevant knowledge and the other of which reflects the net welfare gained from the technical improvements. The two measurements would, of course, be in different units so that subtracting one value from the other would have no intrinsic meaning. However, if the same units were maintained for a number of countries, a ranking of the differences would provide a ranking according to the magnitude of the disparity.

Neither the stock of knowledge nor the derived welfare is capable of direct measurement, so that reliance must be placed upon approximations based upon things which are measurable. Consider how a nation may improve its technology. Advances can be made through inventions (discoveries from first principles) or through innovations (new techniques derived through experience and know-how). In either case the results are achieved from the nation's scientists, engineers, and technicians, the stock of which may be used as a measure of indigenous technology.

A modification is necessary, however, in order to account for the substantial variations in the quality of scientists, engineers, and technical personnel among the various nations. Since the necessary training and experience is costly in terms of the resources and time devoted to the achievement of superior quality, we can presume that the qualitative differences are correlated

with macroeconomic variables such as GNP per
capita.

Technology can also be imported, either under
a licence agreement between two or more parties or
in support of direct investment. With the former,
the cost of the technology can be measured by the
royalties paid to the owner. With direct transfers
to affiliate companies, payment may either be a
royalty or a dividend. Millar (1978, pp.219-222)
indicated that official statistics are not
sufficiently detailed to separate the economic
payment for imported technology from payment for
risk capital. It nevertheless seems reasonable to
assume that technology will follow direct
investment, though not necessarily in a uniform
proportion. Per capita receipt of foreign capital
could therefore be used as an additional
approximation.

While certain types of scientific research may
have applications to both manufacturing and
agricultural activities, we adopt the view that
technology has become increasingly more specialized, so that specific knowledge will tend to
benefit primarily one or the other. Moreover, the
allocation of a nation's resources may favour one
activity at the expense of the other, either
through the market process or through government
policy. We therefore construct separate indices of
technological development and "test" them by
analyzing the correlations with manufacturing and
agricultural performance respectively. We also
assume that agricultural technology is less easily
"purchased" through direct investment by foreign
companies and will be qualitatively different with
greater use of inputs such as tractors, fertilizers
and irrigation.

The second required measurement - the net
welfare gained from technical improvements - is
even more difficult to obtain, primarily because it
is not possible to separate the gains which can be
traced exclusively to technology from those which
are assignable to other influences. We nevertheless assert that nations which rank well in the
technological indices should also achieve a high
ranking in one or more indices of basic fulfilment.
Failure to achieve that status may be attributed to
a large number of reasons. We believe that a
search for those reasons is the most productive
method for obtaining information about the
transfer process. We therefore attach little
importance to the correlations per se, but use them

to develop a list of nations which contribute relatively less to the correlation. Part of that list will consist of nations with a positive disparity between technology and basic needs fulfilment (that is, those for which the basic needs fulfilment is greater, in relative terms, than is predicted from the level of technological development) and part will consist of nations with a negative disparity (that is, those for which a relatively high level of technological development is associated with a relatively poor fulfilment of basic needs).

INDICES OF TECHNOLOGICAL DEVELOPMENT

The procedure for constructing the indices was first used for similar purposes by Harbison (1970). It consists of a calculation of the Euclidean distances from the vectors in multidimensional space, each of which represents the indicator values for a particular country, to the vector representing the largest value for each development stimulant and the smallest value for each development retardant. The stimulants and retardants are established by assumption and the resulting vector is said to be associated with the "ideal" country. Let x_{ij} denote the value of indicator j for country i and let x_{hj} denote the "ideal" score for the same indicator. Hence x_{hj} is associated with the hypothetical country H. The Euclidean distance is called the pattern of development (PD) and is obtained from

$$PD_i = \left[\sum_{j=i}^{n} (x_{ij}) - x_{hj})^2 \right]^{1/2} \qquad (8.1)$$

where the summation occurs across all indicators for country i.

If the values for a given indicator are tightly clustered, the distance component for that indicator will be small nearly identical for all countries. It will therefore be given relatively little weight in the aggregation of all indicators. Similarly, if two indicators are inversely correlated, when combined the resulting distance will add an arbitrary scale factor to each score. One indicator will therefore tend to work against the other, producing a relatively low weight for both. On the other hand, if two indicators are positively correlated then the resulting combination will be nearly equivalent to twice the weighting of either one when used alone. The aggregation weights are therefore determined implicitly from the scatter of indicator values, relative to the "ideal" value, and from the degree of similarity among the selected indicators. Since the indicators have various units of measure, the values are standardized in order to prevent inadvertent weighting according to the numerical magnitude. Each x_{ij} in equation (8.1) therefore represents the original unit minus the arithmetic mean and divided by the standard deviation for the j-th indicator. The "ideal" values are consequently judged from the magnitudes of the standardized units.

In order to assess the relative contribution of specific indicators in the aggregate indices, five indices were constructed to include the following indicators: (1) CAP7, stock of capital per industrial worker; (2) SMRD7, stock of scientists, engineers and technicians per 10,000 population (SCIENCE7), stock of scientists, engineers and technicians engaged in research and experimental development per 10,000 population (SCIRES7), expenditure for research and experimental development as a percentage of GNP (EXPRD7), and proportion of third level enrolment in science and engineering courses (ENROLSC7); (3) TECH7A, SMRD7 plus GNP per capital (4) TECH7B, TECH7A plus total per capita receipt of foreign capital (direct investment and other long-term private capital in SDRs); and (5) AGTECH7, proportion of third level enrolment in agricultural courses (ENROLAG7), use of tractors per 1,000 hectare arable land (TRACTOR7), use of chemical fertilizers per 1,000 hectare arable land (FERTIL7), and percentage of irrigated land (IRRIGAT7). All of the listed indicators were treated as development stimulants and the data were compiled for 1970. The rankings for 126 countries on the basis of the aggregate indices, as well as for selected components of the indices, are shown in the Appendix in this chapter.

The indicators for basic needs fulfilment were compiled for 1980. The ten-year lag was chosen primarily for convenience; further research would be necessary to demonstrate that such a time interval is in some way optimal. In addition to an index of industrial performance (INDUST8) and an index of agricultural performance (AGRI8), five sets of indicators were calculated: nutrition

Technology and Social Development

(NUTRI8), health (HEALTH8), housing (HOUSE8), culture (CULTR8) and a composite of basic needs (BASIC8) for which some (but not all) indicators are included in one of the other sets. A list of component indicators is given after Table 8.3 in the Appendix to this chapter.

The rank correlation coefficients which are shown in Table 8.1 indicate that the relationship between the measures of technological development and the fulfilment of basic needs is greater for the more broadly defined indices: TECH7B and BASIC8. The differences between the correlations produced by TECH7A and TECH7B, however, are relatively small. Moreover, while an inflow of foreign capital is more likely to improve the recipient nation's stock of knowledge than to detract from it, it is not clear whether the improvement will be in the same proportion, relative to the inflow, for all countries. The disparity between the measure of technology and the measure of basic needs fulfilment is therefore taken to be based upon TECH7A, rather than TECH7B, and BASIC8. Foreign capital, which is excluded from TECH7A, can then be used as a possible explanation for possible differences between TECH7A and BASIC8.

Table 8.1: Rank Correlation Coefficients for Aggregate Indices of Technology and Basic Needs (The numeral after the index abbreviation indicates 1970 or 1980 data)

	INDUST8	AGRI8	NUTRI8	HEALTH8	HOUSES	CULTR8	BASIC8
CAP7	0.705	0.259	0.612	0.677	0.690	0.720	0.763
SMRD7	0.712	0.390	0.648	0.704	0.567	0.639	0.722
TECH7A	0.769	0.388	0.695	0.767	0.624	0.712	0.789
AGTECH7	0.593	0.447	0.474	0.582	0.421	0.591	0.586

Note: Abbreviations are defined in the text; indicators comprising the indices are either listed in the text or after the Appendix Table.

The rank correlation coefficients also indicate that agricultural technology (AGTECH) is not as well correlated with either basic needs fulfilment or with agricultural performance (AGRI8)

174

as industrial technology is with BASIC8 and manufacturing performance. Since natural endowments,
such as the quality of land and rainfall, are
likely to be important in the case of agricultural
performance, the impact of that type of technology
may be less easily measured. Moreover, the linkage
between agricultural performance and basic needs
fulfilment appears to be more complicated than the
linkage through the manufacturing sector. For
example, we suggested in a recent paper (Kahn and
Zerby, 1985) that agricultural progress is more
directly related to basic needs fulfilment for
advanced countries than for less developed
countries. These considerations support the
decision to treat agricultural technology
separately.

In order to simplify the analysis of the
countries which display either a positive or a
negative disparity between TECH7A and BASIC8, the
126 countries included in the correlations were
separated into three groups. Group 1 consists of
55 least developed countries, predominantly in Asia
and Africa. Group 2 comprises 38 moderately
developed countries (mostly in Central and South
America), and group 2 contains 33 developed
countries. The grouping was achieved with a
clustering method using 66 indicators for 1970.
[See Zerby and Khan (1983) for a description of the
method and the selection of indicators.] The
respective membership of the groups is given in the
last column of Table 8.3 in the Appendix of this
chapter. A further simplification was achieved by
neglecting all countries for which the difference
in rankings fell within the range from +10 to -10.
The resulting list of countries is shown in Table
8.2.

The six developed countries for which the
ranking according to basic needs fulfilment was
greater than the ranking according to domestically
available technology all received substantial
amounts of foreign capital in 1970 (see Appendix
Table for the rankings according to FORCAP7). The
five countries with a negative disparity are among
the major socialist countries of Europe. While
their ranking according to manufacturing
performance is relatively high (the average ranking
is 4.4), the achievement was not transferred to
basic needs fulfilment (for which the average
ranking of the countries is 25.4). Since the
remaining 22 countries produced similar rankings
for both TECH7A and BASIC8, the two measures appear

Technology and Social Development

Table 8.2: List of Countries which Contribute
Relatively Less to the Correlations. (Rank based
upon TECH7A minus rank based upon BASIC8 lies
outside the range from +10 to −10)

Countries with a positive disparity (difference > +10)		Countries with a negative disparity (difference < −10)	
Highly Developed Countries (total number = 33)			
Austria	+17	Bulgaria	−15
Australia	+12	Czechoslovakia	−12
Canada	+12	Hungary	−27
Denmark	+13	Poland	−23
Greece	+16	Romania	−14
Ireland	+16		
18% of total (mean = +14.3)		15% of total (mean = −18.2)	
Moderately Developed Countries (total number = 38)			
Brazil	+11	Portugal	−14
Columbia	+27	South Africa	−18
Costa Rica	+64	Chile	−15
El Salvador	+22	Dominican Rep.	−23
Mexico	+31	Venezuela	−11
Paraguay	+40	Egypt	−32
Peru	+21.5		
Uruguay	+25		
Fiji	+31		
Jordan	+32.5		
Korea	+13		
Lebanon	+22		
Malaysia	+19		
Philippines	+18		
Sri Lanka	+33		
Thailand	+31		
42% of total (mean = +27.6)		16% of total (mean = −18.8)	

Table 8.2 continues

Table 8.2 continued

Less Developed Countries (total number = 55)			
Dem. Yemen	+16	Afghanistan	-35
Indonesia	+17	Bangladesh	-27
Laos	+31	Burma	-53
Pakistan	+21	Kampuchea	-32
Papua N.G.	+20	Nepal	-13
Algeria	+20	Benin	-38
Botswana	+46	Burundi	-50
Congo	+45	Chad	-11
Liberia	+36	Ethiopia	-24
Senegal	+12	Ghana	-53.5
Tunisia	+18.5	Guinea	-75
Zimbabwe	+18	Lesotheo	-24.5
		Mozambique	-66
		Niger	-74
		Rwanda	-18.5
		Sierra Leone	-37
		Sudan	-17.5
		Togo	-34
		Uganda	-36
		Tanzania	-13.8
		Upper Volta	-24
		Zaire	-11
24% of total (mean = +24.7)		48% of total (mean = -34.7)	

to be reasonably consistent for the developed countries. It should be noted, however, that the intra-group disparities for TECH7A are greater for those countries than for either of the other two groups.[1]

For the moderately developed countries, the most frequent disparity beyond the +10 to -10 range of differences in ranks is positive, indicating that for those countries basic needs fulfilment is accomplished by means other than, or in addition to, indigenous technology. Although that group of 16 countries received more foreign capital, on average, than the six moderately developed countries with a negative disparity, the difference is not statistically significant.[2] The group with a positive disparity tends to rely more heavily on agriculture[3] but only in the case of Malaysia and Sri Lanka are the rankings for AGRI8 relatively

177

high. On the other hand, the six countries with a negative disparity attained higher placings in terms of manufacturing performance than the positive disparity countries, and that difference is weakly significant.[4] Since the negative disparity countries rely more heavily on industrialization, they are evidently similar in this respect to the socialist countries in the previous group: the level of indigenous technology has an apparent effect on manufacturing performance, but the effect is not fully transmitted to basic needs fulfilment. Although 58% of the countries in this group lie outside the designated interval (compared with 33% for the developed countries) the rank correlation between TECH7A and BASIC8 is higher for the moderately developed countries when the rankings are formed separately for each group.[5]

Among the 55 less developed countries 42% show a negative disparity, and with an additional 24% having a positive disparity, the relationship between TECH7A and BASIC8 is the weakest of the three groups. The group with positive disparities is higher placed, on the average, in terms of foreign capital as well as manufacturing performance, agricultural performance and basic needs fulfilment.[6] Consequently, the least developed group, according to these measures, has been the least successful in transferring their domestically available technology to basic needs fulfilment.

SUMMARY AND CONCLUSIONS

A major objective of this chapter was to state the case for a more extensive effort to measure technological development despite obvious weaknesses in the available data. If the results of a measurement process are used and interpreted within the constraints imposed by data limitations, as they always should be, they are nevertheless likely to add more precision to the study of technological transfer than would otherwise be possible. Perhaps of greater importance, each numerical analysis becomes a point of comparison for future efforts. In that way, not only will the shortcomings in the data be made obvious, and hopefully eliminated, but the numerical procedures are also likely to be improved.

A second objective was to indicate that a

nation's supply of scientists, engineers and
technical personnel should form the basis for an
index of technological development. It is, of
course, necessary to adjust for different qualities
of such personnel among the various countries and
to allow for the purchase of technology from other
countries. In this study the use of per capita GNP
and per capita receipt of foreign capital for the
respective adjustments proved useful but not
completely adequate. GNP may have overstated the
differing qualities of scientific personnel and
foreign capital may not accurately reflect the
amount of imported technology. For example, while
FORCAP7 improved the ranking of Australia in terms
of TECH7B to coincide with the ranking according to
BASIC8, the outflow of capital from the U.S.
lowered its technology index to a level which was
well below its basic needs fulfilment.

While the analysis indicated that a more
broadly defined index of technology is likely to be
better than a narrow one, the inclusion of large
numbers of economic performance indicators is
likely to cloud the main issues. The application
of knowledge and experience acquired by a nation's
technical personnel to successful productive
activities is an extremely important part of the
transfer process. If it becomes submerged within
an index which reflects technological potential as
well as its realization, then that part of the
transfer process cannot be examined and compared.
Similarly, to argue that the United States is a
"high-tech" country because it produces and exports
(at least in the recent past) substantial amounts
of commodities with a "high-tech character" is to
explain the effect rather than the cause.

The pattern of correlation among the indices
(and among their major components) suggests that
for the least developed countries technological
progress does not contribute substantially to the
attainment of social development. In particular,
the more broadly defined index (TECH7B) showed
little correlation with most of the social
indicators for the group. As a consequence, it
could be argued that modernization and industrial
development with the help of imported technology
may not be adequate for the fulfilment of basic
needs in the poorer countries. A number of
economists, such as Maitra (1985; also Chapter 2 of
this volume), have put forward such an argument and
suggested that these countries should adopt
labour-intensive, indigenous technology.

Technology and Social Development

Other empirical findings of this study can be summarized as follows: (1) The developed countries in North America and Europe (except Greece, Ireland and Spain) scored well in the two aggregate indices of technological development and have successfully adapted technological knowledge to manufacturing activities. Rankings for TECH7B and BASIC8 are well correlated, but agricultural technology and its transfer to agricultural performance and basic needs fulfilment is much less apparent. (2) Some of the newly industrialized countries such as Israel, South Korea and Singapore also rank well in terms of TECH7A and TECH7B, with Cyprus and Tobago showing a noticeable improvement during the last decade. (3) Kuwait ranks with the countries just mentioned, but the remaining oil-rich nations lag behind in all indices. (4) There are substantial differences between the countries in terms of the level of technological development but the international disparities have diminished slightly over the past ten years. (5) There are relatively more disparities between richer countries than poorer countries in the technology indices. (6) The selected measures of technological development are highly correlated but they are not perfect substitutes. (7) Technological development and its relationship to basic needs fulfilment varies considerably with different stages of development. In the least developed countries, technological progress did not play a consistent role in the fulfilment of basic needs. It undoubtedly contributed, but that contribution was much less noticeable than for the other two groups.

NOTES

1. The difference between the highest and the lowest PD scores for group 3 is 0.673. The same difference for groups 2 and 1, respectively, is 0.2008 and 0.1164. The PD scores, calculated from equation (8.1), are not shown in the table.
2. The difference in average rankings is 9.5 and the associated t-value, using separate variance estimates, is 0.55.
3. In terms of agricultural performance, the average ranking for the group with a positive disparity is 47.6 (compared with 54.3 for the group with a negative disparity) and the average ranking in terms of industrial performance is 59.0 (compared with 53.3 for the group with a negative disparity).

4. The difference is 18.05 and the t-value is 1.96 with separate variance estimates.

5. The rank correlation coefficients for the developed countries (with rankings from 1 to 33) is 0.475 and for the moderately developed countries (with rankings from 1 to 38) is 0.742. When the three groups are combined (so that the rankings range from 1 to 126), the order of the moderately developed group is maintained, but the numerical value of the rankings, and hence the difference in rankings, is substantially higher. One group will have more "outliers" than another if the former is more spread out within the 126 places.

6. The average group rankings are as follows:

	Positive Disparity	Negative Disparity	t-value
FORCAP7	67.0	92.6	−2.79
INDUST8	87.5	105.8	−3.49
BASIC8	84.8	107.1	−4.55
AGRI8	86.7	105.9	−3.60

REFERENCES

Bell, R.M. and S.C. Hill (1978) "Research on Technology and Innovation", pp. 225–274 in F. Bradbury, P. Jervis, R. Johnston and A. Pearson (eds.), **Transfer Process in Technical Change**, Sijthoff and Noordhoff, Alphen aan den Rijn, Netherlands (The paper was first presented at a meeting held at the University of Stirling in July, 1974)

Brown, M. and M. Usui (1974) "Review of Discussions", in pp. 13–112 OECD, **Choice and Adaptation of Technology in Developing Countries**, Organisation for Economic Cooperation and Development, Paris

Elsten, J. (1983) **Explaining Technical Change**, Cambridge University Press, Cambridge

Harbison, F.H., J. Maruhnic and J.R. Resnick (1970) **Quantitative Analysis of Modernisation and Development**, Princeton University Press, Princeton, New Jersey

Hawthorne, E.P. (1971) **The Transfer of Technology**, OECD, Paris

Khan, M.H. (1986) **Socioeconomic Development of**

ASEAN: An International Perspective, Chopmen, Singapore

Khan, M.H. and J.A. Zerby (1985) "Relationships between Agricultural Development, Industrialisation and Basic Needs Fulfilment: A Taxonomic Approach", paper presented at the 19th International Conference of Agricultural Economists, Malaga, Spain

Maitra, P. (1985) "Population, Technology and Economic Development", paper presented at the 14th Conference of Economists, Sydney

Mansfield, E. (1968) **Industrial Research and Technological Innovation**, Norton, New York

Millar, J.S. (1978) "Technological Transfer - The International Dimension", pp. 211-224 in F. Bradbury, P. Jervis, R. Johnston and A. Pearson (eds.), **Transfer Process in Technical Change**, Alphen aan den Rijn, Netherlands

Schumpeter, J. (1961) **The Theory of Economic Development**, Oxford University Press, New York

Stewart, F. (1977) **Technology and Underdevelopment**, Macmillan, London

Szchepanik, E.F. (1975) **Agricultural Policies at Different Levels of Development**, FAO, Rome

UNESCO, (1970) **A Methodology for Planning Technology Development** (Report by Arthur D. Little, Inc. and Hetrick Associates, Inc.), UNESCO, Paris

Zerby, J.A. and Khan, M.H. (1983) "Quantitative Analysis of World Development: A Cluster Analytic Approach", **Pakistan Journal of Applied Economics**, 2, 1, pp. 39-63

Table 8.3: Rankings of 126 Countries According to Various Indicators and Indices

Country	CAP7	SCIENCE7	SCIRES7	EXPRD7	ENROLSC7	SMRD7	GNP7	TECH7A	FORCAP7	TECH7B	INDUST8	BASIC8	AGRI8	Group
Albania	28	59	44	88.5	53	47	29.5	4	33.5	47	46	50	2	2
Austria	25	29	35	68.5	40	37	18	32	11	31	23	15	28.5	3
Australia	7	9.5	18	16.5	33	15	8	13	3	17	24	1	16	3
Belgium	24	17	24	16.5	75	19	11	18	11	17	19	14	38	3
Bulgaria	45	2	7	21.5	3	5	29.5	8	27.5	12	6	23	37	3
Canada	3	10	21	26	44	18	4	15	32	15	22	3	8	3
Czecho-slovakia	60	36	1	1	10	3	29.5	5	27.5	5	3	17	31	3
Denmark	9	9.5	26	75.5	70.5	29	6	22	1	9	28	9	18.5	3
Finland	15	31	25	26	34	28	13	24	54	27	5	16	63	3
France	14	15.5	10	12	68	10	10	11	11	11	20	13	33	3
German D.R.	65	19.5	11	21.5	8	11	29.5	16	27.5	16	1	20	40	3
Germany	18	9.5	13	115.5	13	6	7	4	57	7.5	12	12	22	3
Greece	27	26	62	115.5	81	54	24	41	21	40	39	25	39	3
Hungary	56	3	4	2	11	2	29.5	2	27.5	3	7	29	17	3
Ireland	31	48	30	32	78.5	39	23	38	11	36	32	22	6	3
Italy	33	9.5	32	32	45.5	26	20	23	20	22	10	19	36	3
Japan	11	9.5	6	12	48	7	17	7	11	7.5	9	4	74	3
Netherlands	12	15.5	3	7.5	26	4	12	3	11	4	15	10	5	3
New Zealand	19	9.5	2	32	36	8	14	10	62	13	17	5	1	3
Norway	10	28	22	15	27	20	9	19	11	18	11	11	13	3
Poland	38	1	8	3	5	1	29.5	1	27.5	2	4	24	94	3
Portugal	67	21.5	15.5	102.5	51	27	47	29	55	32	30	43	18.5	2
Romania	37	21.5	27	21.5	12	'7	29.5	20	27.5	37	2	34	68	3
Spain	44	18	60.5	102.5	23	33	34	35	41	37	35	30	61	2
South Africa	30	9.5	19.5	10	66	12	43	17	37	19	18	51	75	2
Sweden	8	9.5	19.5	12	51	13	2	9	11	10	13	7	7	3
Switzerland	13	9.5	23	7.5	35	9	5	6	11	6	14	8	14	3
U.K.	32	30	9	7.5	25	14	15	14	124	23	21	6	26	3
U.S.A.	5	32	5	7.5	59	16	1	12	115	14	8	2	3	3

Table 8.3 continues

183

Country	CAP7	SCIENCE7	SCIRES7	EXPRD7	ENROLSC7	SMRD7	GNP7	TECH7A	FORCAP7	TECH7B	INDUST8	BASIC8	AGRI8	Group
Yugoslavia	34	24	28	39	28	23	29.5	25	68	29	16	32	62	3
Argentina	3	4	34	21.5	77	21	35	26	38	26	37	26	51	3
Bolivia	114	46	59	88.5	91	85	82	88	70	85	92	90	100	2
Brazil	42	59	44	102.5	56	72	53	67	39	61	36	56	93	2
Chile	53	21.5	36	21.5	32	24	39	27	36	28	41	42	83	2
Columbia	62	59	96	122	38.5	90	63	87	76	88	53	60	48	2
Costa Rica	46	59	44	88.5	118	113	49	109	42	96	54.5	45	41	2
Cuba	61	39.5	50.5	4	18	22	51	28	17	25	49	36	4	2
Dominican Republic	52	67	44	88.5	106	103	60	98	49	89	72	75	81	2
Ecuador	83	59	44	102.5	57.5	73	73.5	73	40	64	71	66	58	2
El Salvador	78	52	44	82	102	92.5	68	92	75	93	59	70	66.5	1
Guatemala	87	59	124	115.5	84	108	62	102	99	104	57	97	47	1
Guyana	71	39.5	55	32	14	35	58	39	61	41	56	39	76	1
Haiti	117	88	116.5	62	115	110	114.5	111	100	115	96	112	110	1
Honduras	76	116	44	88.5	76	85	2	85	2	33	66	88.5	77	2
Jamaica	16	39.5	55	122	7	51	44	46	19	43	52	40	118	2
Mexico	49	124.5	92.5	115.5	51	99	46	79	44	69.5	43	48	34	2
Nicaragua	68	59	44	122	22	66	54	64.5	46	63	83.5	58	123	2
Panama	17	39.5	55	32	89	50	45	44	35	44	63	47	45	2
Paraguay	97	59	94.5	88.5	98.5	106.5	79	105	63	102	58	65	108	2
Peru	70	59	44	75.5	103	91	52	82.5	64	76	47	61	109	3
Puerto Rico	6	27	55	21.5	67	34	16	31	27.5	30	27	21	114	2
Tobago	35	39.5	38	102.5	20	49	40	42	22	42	34	37	70	2
Uruguay	73	45	15.5	115.5	113.5	58	38	53	45	51	45	28	59	2
Venezuela	21	21.5	15.5	115.5	73.5	30	25	30	121	38	42	41	72	1
Afghanistan	93.5	115	116.5	62	73.5	80.5	101.5	86	90	108	97	121	82	1
Bangladesh	109	88	116.5	75.5	57.5	83	112	93	113	95	95	120	44	1
Brunei	2	88	70.5	70	70.5	78	22	57	83.5	60	66	52	52	1
Burma	120	88	116.5	26	21	40	114.5	47	113	54	111	100	43	1
Cyprus	50	34	50.5	75.5	29.5	45	37	40	110.5	45	31	33	43	3
Kampuchea	101	88	116.5	62	55	71	105	77	110.5	81	116	109	101	1
Dem. Yemen	96	111	82.5	102.5	124	124	103	124	51	122	109	108	65	1
Fiji	39	69	101	85.5	45.5	80.5	55	75	23	62	83.5	44	35	2
Hong Kong	89	72	55	32	9	36	42	37	17	35	33	31	126	3

Table 8.3 continues

Country	CAP7	SCIENCE7	SCIRES7	EXPRD7	ENROLSC7	SMRD7	GNP7	TECH7A	FORCAP7	TECH7B	INDUST8	BASIC8	AGRI8	Group
India	115	66	89	75.5	108	109	106.5	110	83.5	111	60	101	78.5	1
Indonesia	119	88	70.5	49	98.5	82	117	90	83.5	91	78	73	25	1
Iran	75	88	92.5	102.5	19	65	57	66	122.5	78	67	63	97	1
Iraq	92	88	105.5	75.5	2	62	59	64.5	122.5	75	82	74	46	1
Israel	20	25	29	18	43	25	19	21	5	21	85	18	55	3
Jordan	59	65	101	125	104.5	123	67	121	108	120	89	88.5	80	2
Korea	77	47	58	102.5	17	55	78	59	53	59	26	46	24	2
Kuwait	1	35	15.5	125	100	52	3	34	27.5	34	38	35	27	2
Laos	123	88	88	49	124	119	125	122	83.5	119	90	91	42	1
Lebanon	54	33	87	32	111	60	48	60	17.0	46	54.5	38	32	2
Malaysia	26	53	86	88.5	38.5	68	65	68	47	65	40	49	9	2
Mongolia	51	70	33	88.5	42	56	50	55	33.5	48	48	54.5	115	2
Nepal	55	88	116.5	6.2	92	87	116	97	95	97.5	125	110	91	1
Pakistan	106	120	101	115.5	121	125	91	125	83.5	123	93	104	50	1
Papua N.G.	23	111	82.5	102.5	109.5	114	75	112	51	110	87	92	23	1
Philippines	98	43	60.5	102.5	95	92.5	88.5	96	104	97.5	61	78	54	2
Saudi Arabia	64	88	97.5	82	72	95	41	74	125	125	73	69	122	1
Singapore	29	39.5	52	32	4	32	36	33	4	24	29	27	20	3
Sri Lanka	79	54	70.5	125	93	112	88.5	114	83.5	114	104	81	12	2
Syria	90	44	44	88.5	54	59	70	63	106	68	62	57	10	2
Thailand	40	123	82.5	102.5	97	106.5	90	108	74	106	94	77	57	2
Turkey	66	105	79	49	16	57	61	61	91	66	51	59	86	2
Vietnam	74	88	70.5	102.5	78.5	77	77	71	83.5	72	97	79	28.5	2
Yemen	122	88	116.5	62	124	122	122	123	95	121	124	119	107	1
Algeria	48	111	108	102.5	62	95	64	91	59	84	81	71	95	1
Angola	72	88	70.5	49	112	104	69	100	83.5	100.5	76	107	116	1
Benin	118	88	70.5	49	15	48	109	56	83.5	58	112	94	64	1
Botswana	86	71	105.5	115.5	124	126	96	126	92	124	88	80	125	1
Brundi	126	88	116.5	62	49	69	119.5	76	95	77	107	126	84	1
Cen. Africa Republic	116	88	91	102.5	82	101	104	103.5	102	105	113	105	87	1
Chad	104	88	94.5	75.5	107	111	110	113	107	116	120	124	78.5	1
Congo	69	107	105.5	102.5	109.5	118	84	117	6	92	91	72	117	1
Egypt	107	49	12	39	64.5	31	86	36	118	39	44	68	30	2
Ethiopia	110	88	116.5	62	94	88.5	118	99	105	99	115	123	15	1

Table 8.3 continues

185

Country	CAP7	SCIENCE7	SCIRES7	EXPRD7	ENROLSC7	SMRD7	GNP7	TECH7A	FORCAP7	TECH7B	INDUST8	BASIC8	AGRI8	Group
Ghana	88	64	31	32	90	44	81	49	58	52	99	102.5	99	1
Guinea	84	50	116.5	62	1	38	92	43	113	50	121	118	7	1
Ivory Coast	57	111	90	75.5	80	85.5	73.5	89	51	82	102	86.5	71	1
Kenya	91	88	70.5	39	31	47	97	52	67	56	64	83	104	1
Lesotho	125	111	70.5	49	37	53	121	62	83.5	67	117	86.5	119	1
Siberia	47	111	81.5	102.5	117	120	66	119	48	112	101	83	105	1
Libya	22	88	97.5	82	76	97	21	58	126	126	68	54.5	112.5	1
Madagascar	103	88	101	39	83	64	101.5	70	83.5	71	79	67	89	1
Malawi	113	68	126	49	104.5	100	119.5	103.5	120	107	100	113	21	1
Mali	121	88	116.5	62	101	102	126	106	69	103	126	116	56	1
Mauritania	82	88	70.5	49	124	117	93	118	83.5	117	105	115	112.5	1
Mauritius	95	51	44	49	29.5	46	83	50	69	57	75	53	102	2
Morocco	80	111	70.5	102.5	113.5	116	80	115	103	113	71	64	106	1
Mozambique	58	88	70.5	49	6	41	85	45	65	49	71	111	103	1
Niger	102	88	116.5	62	2	42	106.5	48	71	53	114	122	11	1
Nigeria	99	121	101	75.5	64.5	86	98	95	56	86	70	93	60	1
Rwando	124	122	116.5	62	61	76	123	84	117	87	103	102.5	73	1
Senegal	85	111	82.5	39	120	105	87	107	116	108	98	95	124	1
Sierra Leone	100	88	70.5	49	60	61	94	69	66	69.5	80	106	92	1
Somalia	111	117	125	68.5	116	115	113	120	101	118	123	117	111	1
Sudan	81	118.5	105.5	49	69	77	95	80.5	109	83	122	98	69	1
Togo	108	118.5	70.5	14	96	43	100	51	83.5	55	106	85	66.5	1
Tunisia	63	126	82.5	102.5	47	79	72	80.5	60	74	50	62	96	1
Uganda	112	88	70.5	49	85	74	99	78	98	79	119	114	49	1
Tanzania	36	106	70.5	49	87	75	108	82.5	73	80	74	99	85	1
Upper Volta	93.5	104	109	75.5	86	98	122	101	72	100.5	110	125	53	1
Zaire	105	88	88	49	63	63	111	72	119	73	118	83	88	1
Zambia	4	124.5	37	115.5	119	121	56	116	43	109	85	96	121	1
Zimbabwe	41	88	116.5	120	41	95	71	94	95	94	86	76	120	1

Notes for Table 8.3: List of indicators. INDUST8. ENROL.VO: Prop. of 2nd level enrol. in voc. educ., ENROL.SC: Prop. of 3rd level enrol. in science & eng. courses, SCIENCE: Stock of scientists, engineers & technicians/1000 pop., SCI.RES: stock of scientists, engineers & technicians engaged in R&D/10,000 pop., EXP.R&D: Exp. for R&D as % of GDP, IND.PROD: Index of indust. prod., IND.POP: % of econ. active pop.

Notes for Table 8.3 continues

engaged in indust. activity, IND.ACT: % contri. of industr. activity in GDP, MANUFACT: % contri. of manufact. in GDP, ENERGY: Per cap energy consumption, ELECTRIC: Per cap elect. consumption, STEEL: Steel Consumption/cap., SAL+WAGE: Salaried & wage earners as % of total econ. active pop., MANU/EX: % contri. of manufacturing in exports.

AGR18: Prop. of 3rd level enrol. in agri. courses, LAND/PER: Arable land per person agri., AG/GDP: % contri. of agri. in GDP, AG.PROD: Index of agri. prd., TRACTORS: Use of tractors/1000 hect., FERTILIZ: Use of chem.fertiliz./1000. hect., AG/EX: % contri. of agri in expt. IRRIGAT: % of irrigated land, AG/IMP*: % contri. of agri. in impt., FOOD.PRO: Index of food prod., CROP.PRO: Index of crop prod., LIVESTOCK: Index of livestock prod., CER.PROD: Index of cereal prod., FORESTRY: roundwood prod./cap., FISHERY: Fish catches/1000 pop.

BASIC8: POP.GRO*: Annual rate of growth of pop., HOSPITAL: Hospital beds/10,000 pop., INFANT*: Infant mortality rate, LIFE.EXP: Expect. of life, DISEASE*: Death rate due to infect & other diseases/100,000 pop., DIETARY: Dietary energy supply in relation to nutri. req., CALORIE: Cal. consumption as % of req., PROTEIN: Protein consumed/cap./day, ADUL.LIT*: % of illiteracy of adult pop., ENROL.1: 1st level enrol. ratio, ENROL.2: 2nd level enrol. ratio, EXP.ED: Govt. expd. on educ. as % of GNP, TOILETS: Dwellings with toilet as % of dwell., WATER: Dwellings with piped water as % of all dwell., LIGHT: Dwellings with elec. as % of all dwell., CONS.DWE: Dwelling constructed/1000 pop., GDP/CAP: GDP/cap in US$, DAILIES: Circulation of daily newspapers/1000 pop., RADIOS: No. of radio per 1000 pop., TELEPHONE: No. of telephones per 100 pop.

Sources: Various UN publications.

* Indicators which are treated as 'retardant' to development.

187

Chapter Nine

SUSTAINABLE   RESOURCE   USE   AND   DEVELOPMENT:
UNCERTAINTY, IRREVERSIBILITY AND RATIONAL CHOICE

Anthony H. Chisholm

INTRODUCTION

Preservation versus development of rare natural
environments, the protection of endangered species,
and the sustainability of biologically-based
productive systems like agriculture are issues of
concern to societies in both developed and
developing countries. From a conceptual viewpoint,
the above issues are closely linked by two key
concepts: irreversibility and uncertainty. Ecosystems, natural populations of flora and fauna,
and most land used for agriculture are the products
of geomorphologic and biological processes that
represent a time frame measured in aeons. If they
are destroyed or too severely degraded, they cannot
be reproduced or restored by man. There is thus a
basic irreversibility.
    Uncertainty is pervasive in economic life, but
more than the usual degree of uncertainty surrounds
the potential future benefits from conserving ecosystems or questions of sustainable resource-use.
The introduction of uncertainty into a decision-
making model requires a clear specification of the
nature and source(s) of uncertainty. The goal of
'sustainability' has been strongly advocated by
ecologists and biological scientists. This goal is
usually stated in very general terms and needs to
be defined more precisely for purposes of economic
analysis.
    This chapter examines the problem of rational
social choice for the above class of resource
policy problems. Ultimately, most policy decisions
relating to competing uses for natural resources,
and the management of biologically-based production
systems (e.g., agriculture), are made under
circumstances of risk aversion and a high degree of

unresolved uncertainty. Expected utility theory provides the conventional framework for rational individual choice under uncertainty. However, a number of researchers have questioned the relevance and applicability of expected utility theory to the above class of problems. Alternative theories of rational choice have been proposed which place greater weight on risk conservatism, including regret theory and the strategy of safe minimum standards of conservation. The expected utility and regret theories are reviewed briefly and a more detailed analysis is made of the safe minimum standards approach and of the research approach largely associated with Resources for the Future. The relationship between these latter approaches and the goal of sustainability are then examined.

Most important preservation-development questions involve long planning horizons and the rate of discounting used typically has a significant effect on the results. It is beyond the scope of this chapter to attempt to survey the substantial literature on the social rate of discount. However, some seemingly important issues are raised which have received no, or little, attention in the mainstream debate on the choice of a social discount rate.

This chapter attempts to cover a lot of ground, but there are important things it does not do that should be stated at the outset. The major purpose of this chapter is to find and examine conceptual frameworks which lead us to ask the right questions and within which the questions can be usefully investigated, rather than attempt to reach firm conclusions on specific questions. However, it is not possible in a single chapter to consider all interesting frameworks for thinking about resource and environmental issues, or to exhaustively analyze the foundations of the particular framework(s) that are presented. The main framework examined is that of benefit-cost analysis (CBA) and the associated decision-rule for efficient choice of potential Pareto improvement. This chapter does not examine the philosophical basis of utilitarianism underpinning CBA (e.g., see MacIntyre 1977) and it only touches upon the literature on environmental ethics (e.g. see Kneese and Schultz, 1985). The implications for resource and environmental questions of other notable decision-rules, such as the ethically-based decision rule proposed by Rawls (1971), are not discussed.

189

IRREVERSIBILITY AND UNCERTAINTY

The strong concern that many people feel for the fate of threatened environments presumably reflects a perception that loss will be irreversible. Many of the biological impacts of man's development activities can be extremely difficult to reverse over any measure of time that has any meaning for human societies. There is a basis for social decisions which are more than usually careful if environmental modifications are technically irreversible, or if restoration of an environment to its original state is excessively costly in resources or time. Failure to take particular actions may also lead to irreversible consequences. For example, a pollution abatement program may be needed to prevent extinction of a species, or a soil conservation program may be required if irreversible land degradation is to be avoided.

There is a substantial literature on the role of irreversibility in the approach society should take towards economic development and environmental preservation.[1] The principal conclusion that emerges from most analyses of irreversibility is one which accords with intuition: Resources should be developed less extensively where there is downward irreversibility, e.g., wilderness areas which once developed cannot be restored to their original state. Similarly, greater emphasis should be placed on investments in environmental quality in cases where 'not investing' has irreversible consequences.

For irreversibility to generate different optimal decisions than in the reversible case, there must be some change over time in the attractiveness of policy choices. For example, if future generations value environmental amenities more highly (relative to produced goods and services) than does the present generation then lower rates of development will be desirable when the development is irreversible. If development were completely reversible, future generations could increase the supply of environmental amenities by switching back to a less developed state. However, when the biological impacts of development are irreversible, it is socially desirable to accept less than the 'ideal' current extent of development to preserve more environmental amenities for the future when demand is higher. Clearly, irreversibility would pose no special problem if the 'in situ' resources of an environment were expected to decline in value relative to the value of, say, the extractive resources on the site.

The view that unique natural environments are likely to appreciate in value relative to the value of goods and services they might yield if developed is crucially dependent on an assumption of asymmetric technological change made by Krutilla (1967). That is to say, while a steady stream of technological change will expand capacity to produce ordinary goods and services, it will not produce rare natural environments that are fixed in supply. It is also usually assumed, that through time, the income elasticity of demand for the environmental amenities will grow relative to the income elasticity of demand for goods and services produced by development of environmental sites. Some may argue that this is an unduly 'technological determinist' view of the world, particularly for many developing countries. We cannot assume that future technological advance will be sufficient to cause the value of food and extractive resources to decline over time relative to the value of environmental amenities. There is too much social and economic uncertainty about future time paths for technological change, population growth, income levels, ethical values and tastes, and other variables which influence future demand for natural resources.

Another kind of uncertainty about the future benefits of preservation is the largely unknown future usefulness of particular indigenous species of flora and fauna as, say, a valuable source of a new medical drug or as genetic material for an improved crop species. It is this kind of uncertainty that Fisher and Krutilla (1985) have in mind when they introduce their concept of quasi-option value.

Quasi-option Value
A requisite for rational decision making is first to seek out and evaluate all possible strategies that will yield information and reduce uncertainty. The concept of quasi-option value describes the expected social value of information from this process. For example, if uncertainty is due to lack of information about preservation benefits of a natural environment, say the value of genetic material contained in some indigenous species, then knowledge may be obtained by delaying irreversible

development of the habitat. Quasi-option value is then simply the expected value of information conditional on delay of development. If a policy maker ignores the prospect of better information then development strategies which allow greater opportunities for flexibility and adjustment to new information will be given insufficient weight, assuming that the development process itself does not generate any useful information. If the resolution of uncertainty depends on some positive level of development of a natural resource, then some development may be optimal solely for the purpose of providing information even where this may have irreversible consequences that turn out to have been a mistake.

Up to this point it is has been assumed that it is known with certainty whether or not a particular development project has an irreversible biological impact. However, in some situations there may be uncertainty about whether the consequences of development are irreversible. In these circumstances, development of a small area may be desirable to obtain such information. This may include, for example, experimentation with various forms of agricultural and pastoral land use to determine whether they are sustainable and, if they are not, whether irreversible land degradation is the result.

It is apparent that quasi-option value is quite explicitly a time-sequenced (dynamic) concept and also that its existence does not require an assumption of risk aversion. These characteristics distinguish the Fisher-Krutilla concept of quasi-option value from the earlier concept of option value originally advanced by Weisbrod (1964).

Option Value

Weisbrod argued that an individual who was unsure of whether she/he would visit a site, such as a national park, would be willing to pay something for the option to visit the park in the future. The amount a person would be willing to pay to guarantee that the site would be available in the future would be a sum in excess of their expected consumer surplus. Since Weisbrod's original article much has been written on the option value question and it has become embroiled in a complex technical debate. Bishop (1982) provides a good survey of the issues.

Sustainable Resource Use and Development

Cicchetti and Freeman (1971) showed that option value stems from the combination of the individual's uncertainty about their future demand for the site and uncertainty about its future availability. However, until recently all the analyses of option value have focused exclusively on demand uncertainty. Option value is here a risk aversion premium which exists because consumers are uncertain about their future demand for an environmental amenity. If an individual knows their future demand perfectly there is no uncertainty and option value is zero.

Before the publication of a paper by Schmalensee (1972) it was believed that option values would always be positive and that the measurement of user benefits alone would therefore provide an unambiguous underestimate of the total benefits of, say, maintaining a national park. This result was important because few economists are very optimistic about measuring option value. However, Schmalensee's analysis showed that under plausible assumptions option value may be positive, negative or zero for a risk-averse individual. Thus user benefits could overstate total benefits. Previous writers had considered only the risk associated with not buying the option and the associated future possibility that visits will be demanded but unavailable. But there is also a risk associated with buying the option and having it turn out to be useless because an individual decides he does not want to use the option. The way an individual views these alternative risks determines the sign of the option value.

In many natural resource situations it is the future availability (supply) of the resource which is in doubt. The impact of human activities on biological and natural processes is commonly poorly understood and there are risks of irreversible degradation. Supply-side option value depends on ignorance. Where future supply of the resource is uncertain, but demand is certain, consumer surplus alone would underestimate total benefits of maintaining supply by an amount equal to option value. As with option value arising from demand uncertainty, supply-side option value is also a risk-aversion premium. However, unlike the former, supply-side option value appears to be unambiguously positive. Considering both demand and supply-side option value, the overall value is more likely to be positive and significant when uncertainty is largely on the supply side and the

193

resource provides services that are unique or for which there are very limited substitutes.

The notion of option value needs to be distinguished from two related concepts. Firstly, there is the concept of existence value which refers to a willingness to pay merely for the knowledge that, say, blue whales continue to exist. Secondly, there is the concept of bequest value which refers to the collective willingness of the present generation to conserve resources for future generations. The latter concept is closely linked with the question of the social discount rate which is discussed later.

ALTERNATIVE DECISION-RULES

The focus of the discussion now turns to alternative decision-rules or procedures for guiding social choice in an uncertain environment. As with conventional benefit-cost analysis, the application of these decision-rules requires that costs and benefits are expressed in present value terms. The decision-rules and procedures may be viewed as alternative modifications or extensions to conventional benefit-cost analysis.

The first approach is largely attributable to research at Resources of the Future (RFF), particularly by Krutilla, Fisher and Smith.

RFF Approach
The point that a development project that passes a conventional benefit-cost analysis might not pass a more sophisticated one that recognizes the above concepts may be illustrated by considering an endangered species that would become extinct if a water resource project were undertaken. Let B_p equal the gross social benefits of preservation minus the associated costs directly involved in preservation. Similarly, let B_d equal the gross benefits of constructing the water project minus direct costs. All benefits and costs are expressed in present value terms. While only a part of B_p can be measured, it is assumed that B_d can be adequately measured. B_p^m represents measurable benefits of preservation net of direct costs.

The expected present value of measurable net development benefits $(NB_d) = B_d - B_p^m$. If $B_d < 0$ or $B_d < B_p^m$, then clearly preservation is the efficient choice.[3] However, if $B_d > B_p^m$ (i.e. NB_d

194

is positive) preservation may still be the efficient choice. The question facing the decision maker is whether option value, quasi-option value, existence value and the like are sufficient to make $B_p > B_d$ even though $B_p^m < B_d$.

Expected Utility

The expected utility (EU) approach involves assigning a numerical value and subjective probability estimates to state-contingent outcomes. The theory is based on a small number of basic axioms which are widely believed to represent the essence of rational behaviour under uncertainty. The theory is fairly robust under a wide variety of circumstances and it is generally held to provide a more rigorous and powerful basis for economic analysis under uncertainty than the simpler mean-variance approach, especially with respect to its explicit incorporation of risk aversion. However, it is now well known that under some circumstances people behave in ways that systematically violate the axioms, particularly the independence axiom. Attempts have been made to develop models in which the independence axiom is either relaxed or abandoned; e.g., Machina (1982, 1983) and Quiggan (1982). These later models are more complex than the original EU models, largely because there is a problem of avoiding violations of dominance in which one prospect is preferred to another which first stochastically dominates it.[4]

A major feature of most differences between 'rational' choices based on EU theory and observed choices, made by individuals, in carefully constructed experiments, is that people place greater weight on low-probability outlying events. In other words, a common violation of EU theory is the apparent overweighing of outlying events.[5] This result is particularly relevant to the group of environmental problems that are the focus of this chapter.

The above considerations have led a number of theorists to challenge the idea that the framework of expected utility theory constitutes the only acceptable basis for rational choice under uncertainty. Most of the alternative theories of choice under uncertainty emphasize various forms of 'risk conservatism' beyond that usually found in the EU model (Page and MacLean, 1983). It is argued by Loomes and Sugden (1982), for example, that conventional EU theory represents an unnecessarily

restrictive notion of rationality and that it is no
less rational to act in accordance with regret
theory. They also suggest that approaches like EU
theory that are based on reference functionals with
a single argument do not adequately capture important elements of choice.

Regret Theory

Loomes and Sugden's concept of regret has some
similarities to Savage's (1951) notion, but their
theory is rather different from his minimax regret
criterion. Like EU theory, a choice problem cannot
be analyzed in their theoretical framework unless a
matrix of state-contingent outcomes can be
specified. They limit state-contingent consequences to two: 'what is' and 'what might have
been'. People rejoice if their choice turns out to
have been the correct one and feel regret if, with
the benefit of hindsight, their choice was a
mistake. Maximization of EU is included as a
limiting case in which a person experiences neither
regret nor rejoicing. When people experience
regret or rejoicing the objective is to maximize
the expectation of 'modified' utility.

Loomes-Sugden acknowledge that their model
explicitly involves the possibility of intran-
sitivity in preferences, but they argue that
transitivity is not a necessary condition for
rational choice under uncertainty. However,
Quiggan (1986) also shows that when more than two
state-contingent outcomes are allowed their regret
model displays systematic violations of dominance.
Violations of first stochastic dominance are widely
held to be a fatal flaw in any general theory of
choice under uncertainty. Quiggin also suggests
that while regret-rejoicing is commonly a real
feature of human experiences, it may not be a
wholly rational one. 'To a large extent regret
consists of crying over spilt milk, which, as the
proverb says, is not the way to optimise.' However, regret theory does provide a reasonable
description of the way in which choices are made in
some uncertainty settings. As confidence in probability estimates declines and in circumstances
where some probabilities are more uncertain than
others, it seems likely that greater weight will be
given to maximin or minimum-regret rules of the
type advocated by Savage and Loomes and Sugden.

Individual and social choices[6] are also likely
to display greater 'risk conservatism' when the

option of avoiding the worst consequence (risk) is available; when the stakes are high; and/or when there is some degree of incommensurability (e.g., across generations) between alternative prospects (Page and MacLean, 1983). In these types of circumstances, which apply to a number of our most important resource and environmental policy questions (endangered species, land degradation, pesticides and toxic chemicals), suggestions for safe minimum standards of conservation have been made by some economists. The approach of safe minimum standards has some similarities both with regret theory and with the goal of sustainability advocated by ecologists.

Safe Minimum Standards
The safe minimum standard (SMS) of conservation proposed by Ciriacy-Wantrup (1968) refers to a state of conservation which avoids a threshold or critical zone beyond which further depletion of a resource is irreversible. It is thus a positive descriptive term relating to the physical and biological condition of a resource, e.g., endangered species, threat of irreversible land degradation etc. The SMS approach advocated by Bishop (1978, 1979) on the other hand, is a normative framework for deciding whether or not a SMS should be established. The SMS approach derives from the minimax principle of game theory. The minimax principle, indicating society should always choose the strategy that minimizes maximum possible losses, has the obvious defect that the social costs of avoiding uncertainty may be too great. The basic decision rule of the SMS approach states that the SMS should be adopted unless the social costs of doing so are unacceptably large. How much is 'unacceptably large' is seen ultimately to involve a political judgement.

The SMS approach explicitly assumes that for a number of important resource policy questions the probabilities of alternative outcomes are unknown and also that the 'natural' and 'social' uncertainty is often so great that the outcomes themselves and the associated losses are usually poorly understood.

Bishop (1978), building on the earlier research of Ciriacy-Wantrup, illustrates how the problem of uncertainty about the prospects of large losses through extinction of species can be portrayed as a 'two-person game against nature'

197

with the contestants being 'society' and 'nature'. Nature is assumed to choose its strategy by some unpredictable (random) mechanism.

Returning to the water resource example outlined earlier, society now can be viewed as having two strategies: E (for extinction), which involves building a dam, and maintaining a SMS by leaving the site unflooded. The game is shown in Table 9.1.

In state 1, there are no significant losses to society if the species becomes extinct. In state 2, the species turns out to be very valuable to society, say, as a cure for cancer. If the size of the maximum possible loss from extinction, Y, exceeds the cost, X, of maintaining a safe minimum standard a minimax strategy (minimizing maximum possible losses) would select the SMS. Bishop claims that the cost of preserving many species is very low in relation to the potential losses from not saving them.

The minimax strategy is an extremely conservative rule. If the costs of implementing a SMS are only slightly less than the social losses that would be incurred under the worst conceivable future state strict adherence to the minimax strategy will likely result in inferior social choices. A further problem arises if all that is known about Y is that it could be large. In these circumstances it is unclear whether E or SMS is the minimax strategy.

Table 9.1: Matrix of Losses

| | States | | |
Strategy	1	2	Maximum losses
E	0	Y	Y
SMS	X	X−Y	X

What is clear is that the lower costs of the SMS, ceteris paribus, the more likely the SMS strategy represents a rational social choice. These are the grounds for Bishop's (1978) modified minimax decision rule: 'adopt the safe minimum standard unless the social costs are unacceptably large' (p.13).

How does the SMS approach compare with the RFF approach? The answer to this question is open to dispute as shown in the interchange between Bishop (1979) and Smith and Krutilla (1979). Recall that under the RFF approach measurable net development benefits, NB_d, are equal to gross benefits of development net of direct costs, B_d, minus measurable benefits of preservation net of direct costs, B_p^m; i.e. $NB_d = B_d - B_p^m$. Bishop views NB_d as a measure of the social cost (SC) of maintaining a SMS. If $B_d < 0$ or $B_d < B_p^m$, then preservation is clearly the efficient choice under both the RFF and SMS approaches. Under the SMS approach this is equivalent to saying that the social costs of maintaining a SMS of conservation are negative. In the more difficult situation when $NB_d = SC > 0$, under both approaches a decision maker is attempting to judge whether $B_d = B_p^m$ is 'too large' to justify preservation. As was indicated earlier, the question with RFF approach is whether option value, quasi-option value, existence value and the like are sufficient to make $B_p > B_d$ even though $B_p^m < B_d$. On the other hand, with the SMS approach the decision maker is essentially being asked to express the collective willingness of society to absorb social costs to avoid possible high losses (forgone gains) that would fall largely on future generations.

Advocates of the SMS approach stress the great natural and social uncertainty about the long-run effects of phenomena such as extinction of a species. And Bishop claims that the SMS approach deals more realistically with pure uncertainty than the RFF approach. Essentially, the SMS approach explicitly abandons the notion that optimal policies relating to many preservation/development issues can be identified using economic techniques alone. The approach is more akin to the cost-effectiveness approach than a fully-fledged benefit-cost analysis. That is to say, the implied function of economists is largely to advise on cost-effective ways of attaining policy objectives. The RFF approach, by contrast, is based fairly explicitly on the Pareto efficiency framework. Policy objectives with the SMS approach, e.g., to save a species from extinction or to attain a 'socially optimal' level of land conservation/degradation, will be influenced by economic considerations only insofar as the estimated costs of meeting a given objective are considered by the policy maker to be 'too large'. If the social costs of attaining the policy objective (SMS) are judged to be too large the objective will be abandoned or revised.

The SMS approach would appear to be more closely aligned with that of many ecologists and biologists than other economic approaches. Tisdell (1983, 1985a, 1985b) has written a series of papers in which he reviews and critically evaluates the World Conservation Strategy (WCS) and the research on sustainable systems undertaken by ecologists and biologists. He suggests that the SMS approach could provide 'a bridge' between economists and ecologists. The following discussion draws upon Tisdell's research.

Many ecologists, including those who assume a prominent role in the drafting of the World Conservation Strategy (1980), advocate that a dominant goal of mankind should be sustainable development of '... living and non-living resources to satisfy human needs and improve the quality of life'. Towards this end, conservation is defined as 'the management of the human use of the biosphere so that it may yield the greatest sustainable development to present generations while maintaining its potential to meet the needs and aspirations of future generations'. Sustainable economic development is seen as requiring:

1. the maintenance of essential ecological processes and life-support systems (e.g., agricultural systems, forests and coastal and freshwater systems);
2. the preservation of genetic diversity; and
3. sustainable utilization of species and ecosystems.

The World Conservation Strategy (WCS) proposals are cast in too general terms to be much help as a guide to policy action and the document is perhaps best interpreted as a vehicle for focussing attention on issues and encouraging countries to formulate more specific national and regional conservation strategies. Many countries have now formulated national and/or state (regional) conservation strategies.

The WCS also expressed concern about the sustainability of a productive system like agriculture with its growing dependence on an increasingly narrow genetic base. A number of

ecologists have carried out more detailed research
on sustainability of productive systems, e.g., the
work by Conway (1983) on agricultural systems. In
addition to sustainability of yield (or net
income), Conway lists productivity, stability, and
equitable income distribution as being desirable
properties of an agricultural system.

Sustainability is probably the single most
important criterion advanced by ecologists and
biologists for judging the effectiveness of
productive systems and for generally guiding
decisions on preservation/development issues. The
central role given to the criterion of sustainability is not restricted to ecologists and
biologists. Most conservation pressure groups are
also strong advocates of sustainable systems and a
sustainable society.[9] Yet, sustainability is a
criterion which economists, at least explicitly,
have generally paid scant attention to. There are
of course exceptions, such as Georgescu-Roegen
(1975) and Daly (1980) who have argued that the
most important goal for mankind is to ensure the
continued existence of the species and that the
optimal strategy for attaining this goal is to move
to a steady-state economy in which per capita
consumption is constrained and there is zero
population growth. Even if it is accepted that
this should be the goal of mankind, Tisdell (1985b)
argues that it is not at all obvious that the
policy prescription is the correct one. It is also
pertinent here to note two observations made by
Tisdell relating to the WCS[10] and more generally to
the work of ecologists. First, given the
importance that ecologists and biologists attach to
the concept of sustainability it is surprising that
the concept is not more precisely defined and
measured by them. Second, trade-offs of some form
are usually unavoidable because not all objectives
can be simultaneously achieved. But ecologists
typically pose problems as though trade-offs did
not exist and they generally offer little guidance
on the desirability of different forms of trade-
offs, e.g., between productivity and sustainability
of yield of an agricultural crop, or the accept-
ability, if any, of trade-offs between present and
future generations. While many ecologists and
biologists are sceptical and even hostile toward
discounting procedures they do not provide any
explicit criterion, such as the net present value
measure, for evaluating the desirability of
different income flows in time. The advocacy by

some non-economists that all generations should be
treated equally by using a zero rate of discount
combined with an infinite time horizon is discussed
in the final section of the chapter. The main
conclusion is that the advocates of this procedure
have not recognized its implications and that these
would be unacceptable to society.

The approach of ecologists and biologists
outlined above involves many unresolved conceptual
issues and is of limited usefulness in guiding
'real world' social choices and policy making; but
clearly biophysical information and knowledge of
the characteristics of ecosystems is an essential
ingredient in any rational social choices involving
environmental issues. Furthermore, the approach
taken in the WCS and by some ecologists is firmly
rooted in humanism and a balance is explicitly
being sought between preservation and sustainable
development to satisfy human needs. In this
respect the approach is more specific and closer to
an economics approach than the naturalistic ethical
ideas which propose that strict adherence to
humanism be abandoned and moral consideration be
explicitly extended to non-human species. Short of
according moral consideration to everything in
existence, however, there appears to be no logical
point at which to draw a line once a start is made
down this path. Moreover, most of the naturalistic
ethical ideas are in a very general and abstract
form, e.g., 'A thing is right when it tends to
preserve the integrity, stability and beauty of the
biotic community. It is wrong when it tends
otherwise' (Leopold, 1949). Clearly, such ethical
ideas are presently in too abstract a form to mesh
with economic concepts and actual policy making
other than in a most general manner. Some
economists may also question the authority by which
a naturalistic philosopher says something is
morally right or morally wrong. There is no doubt
though that naturalistic ideas are moulding the
values and goals of significant numbers of people
in society and that they may have an even greater
influence in the future. It is also important that
economists who are concerned with environmental
issues keep abreast of the main ideas emerging from
the naturalistic ethical literature.[11] Most economists, including this writer, have been remiss, at
least in the past, in generally paying scant
attention to this area of literature. Among other
things, this probably explains, in large part, why
communication and understanding between economists

and environmentalists is commonly so poor.

It is pertinent now to consider the question posed by Tisdell, namely: to what extent does the SMS approach and related approaches provide a bridge between economists and ecologists? Clearly, ecologists would support Ciriacy-Wantrup's concept of a SMS; that is, a state of conservation which avoids a threshold or critical zone. However, it should be kept in mind that Ciriacy-Wantrup's concept of a SMS is a positive (physical) concept rather than a normative concept, although some of his remarks could be interpreted as advocating that the strategy of a SMS should be implemented. Adopting this strategy would accord closely with the position taken by many ecologists as it is based solely on biophysical factors. Moreover, a SMS strategy would appear to be strongly correlated with a goal of sustainability in the sense that so long as critical zones are avoided a system will continue to be sustainable.

A 'threshold' may be defined as a point beyond which marginal physical damages rise sharply. Usually there will be a close relationship between the direction of movement of marginal <u>physical</u> and marginal <u>value</u> damages. Consequently, in situations where biophysical thresholds can be clearly identified, conventional economic criteria, such as the net present value (NPV) criterion, will commonly indicate that these critical zones should be avoided. In these cases, the NPV goal is quite compatible with that of sustainability. However, in many important situations requiring social choice the value placed on damages may be very small even when a threshold is passed, or the estimated economic costs of avoiding the critical zone may be large and exceed the damages. Strict adherence to the NPV criterion in these cases may justify a development project that results in the extinction of a species, or the exploitation of, say, a fish species beyond the point of a sustainable population, or the deliberate mining of soil to the point where it becomes uneconomic for agricultural use. In these cases, the SMS approach advocated by Bishop - that is, adopt the safe minimum standard unless the social costs are unacceptably large - clearly does provide a bridge between economists and ecologists. Although ecologists may be no happier, having the judgement of whether or not social costs of conservation are too large made by politicians than by economists.

It is not clear where mainstream economists

stand on the desirability of sustainability. Most economists do not seem to see sustainability as a desirable goal in itself. At the same time, many economists are fundamentally uncomfortable with actions, or lack of them that results in the extinguishing of a species or the destruction (complete mining) of a renewable resource, e.g., soil, even when decision rules such as the NPV criterion point clearly in this direction. For many, there is perhaps an underlying belief that it is ethically defensible to exploit and steadily reduce the stock of a non-renewable resource because it cannot be utilized in any other way. But, by definition, a renewable resource is different because it has the potential to sustain a flow of services indefinitely without the resource stock being reduced if it is utilized in an appropriate way.[12]

In many situations, of course, there will be a range of feasible sustainable yields and the issue of the socially optimal sustainable yield is then raised. Ecologists have a preference for a natural renewable system, e.g., a fishing ground, to operate at a level near maximum physical sustainable yield. In these circumstances, a SMS of conservation is better than allowing the fish species to become extinct, but ecologists would prefer the standard to be much higher. However, as far as the author is aware, ecologists have not proposed decision-rules for selecting levels of 'optimal' sustainable yield.

SOCIAL DISCOUNT RATE

The rate of discounting used in benefit-cost analyses to evaluate preservation versus development alternatives commonly has a quite decisive effect on the result given the typically long time horizons involved. It is beyond the scope of this chapter to attempt to review the very substantial literature relating to the choice of a social rate of discount.[13] Some points are made here and issues raised, however, which the author believes to be important, but which have received no, or little, attention in the mainstream debate.

One question relates to the adequacy of investment funds for long-lived private investments designed to protect the environment or to ensure sustainable agricultural production. It may be argued that the aggregate level of saving and investment by the community is too small and this causes investors to be unduly myopic and thus discriminates against longer-lived investments such as soil conservation. One well-known force operating in this direction is an income tax which reduces the rate of return on savings and thus discriminates against saving (future consumption) relative to present consumption. A second force which has been identified as a type of market failure, essentially arises from a free-rider problem, which exists for a community that desires to save for future generations. It has been shown that the amount provided for future generations, if everyone acts in an individual capacity in the market place, is less than all individuals, taken together, would collectively desire. It could be argued that these two forces provide a case for subsidizing long-lived investments.

A further complication arises, however, when it is recognized that a form of market failure analogous to that causing inadequate saving for future generations exists with respect to charitable giving to the poor to augment their present consumption. People acting in an individual capacity will exhibit some degree of 'free-rider' behaviour and will consequently make a smaller aggregate charitable gift to the poor than is collectively optimal. Insofar as one form of market failure points towards too little saving for future generations, and the other towards too little charitable giving to augment present consumption by today's poor, we cannot unambiguously conclude that there is too little of one or the other. So far as the author is aware, this point has not been made in the theoretical literature on optimal social discount rates, or elsewhere.[14]

Olson and Bailey (1981) claim that economists have largely taken for granted a positive time preference, rather than providing convincing theoretical and empirical evidence for it, though there have been some notable exceptions such as Ramsey (1928). In particular, they point out that it is erroneous to use positive real interest rates as supporting evidence for a positive rate of time preference. Capital goods can be useful in production and the existence in society of profitable investment opportunities implies that the sacrifice of one dollar of present consumption will allow more than one dollar increase in future consumption. This opportunity could generate a positive

interest rate even when there was no underlying
preference for present over future consumption
(i.e., a zero rate of time preference). A careful
reader may protest at this point that if we adopt
the convention of defining the rate of 'time
preference' as being the marginal rate of substitution between consumption between any two periods
that this must be equal in equilibrium to a
competitive market interest rate. This statement
is true, but the author concurs with Olson and
Bailey that it is more meaningful to define the
rate of 'time preference' so as to exclude the
effect of any differences in marginal utility
arising from anticipated higher levels of consumption in the future than in the present. These
differences are attributable to an underlying
assumption that there is diminishing marginal
utility to consumption in each period. True 'time
preference' then includes only any preferences for
present over future consumption which are due to
other causes. A component of discounting which
derives solely from an assumed growth of incomes
and real consumption may be a valid procedure over
fairly short periods of time, but it is a question-
able assumption for the long time horizons relevant
to most environmental and natural resource issues.

The concept of time preference adopted by
Olson and Bailey, and by me, is well summed up in
Bohm-Bawerk's (1959) original account:[15]

> We must now consider a second phenomenon of
> human experience – one that is heavily fraught
> with consequence. That is the fact that we
> feel less concerned about future sensations of
> joy and sorrow simply because they do lie in
> the future, and the lessening of our concern
> is in proportion to the remoteness of that
> future. Consequently we accord to goods which
> are intended to serve future ends a value
> which falls short of the true intensity of
> their future marginal utility. (p.273)

The question at issue then is, regardless of
whether future generations are expected to be
richer or poorer, do (and should) present
generations discount future utilities? A logical
point of departure, following Olson and Bailey, is
the observation that finite time horizons imply
positive time preference since whatever happens
after the end of the time horizon is discounted to
the point that it is given a zero value to any

income and consumption beyond a certain point in time. Therefore the most relevant question is whether there is positive time preference within an infinite time horizon.

An infinite time horizon and a zero rate of time preference, together with the expectation of continuing positive interest rates, implies that people would reduce present consumption to subsistence levels in order to reap the enormous gains in future consumption that compound interest on their savings would make possible.[16] Subsistence levels of consumption would stop only when income had become so high that the marginal utility of future consumption had fallen toward zero, or alternatively there was so much capital accumulation that the interest rate was no longer positive.

The fact that we observe both positive rates of interest and levels of current consumption substantially above subsistence levels is compelling evidence of positive time preference.[17] As Olson and Bailey state:

> We doubt that the proponents of a zero time preference and an infinite time horizon have understood the implications of their argument and conclude that their argument surely cannot be a proper basis for national policy. (p.13)

The above statement, of course, does not imply that the present generation has no desire to make bequests to future generations. The substantial social saving by past generations, in large part, can be explained only in terms of a desire to bequeath increased consumption opportunities to descendants. Indeed, it can be argued that people who believe that they will have a continuing line of descendants with the same desire to make bequests to their children as they have will act as if the time horizon was infinite even though they may give no conscious thought to such a long time horizon. However, past and present generations are clearly not prepared to 'impoverish' themselves to give to future generations, which is what a zero rate of time preference implies. Similarly the fact that developed (high income) countries transfer some of their income to developing (low income) countries, but not sufficient to substantially reduce their own high consumption levels, also implies a discount rate significantly greater than zero.

It is helpful now to briefly consider the

issue of discounting from another perspective. The point is often made that, with discounting, providing the damages we inflict on future generations lie sufficiently in the future, the present value calculation of these damages will be trivially small. This is true, but it is only one side of a coin. The other side of the coin is that over very long time periods, say 500 years, a trivially small sum of money invested now at a modest real rate of compound interest will grow to be a very large sum at the end of 500 years. Providing that a cost-benefit analysis correctly identifies that if a particular project proceeds the present value of the benefits will exceed the present value of the costs (including damages inflicted on future generations) there is a potential Pareto improvement. A sum of money could be set aside (invested) to fully compensate future generations for damages and any present losers from the project could also be fully compensated and there would be a clear overall gain to society. The issue of how much compensation is actually paid is an equity question involving a value judgement. Some would argue that, especially for actions by present generations which knowingly inflict damages on the as yet unborn, compensation should always be paid. But, however the question of compensation is resolved in particular cases, discounting of future damages and benefits is required for efficient social choices. In some cases it may be claimed that no practical vehicle for paying compensation exists. Clearly, in such cases a government would not necessarily proceed with, say, a development project that showed a potential Pareto improvement.

The discussion to this point, and the whole debate on optimal social discount rates, has been implicitly based on the premise of a well-functioning political process and a benevolent government that would take an appropriately long-term perspective and use optimal social discount rates in its decision-making calculus. There is evidence, however, that a limited time perspective is exhibited in collective (government) choice. A familiar reason advanced for government adopting a limited time horizon has to do with electoral term limits.

Brennan and Buchanan (1985) have advanced another quite different reason. Their concern is with the choice behaviour of an individual who participates in some group decision process as one member (one voter) among many and who expects that his/her expressed preferences (choices) will be counted and amalgamated with those of others through the operation of a known rule (e.g., majority voting) that will generate a single collective (public) outcome. Importantly, choices made in one period affect the options available and thus the choices made in future periods.

Their major conclusion is that there is a disparity between the discount rate embodied in the choices made by individuals in their separate roles as private and public decision makers. As a consequence, the 'social discount rate' generated by majoritarian political decision-making institutions will be higher than that rate of discount exhibited by persons in their private behaviour. The discount rate that informs the body politic is also higher than the actual market-determined rate of interest.

The problem has its origins in the attenuation of each individual's control over future collective-choice options. An individual is unable to know why other persons order alternatives, which affect the options available in future periods, as they do. The individual will therefore tend to make voting choices in terms of a shorter time horizon than that reflected in his private choices. That is to say, each individual in his capacity as a voter will exhibit less desire in selecting 'current options with future periods in prospect'. Brennan and Buchanan's line of reasoning is illustrated in their debt trap example.

> The participant in ordinary politics may recognize that debt (public) retirement now will benefit the whole community in the long run, but given nonfiscally constrained democratic decision processes, there is no means of guaranteeing that debt retirement now will, indeed, have the long-term effects that are preferred. (p.64)

A political coalition in a subsequent period may completely undo any effects of fiscal prudence in the current period. The solution is seen to lie in terms of constitutional commitments or constraints whereby members of a body politic can incorporate long-term considerations into current-period decisions. That is to say, governments can be induced to take the long view only if they are appropriately constrained by constitutional rules that at present do not exist.

At this point, a distinction should be drawn between constitutional constraints on the power of the collectivity as a unit (government) to act and possible precommitments that individuals may make with respect to their private behaviour. An individual recognizing the temporal independence of choice may find it rational to make a precommitment even with respect to purely private behaviour. By precommiting some future choices, an individual may avoid the risk that a pattern of purely situational responses will prevent the attainment of a long-run plan. The classic example of precommitment is given by Elster (1971) in his book **Ulysses and the Sirens.** Ulysses does not trust his ability to resist the temptation of the Sirens and he knows that if he succumbs the larger purpose of his voyage will be undermined. He therefore requests to be bound to the mast of his ship as it approaches the Sirens' shore.

In the setting of pure private behaviour, an individual knows that any precommitment will constrain his ability to satisfy personal preferences (desires) in the future. In other words, there is a clear trade-off between precommitment and liberty. In the collective (public-choice) setting there is no such trade-off in the problem analyzed by Brennan and Buchanan. The boundaries imposed, by any new constitutional rules, on the range of collective choices are designed to permit individuals through voting choices, to express their true preferences for society (government) to take an appropriately long-term perspective.

Intergenerational questions are not discussed by Brennan and Buchanan, however, parts of their analysis are relevant to these issues. First, with respect to future generations and the non-human components of the Earth's ecosystems the preferences of existing generations must govern. Existing generations, in this sense, have dictatorial powers thrust upon them. But these powers are not absolute. Existing generations may plan to make sacrifices now with a long-range plan in mind for the Earth's indefinite future. However, the present generation has no guarantee that some succeeding generation will not undo (exploit) the 'conservation good' that it hopes will benefit many generations to come. It seems that existing generations would be willing to conserve more if they knew that all future generations were bound to do likewise. This point is conceptually distinct from the concern expressed by some about allowing the unfettered desires and preferences of existing persons to rule when considering questions that effect future generations. This concern, I believe, is the 'collective' analogy to <u>Ulysses and the Sirens</u>. The present generation may be prepared to make a precommitment, in order to resist the temptation of 'excessive' current consumption, and so achieve the larger purpose of ensuring that it preserves equitable <u>opportunities</u> for future generations.[18] The vehicle for ensuring a binding precommitment by the present generation, and likewise by future generations, would probably need to be a set of constitutional rules.

NOTES

1. See Krutilla (1967), Arrow and Fisher (1974), Krutilla and Fisher (1975), and Fisher and Krutilla (1985).
2. Since writing this chapter, the author has read a paper by Gallagher and Smith (1985) which provides an analysis of the benefits of a change in the probability distribution of access to an un-certain environmental resource. A major conclusion is that conventional measure of compensating or equivalent surplus do not necessarily bound an individual's valuation of change in access to an environmental amenity with uncertain availability. They argue that the appropriate measure is the change in an individual's income that would be required to maintain a given level of expected utility as the probability distribution associated with the supply of the environmental resource changes.
3. Preservation may not be the efficient choice in this case if option value is believed to be negative.
4. A distribution of state-contingent out-comes first stochastically dominates another when for any outcome x, the probability of a worse outcome is greater under the second distribution.
5. Quiggan's theory of anticipated utility is designed to overcome this apparent shortcoming of utility theory.
6. Nearly all the theoretical work on expected utility theory and regret theory is based on the problem of individual choice. More research is required to determine to what extent the main

211

results carry directly over to issues of social choice.

7. The term land degradation covers an array of biophysical processes affecting land quality that result largely from the activities of man. The main forms of degradation include: soil erosion, irrigation-induced salinity, dryland salinity, soil acidification, desertification, and destruction of natural flora and fauna habitats. Papers on land degradation by researchers from both physical and social science disciplines are contained in A.H. Chisholm and R.B. Dumsday (eds) **Land Degradation: Problems and Policies**, Cambridge University Press (1987).

8. The bald statement does not do justice to the contribution of Ciriacy-Wantrup to conservation economics. Krutilla (1967) acknowledged this contribution when he wrote, 'It must be acknowledged that with sufficient patience and perception nearly all of the arguments for preserving unique phenomena of nature can be found in the classic on conservation economics by Ciriacy-Wantrup' (p.778, f.3).

9. See, for example, Brown and Shaw (1982).

10. Tisdell (1985b) focuses particularly on the work of Conway.

11. For a good review of environmental ethics from an economics perspective see Kneese and Schultz (1985).

12. The problem of land degradation provides a good vehicle for illustrating these conceptual issues in a more specific setting. For a discussion of these issues in the context of land utilization see Chisholm (1987).

13. An excellent collection of papers on this topic is contained in Lind (1982).

14. This issue was first posed by the author in Chisholm (1987).

15. The first phenomenon proposed by Bohm-Bawerk as being capable of producing a difference in value between goods at different points in time was "... if a person suffers in the present from appreciable lack of certain goods, or of goods in general, but has reason to be more generously provided for at a future time, then that person will always place a higher value on a given quantity of immediately available goods than on the same quantity of future goods" (p.265).

16. Hirschleifer (1970, p.96) reaches a similar conclusion when he concludes that zero time

212

[2][1]3

preference would imply infinite deferral of all consumption.

17. Only a drastically diminishing marginal utility of consumption could possibly make positive rates of interest and current consumption levels substantially above subsistence levels compatible with a zero rate of time preference.

18. The notion of intergenerational justice based on preserving opportunities for future generations is proposed by Page (1977) and is related to the ideas of Rawls.

19. A part of the research for this chapter was undertaken while the author was a visiting fellow at the Centre for Resource and Environmental Studies, Australian National University. The revision of the 1986 conference paper on which this chapter is based has benefited from comments of the two discussants.

REFERENCES

Arrow, K.J. and Fisher, A.C. (1974) 'Environmental Preservation, Uncertainty, and Irreversibility', **Quarterly Journal of Economics**, 88, pp. 312-19

Bishop, R.C. (1978) 'Endangered Species and Uncertainty: The Economics of a Safe Minimum Standard', **American Journal of Agricultural Economics**, 60, pp. 10-18

Bishop, R.C. (1979) 'Endangered Species and Uncertainty: A Reply', **American Journal of Agricultural Economics**, 61, pp. 376-79

Bishop, R.C. (1982) 'Option Value: An Exposition and Extension', **Land Economics**, 58, pp. 1-15

Bohm-Bawerk, Eugen von (1959) **Capital and Interest**, 2, **Positive Theory of Capital**, Libertarian Press, South Holland, Illinois

Brennan, G. and Buchanan, J.M. (1985) **The Reason of Rules**, Cambridge University Press, Cambridge

Brown, L.R. and Shaw, P. (1982) **Six Steps to a Sustainable Society**, Worldwatch Institute, Washington

Chisholm, A.H. (1987) 'Rational Approaches to Environmental Issues', pp. 341-58 in Chisholm, A.H. and Dumsday, R.G. eds., **Land Degradation: Problems and Policies**, Cambridge University Press, Sydney

Chisholm, A.H. and Dumsday, R.G., eds., (1987) **Land Degradation: Problems and Policies**, Cambridge University Press, Sydney

Cicchetti, C.J. and Freeman, A.M. (1971) 'Option

Demand and Consumer Surplus: Further Comment', **Quarterly Journal of Economics, 85,** pp. 528-39

Ciriacy-Wantrup, S.V. (1986) **Resource Conservation: Economics and Policies,** 3rd ed., University of California Div. Agr. Sci., Berkeley

Conway, G.R. (1983) **Applying Ecology,** Centre for Environmental Technology, Imperial College, London

Daly, H. (1980) **Economics, Ecology and Ethics,** Freeman, San Francisco

Elster, J. (1971) **Ulysses and the Sirens,** Cambridge University Press, Cambridge

Fisher, A.C. and Krutilla, J.C. (1985) 'Economics of Nature Preservation' pp. 165-89 in Kneese, A.V. and Sweeney, J.L., eds., **Handbook of Natural Resource and Energy Economics,** vol. 1, North Holland, Amsterdam

Gallagher, D.R. and Smith, V.K. (1985) 'Measuring Values for Environmental Resources under Uncertainty', **Journal of Environmemtal Economics and Management, 12,** pp. 132-43

Georgescu-Roegen, N. (1975) 'Selections from "Energy and Economic Myths"', **Southern Economic Journal, 41,** pp. 347-81

Hirschleifer, J. (1970) **Investment, Interest and Capital,** Prentice Hall, Englewood Cliffs, New Jersey

Kneese, A.V. and Schultz, W.D. (1985) 'Ethics and Environmental Economics', pp. 191-220 in Kneese, A.V. and Sweeney, J.L., eds., **Handbook of Natural Resource and Energy Economics,** vol. 1, North Holland, Amsterdam

Krutilla, J.V. (1967) 'Conservation Reconsidered', **American Economic Review, 57,** pp. 777-86

Krutilla, J.V. and Fisher, A.C. (1975) **The Economics of Natural Environments: Studies in the Valuation of Commodity and Amenity Resources,** John Hopkins University Press, Baltimore

Leopold, A. (1949) **A Sand Country Almanac and Sketches Here and There,** Oxford University Press, New York.

Lind, R.C. (1982) **Discounting for Time and Risk in Energy Policy,** Resources for the Future, Inc., Washington, D.C.

Loomes, G. and Sugden, R. (1982) 'Regret Theory: An Alternative Theory of Rational Choice under Uncertainty', **Economic Journal, 92,** pp. 805-24

Machina, M.J. (1982) 'Expected Utility Analysis, Without the Independence Axiom', **Econometrica, 50,** pp. 277-323

Machina, M.J. (1983) 'The Economic Theory of Individual Behaviour Toward Risk: Theory, Evidence and New Directions', **Technical Report** No. 433, Center for Research on Organizational Efficiency, Stanford University, Palo Alto, California

MacIntyre, A. (1977) 'Utilitarianism and Cost-Benefit Analysis: An Essay on the Relevance of Moral Philosophy to Bureaucratic Theory' in Sayre, K., ed., **Values in the Electric Power Industry**, University of Notre Dame Press

Olson, M. and Bailey, M.J. (1981) 'Positive Time Preference', **Journal of Political Economy**, 89, pp. 1-25

Page, T. (1977) **Conservation and Economics Efficiency**, John Hopkins Press for Resources for the Future Inc., Baltimore

Page, T. and MacLean (1983) 'Risk Conservatism and the Circumstances of Utility Theory', **American Journal of Agricultural Economics**, 65, pp. 1021-26

Quiggan, J. (1982) 'A Theory of Anticipated Utility', **Journal of Economic Behaviour and Organisation**, 3, pp. 323-43

Quiggan, J. (1986) 'Violations of Dominance in Regret Theory', **Centre for Resource and Environmental Studies**, Australian National University, Canberra (mimeo)

Ramsey, F.P. (1928) 'A Mathematical Theory of Saving', **Economic Journal**, 38, pp. 543-59

Rawls, J. (1971) **A Theory of Justice**, Harvard University Press, Cambridge

Savage, L.J. (1951) 'The Theory of Statistical Decision', **Journal of the American Statistical Association**, 46, pp. 55-67

Schmalensee, R. (1972) 'Option Demand and Consumer's Surplus: Valuing Price Changes Under Uncertainty', **American Economic Review**, 62, pp. 813-24

Schultz, T.W. (1974) 'Is Modern Agriculture Consistent with a Stable Environment', in **The Future of Agriculture: Technology, Policies and Adjustment**, Papers and Reports, 15th International Conference of Agricultural Economists, Oxford Agricultural Economics Institute, Oxford

Smith, V.K. and Krutilla, J.V. (1979) 'Endangered Species, Irreversibilities, and Uncertainty: A Comment', **American Journal of Agricultural Economics**, 61, pp. 371-75

Tisdell, C.A. (1983) 'An Economist's Critique of the World Conservation Strategy, with Examples from the Australian Experience', **Environmental Conservation, 10**, pp. 43-52

Tisdell, C.A. (1985a) 'Economics, Ecology, Sustainable Agricultural Systems and Development', **Development Southern Africa, 2**, pp. 513-21

Tisdell, C.A. (1985b) 'Sustainable Development: Conflicting Approaches of Ecologists and Economists, and Implications for LDCs', **Research Report No.** 112, Department of Economics, University of Newcastle, Australia

Weisbrod, B. (1964) 'Collective-Consumption Services of Individual Consumption Goods', **Quarterly Journal of Economics, 78**, pp. 471-77

World Conservation Strategy (1980) IUCN, Glands, Switzerland

Chapter Ten

THE CHANGING ROLE OF THE HOUSEHOLD ECONOMY IN A
WORLD OF EXPANDING TECHNOLOGY

David Darton and Gerard O'Neill

INTRODUCTION

This chapter analyses some of the results from the
Henley Centre's[1] 'Planning for Social Change' (PSC)
survey to identify how the role of the household
economy in Britain may change in the future. We
shall limit ourselves to considering the current
behaviour, attitudes, and expectations revealed in
the survey in the context of demographic, economic,
political, and technological changes that are
likely over the next few years. We will refrain
from explicit comment on the wealth of work carried
out on the informal economy in Britain by Gershuny
(1983), Pahl (1984) and Toffler (1983) in order to
concentrate on this.
    The PSC survey is carried out each year as
part of the Centre's social research programme.
Although some questions are repeated at regular
intervals, each survey is designed to cover topical
issues that are related to the general research
that is in progress during a particular year. The
1985 survey was concerned particularly with the
role of the home and family in people's lives and
therefore, provides data that allow us to examine
the changing role of the home in Britain's economy.
    In 1985, the PSC survey was carried out in May
among 1,750 adults (aged 16 and above). The sample
was chosen to be representative in terms of age,
sex, and class in each of the standard planning
regions. Interlocking quotas were not used and the
data have not been weighted in any way.
    We shall begin with a very brief historical
perspective; then discuss the extent to which
people use their home and the extent of family
activity as opposed to individual activity. Within
this context we will then examine the impact of

217

technology, including specifically information technology. From this base we will offer a view of how the role of the household economy may change in the future.

THE HOUSEHOLD AND THE MARKET

The household as a source of material resources considerably predates the modern market economy. That the latter is now perceived to be the sole or major source of these resources is the culmination of a lengthy historical process (Brown, 1982). However, this process, as we see below, is still not complete. Indeed, if present trends continue, the proportion of total economic activity carried out within the household may well come full circle back to that which prevailed in pre-industrial times.

The relationship between production in the household economy and that in the market or formal economy has evolved in two fairly distinct stages:

1. Industrialization transferred the production of basic goods, such as food and clothing, from the household economy to the increasingly more efficient market economy.

2. At a later stage, the advent of mass production and urbanization transferred the production of other goods and services to the market economy, particularly new goods and services impossible to produce in the home (e.g., electricity).

Of course, the household has retained several key economic roles throughout this process, including the education of children (to some extent) and the 'servicing' of the predominantly male labour force in the market economy (Becker, 1981). Nevertheless a major characteristic of this century has been the continued development of the formal or market economy.

The evolution of the production process, and the changing interplay between the formal/market economy and the informal economy is examined in Figure 10.1, which illustrates two key themes:

1. More capital-intensive, 'high-tech' productive processes have accounted for a growing share of the formal economy.

2. The declining importance of household economic activities in the informal economy has been accompanied by an increase in activities in the black economy, i.e., economic activities, often

illegal, which are not measured as being part of the formal economy.

The decline in the importance of the household economy has not of course meant that no new functions have been undertaken within the home. The continued march of technology through people's front doors has been expanding the range of activities possible within the home for some years. But what may be happening in the 1980s in Britain is that the historical process of growth in the market economy outweighing growth in the household economy may be being reversed.

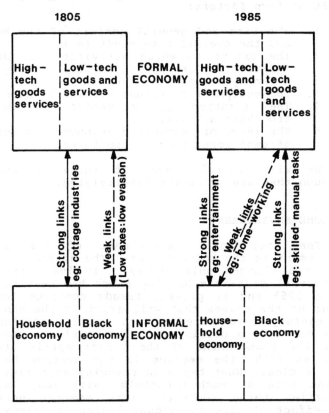

Figure 10.1: The changing economy – a representation of the past

The rise in household economic activities recently would certainly seem to outweigh growth in other areas of the economy, though of course

accurate measurement is very difficult. It may be
that this is a short-term function of a
particularly severe recession together with
changing income distribution and relative prices.
We suggest below, however, that the nature of the
household economy and its importance in the British
economy may be fundamentally changing. If this is
so, the interesting question for debate is whether
this is a phenomenon peculiar to Britain or an
inevitable result of development.

The number and range of activities taking
place within the household in Britain are largely a
result of five factors:

1. The size and general comfort of the home
   and the overall time spent in it.
2. The extent to which activities are done
   individually as opposed to collectively as
   a family or household unit.
3. The equipment contained within the home.
4. The relative attractiveness of away-
   from-home activities.
5. The level of economic development in terms
   of employment/income structures.

We will consider each of these in turn,
although they are of course interrelated.

THE HOME ENVIRONMENT

The most basic determinant of the home
environment is the house itself. The housing stock
of course changes only slowly. In 1980, three-
quarters of Britain's housing stock had been built
before 1965 and if present trends continue four-
fifths of the houses that will exist at the end of
the century have already been built. Although
there has been a decline in the size of new houses
since the abandonment of the Parker Morris standards in 1979, the decline in the average house
size is slow. What has been changing more rapidly
is the size of each household, with many large
properties being converted into smaller units.
(The effect of more individual living is discussed
below.)

Despite the very slow change in the housing
stock, the home living environment has changed
rapidly with the house proving very flexible in
accommodating aspirations for comfort and
convenience. Old houses are fitted with double

glazing, central heating, modern plumbing, electricity, etc. According to the PSC survey over two-thirds of houses now have central heating and more than a third are double-glazed. Many of the improvements in the home require substantial investment and the rise in the comfort of the home partly reflects the rapid rise in home ownership over the last few years. Owner occupation now stands at about 65% in Britain, which is considerably higher than most other countries. A number of surveys indicate that the aspiration for home ownership remains strong and it is likely that the individual's investment in housing will continue to rise. The home-centredness of many people is shown in the responses to the PSC question, 'How much do you feel you know about what makes a house stylishly furnished and decorated? Only 16% said they 'know only a little' while 56% said they 'know some' and 27% 'a lot' about it. Of most interest is the fact that of those who know only 'some' or 'a little' nearly a third want to 'find out a lot more' about how to furnish a house stylishly. A similar proportion wanted to find out a lot more about DIY (do-it-yourself) and of the various activities asked about, only organizing one's savings and knowing what is good for your health had a higher proportion of people saying they wanted to find out a lot more about them.

Increased investment in the house and greater concern with home decor is resulting in more comfortable homes in which to do a wide variety of activities. The majority of people surveyed, 59%, said that they were spending more time at home now compared with 5 years ago. In the case of some respondents this is mainly attributable to life-cycle factors:

1. Two-thirds of 25-34-year-olds said they were spending more time at home (mainly because of the presence of their children).
2. Nearly four-fifths of those aged over 60 were at home more often (partly due to increased fraility).

The life cycle is only one factor in the trend towards increased time spent at home. Other significant factors are:

3. Social Class: Significantly more manual workers are spending more time at home than professional workers.

4. Employment status: Significantly more economically inactive people are spending more time at home than part-time employees (reflecting recent trends in employment).

5. Marital status: Significantly more married people than single people are spending more time at home, though of course this includes the effects of life cycle factor.

When respondents who said they spend more time at home were asked why, 68% cited a lack of money. (We will consider some of the other reasons given below). Britain will become more affluent during the rest of this century (the Centre forecasts an average annual rise in personal disposable income of just under 2%), while there will be a continuation of the migration to smaller towns and the countryside. This would tend to suggest that less of the population would be spending an increasing amount of time at home in the future. However, the trends toward owner-occupation, greater investment in the home, and more knowledge about the home environment, suggest that people will become more home-centred overall, even if the direct effect of rising personal discretionary incomes is to reduce the rate at which activities are switched toward the home.

We should note at this point that the Centre expects the average amount of free time availability to increase (partly as a result of increased penetration of white goods within the home). Table 10.1 illustrates these trends by gender and economic status.

The greater amount of free time available and increasing affluence is stimulating greater expenditure on leisure. Trends and projections for leisure expenditure are indicated in Figure 10.2. There are signs in the eighties that one of the major areas in which activities are being switched to the home is that of leisure. Defining in-home leisure spending to be spending on 'viewing and screen-related equipment and software', 'listening equipment and software except for 20% of equipment', 'DIY (do-it-yourself) and gardening', arts and crafts, musical instruments, pets, toys and games, half of that on photography, and two-thirds of that on reading material, the Centre expects a continued switch in spending to goods and services related to in-home leisure. At the same time, the role of the household economy will be changed by the increased penetration of certain durables related to the demand for convenience and individual activity. We will next look briefly at the latter before turning more specifically to the impact of new durables on the household economy.

Table 10.1: Time Use in a Typical Week (Hours) in Britain

	Full–Time[2]				Part–Time[2]							
	Men		Women		Men		Women		Housewives		Retired	
Year	1985	1990	1985	1990	1985	1990	1985	1990	1985	1990	1985	1990
Employment[1,2]	45.0	41.5	40.8	36.8	24.3	19.0	22.2	21.7				
Essential Activities[1]	33.1	35.3	45.1	40.2	48.8	51.0	61.3	56.3	76.6	74.6	49.8	49.2
Sleep[1]	56.4	56.4	57.5	57.5	56.6	56.6	57.0	57.0	59.2	59.2	60.2	60.2
Free Time[1]	33.5	34.8	24.6	33.5	38.5	41.4	27.5	33.0	32.2	34.2	58.0	58.6
per weekday	2.6	2.8	2.1	2.9	4.5	4.9	3.1	3.3	4.2	4.4	7.9	8.0
per weekend day	10.2	10.4	7.2	9.6	7.8	8.5	5.9	8.3	5.6	6.1	9.1	9.3

Notes: [1] Whole Week   [2] Includes Travel to/from work
[3] Excludes Self–Employed.
Source: Based on Planning for Social Change Survey (PSC), Henley Centre for Forecasting, London.

INDIVIDUALISM WITHIN THE HOME

The 'typical' British household is still often thought of as a family comprising a married couple with a father in employment and mother at home with two dependent children. In fact such families represent only one in twenty households. This is rather a strict interpretation of the typical family. Three in ten households are two-parent with one child or more. Moreover the vast majority of people pass through a household of this type at some stage in their lives. Nevertheless, the importance of individual activity is clear with 23% of households being a single person household in 1982, up from 17% in 1971. The rise has occurred at both ends of the age structure.

Divorce has had a considerable impact on household structure. The divorce rate has risen by 500% since 1961, with the result that one in three

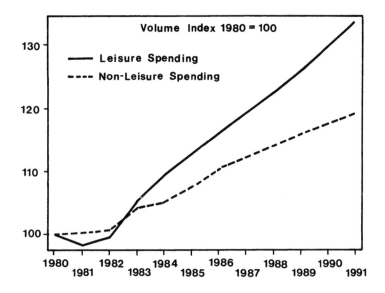

Figure 10.2: Trends in expenditure on leisure commodities (leisure-spending) and non-leisure spending

marriages today will end in divorce. There has therefore been a substantial increase in the number of one parent families from 0.5 million in 1971 to about 1 million today.

Other changes in family structures have arisen from greater affluence and longevity. Rising real incomes during the postwar period have meant that families have been under less pressure to stay together as a matter of economic necessity. The growth in the earning power of young workers, together with expansions in higher education, has increased the propensity for young adults to live away from their parents. In 1980, 10% of 16-19-year-olds lived away from their parents although only 4% were married.

At the other end of the age spectrum, greater affluence among the majority of retired people, together with a growing acceptance that support for the old is a public rather than a family responsibility, has meant that old people increasingly form separate households.

These changes in household structure in themselves raise the amount of individual activity within households but as noted above the family household remains important with:

- the great majority of men and women marrying (only 8% of females and 14% of males will not marry at any time).
- 88% of children living with both their natural parents.
- the majority of divorcees subsequently re-marrying.

It is therefore the extent to which sovereignty has been transferred from the family to the individual within the family household that is as important as the change in household structure.

The PSC survey does suggest that such a transfer of sovereignty is occurring, with more individual activity going on within the family household. In response to the question, **'Some people say that families spend less of their time together as a unit. Why do you think this might be?'** only 19% said, 'I do not think this is happening.' When asked, **'Does your family spend more or less time as a group in your main living room than a similar family would have done 10 years ago?'** 49% said less, more than double the 23% that said more. The perception that families spend less time together than in the past is thus strong, as is an expectation that the trend toward greater individualism in the home will continue into the future. Three-quarters of respondents said that **'members of families will become more independent of each other'**, while only a quarter felt that **'families in the future are likely to do more things together'**.

It is interesting to note that 51% of those saying that they spend less time as a family in their main living room state that instead they spend more time in their own rooms, suggesting that each room within the home is becoming a multi-activity centre. A duplication of equipment is therefore likely and this is one of the most direct links between greater individualism and the household economy. There is much data to support the hypothesis of greater duplication. For example, small-screen second televisions have been the most buoyant sector of the television market for much of the eighties. Indeed, a third of respondents to the PSC survey said that **'Central heating, two TV sets in homes and all those gadgets encourage people to be off in different places doing their own thing**, as a, reason for families spending less time together.

As well as being reflected in duplicate durable ownership, greater individualism and the household economy are also linked because different types of equipment are more important for enabling individual activity. For example a video recorder allows individuals to watch programmes at different times as opposed to watching them as a family at the same time. Similarly a microwave oven makes eating individually as opposed to as a family group easier. We will now turn to the impact of home technology on the household economy.

HOME TECHNOLOGY

A substantial minority (43%) of those spending a different amount of time at home described **'getting more equipment in the home'** as an important reason for the change. This rises to 53% for those aged 25-44, but even in the case of the over-sixties the figure is still as high as 31%.

A growing number of household durables pre-empt value-added from the formal/market economy. New household durables are generally used to obtain goods and services previously only available outside the home. An obvious example is the video recorder - whereas individuals wishing to see a new film would previously have had no choice but to go to a cinema, they can now see new releases in their homes on video.

PSC data on durable ownership indicates areas in which value-added is increasingly pre-empted by the household economy. The areas of food storage and preparation particularly have experienced this process of pre-emption (see Table 10.2).

Of course the motivation behind the ownership of these durables is not simply because people want to do more in their homes, but because things are made cheaper and more convenient. To the extent that the real prices of both white goods and entertainment durables are forecast to fall, we can expect the increases in penetration of these durables to continue. Another sense in which value-added is being pre-empted from the formal/market economy is the rise in the amount of, and sophistication of, DIY activities. More than half of PSC respondents say that they own a comprehensive tool set and this rises to more than two-thirds of 35-44-year-olds. As this group is unlikely to discard these tools, and with the continued rise in owner-occupation (which encourages DIY activities according to the survey) we can expect overall involvement in DIY activities to continue to rise.

Table 10.2: Percentage of Individuals by Age-Group Owning Food-Related Durables in Britain, 1985

Item Age:	16-24	25-34	35-44	45-59	60+	ALL
Freezer	71	81	83	83	70	77
Microwave Oven	20	18	23	22	9	18
Food Pro-						
cessor/Mixer	48	59	61	58	50	54
Dishwasher	5	3	8	6	3	5

Source: Planning for Social Change Survey (PSC), Henley Centre for Forecasting, London.

Figures 10.3 - 10.5 show the importance of owning equipment for those who already own it and the importance of obtaining it for those who do not. The scale is an importance scale of the mean response where very important is 'scored' as 300, quite important as 100, not very important as zero, and not at all important as -100. The last chart shows the difference in the importance 'score' between those already owning the equipment and those who do not. There are several points to note from these figures.

    - The relatively higher importance attributed to owning goods that potentially contribute to the home environment.

    - The very high importance of owning a car and relatively high importance attached to obtaining one. This is significant given that one reason for the increase in home-based activity in Britain is increased fear of the safety of the streets.

    - The moderately high importance attached to obtaining labour-saving kitchen equipment (with the exception of dishwashers).

    - The relatively low importance attached to owning or obtaining home entertainment and communications equipment except the telephone (with over 90% penetration the importance of television is assumed).

    - The generally high difference between the

importance attributed to a good by those already owning it, as opposed to those that have yet to obtain it. The high differences indicate that it would be wrong today to assume that people necessarily have strong aspirations to own things that they don't own already.

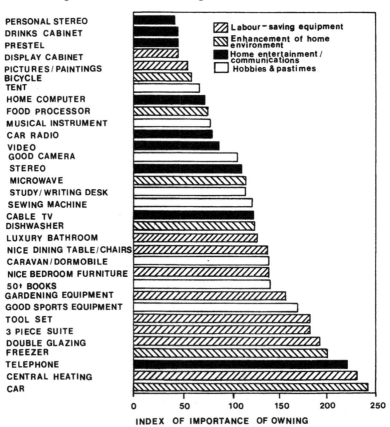

Figure 10.3: Rated importance of owning items of household equipment by owners in Britain, 1985

More and more, it is a specific lifestyle that makes a product or service more attractive, while another lifestyle makes the same product or service relatively unimportant. Products to the left in Figure 10.5 can be thought of as being more 'lifestyle specific', while those to the right have a more general importance (or unimportance) for

everyone.   Increasingly   lifestyles   are   not
determined by the desire to obtain a level of
ownership, but by other criteria, with ownership
sometimes being instrumental to the desired
lifestyle, but not its objective.

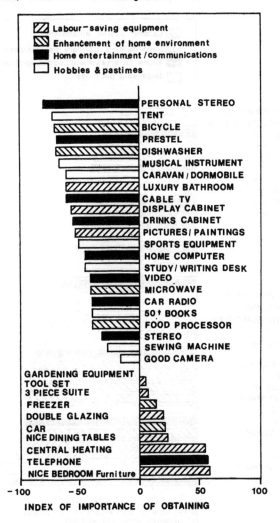

Figure 10.4   Rated importance of obtaining items
of household equipment by non-owners in Britain,
1985

The prevalence of household equipment which pre-empts goods and services previously provided in the formal economy has been illustrated above. Most of this equipment is of a type which has allowed a 're-appropriation' of those goods and

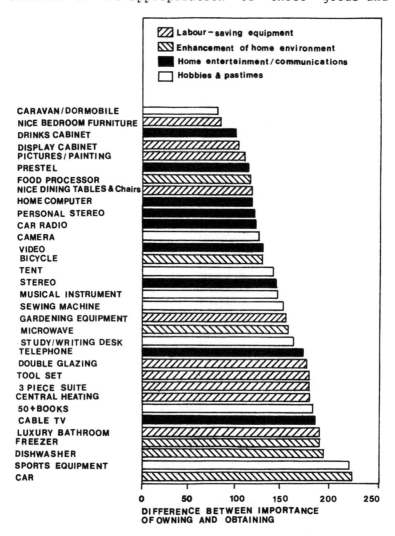

Figure 10.5: Estimated difference between importance of owning and obtaining items of household equipment in Britain, 1985

services originally transferred from the household economy to the low-tech sector of the formal economy during the early stages of industrialization (e.g., food production and preparation).

But what of the high-tech sector? An increasingly important element in the high-tech sector of the formal economy is the communications and information-processing industry. The penetration of 'information-related' equipment into the home will be key in determining the extent to which the household economy impinges on the high-tech sector of the formal/market economy. With the exception of the home computer, the ownership levels of the newer information-related durables in Britain are very low (See Tables 10.3 and 10.4).

Table 10.3: Percentage of Individuals Owning Information-Related Durables in Britain, 1985

Age:	16-24	25-34	35-44	45-59	60+	ALL
Telephone	77	86	86	90	85	84
Cable Television	3	4	3	4	5	4
Home Computer	16	21	39	13	2	17
Prestel	5	2	4	3	2	3

Source: Planning for Social Change Survey, Henley Centre for Forecasting, London.

Even home computers are not particularly prevalent, with fewer than two-fifths of 35-44-year-olds owning them and only a fifth or less of other age groups having them. The data would therefore suggest that the household economy is having little impact at the moment on the high-tech formal economy. In addition, a relatively low proportion of non-owners think that it is very or quite important to acquire information-related durables in the future.

With the exception of the telephone, the overwhelming majority of individuals do not own the new information-related durables, nor do they think it important that they acquire them in the future. Where there is a feeling that the future ownership of the durables is important, it is mainly among younger individuals. Thus, evidence that potential future acquisition of those durables is central

Changing Role of the Household Economy

to the development of the 'information economy'
would suggest that its development will be slow or
non-existent, despite even the marginally higher
preferences of younger people.

Table 10.4: Percentage of Individuals Not Owning
Information-Related Durables in Britain, 1985 Saying
Acquisition is Important

Age:	16–24	25–34	35–44	45–59	60+	ALL	Non–Owners % of Total Sample
Telephone	50	56	42	38	26	44	16
Cable Television	12	7	5	3	2	6	96
Home Computer	15	25	20	7	3	12	83
Prestel	4	6	2	4	2	4	97

Source: Planning for Social Change Survey, Henley Centre
for Forecasting, London.

Such a pessimistic conclusion, however, would
be premature. Evidence about peoples' attitudes to
doing particular activities from the home if new
durables made it possible, suggests that there is a
potential for a sharp increase in the penetration
of some of these durables. Table 10.5 shows the
proportion of respondents who replied that they

Table 10.5: Percentage of Individuals Who Would Do
Selected Activities From Home in Britain, 1985

Activity	Social Class: AB	C1	C2	DE	Total
Everyday Shopping	33	32	28	33	31
Banking	59	56	50	34	48
Minor Legal Advice	44	44	46	41	44
Minor Medical Advice	46	53	51	52	51
Choosing a Holiday	40	35	40	34	37

Source: Planning for Social Change Survey, Henley
Centre for Technology, London.

232

would do selected activities from the home if it were possible.

A majority of the sample would obtain minor medical advice from the home using communications technology. Banking would also be a popular activity to be done from the home. Table 10.5 suggests that there is a strong, latent demand among all social classes for providing more services in the home.

Indeed historically we can see a trend in Britain toward a self-service rather than a service economy. In real terms the share of consumer spending on services has not risen significantly. What has risen has been spending on household durables, which allow us to provide services ourselves within the home rather than pay someone in the formal economy to do it. Already providers of entertainment services in the formal market economy have lost out to this phenomenon - as witness the decline of the cinemas and the pubs, compared to the rise in video recorder ownership and home brewing. The question is whether or not the more 'essential' services highlighted in Table 10.5 will be the next to be transferred to the home. The answer is probably yes despite the low priority on obtaining information-related durables discussed above. The reason is that as people continue to become more home-centred and demand individual as opposed to collective activities, their attitudes to these home durables will change. We have discussed the increasing home-centredness in terms of the home environment and the increasing penetration of certain durables, but of course the extent to which away-from-home activities can meet the needs of people will also determine the degree to which activities within the home continue to increase in importance. We will look at this very briefly before concluding.

ATTRACTIVENESS OF AWAY-FROM-HOME ACTIVITIES

Many away-from-home leisure facilities have seen sharp declines in their use in recent years. Notable are the more passive entertainment sectors such as the pubs, the cinema, the theatre, betting shops and bingo halls. While the eating-out market still shows some growth, it is slow given the rise in overall leisure spending. Many of the problems of these destinations arise from increased competition with the home. The Henley Centre's

quarterly time-use survey shows high and increasing
incidence of home entertaining, and substantial
proportions of people would rather do a variety of
things in the home that not so long ago were mostly
done outside the home, as these PSC results
indicate.

The away-from-home activities that are doing
relatively well are those that are offering an
experience which cannot easily be repeated at home
in addition to the basic service of, say, pouring a
drink, which can very easily be duplicated within
our now very comfortable homes. These are often
destinations that require a long trip away from
home as people will increasingly only leave their
home for a really 'worthwhile' trip. As people
still often have to travel together in a car shared
by more than one member of the household, but want
to act more as individuals once they reach their
destination, multi-activity destinations such as
theme parks and mixed shopping-activity centres are
particularly attractive.

Table 10.6: Percentage of all Individuals in
Britain Preferring to Do Specified Activities in
the Home Rather than Outside

Watch a film	64
Listen to music	56
Eat a lavish meal	34
Have an alcoholic drink	26
Exercise	16

In the next few years, the constraints on
leaving home due to the lack of facilities for
children or baby-sitting services is likely to
become more acute in Britain as the number of young
families will rise significantly as the 60s baby
boom reaches the peak family formation age group.
Although business and local authorities are
beginning to respond to the needs for multi-
activity centres, the process of increasing their
supply is slow. The Centre's analysis of the law-
and-order question and the relationship of
perceptions to reality as far as safety goes both
suggest that fear of the safety of the streets will
be a significant deterrent to leaving the home
during the next ten years or so.

Our conclusion is that there will continue to
be a relative rise in home-based activities in

Britain over the next ten years. The concomitant increase in home-centredness will occur at a time when the new information durables are being made available on an increasing scale. With the orientation of activities shifting toward the home we would expect the household penetration of many of these durables to rise steeply as it becomes clearer what it is that they would allow people to do from the home.

THE FUTURE ROLE OF THE HOME ECONOMY

As information durables in particular, but also other durables, continue their invasion of the home and people continue to become more home-centred, expanding the range of activities that they undertake at home, there could be a fundamental restructuring of the economy. This is illustrated in Figure 10.6.

By the end of the century, the formal/informal distinction within the economy could well have vanished. Instead a new dichotomy will arise – that between the information and the casual economies. The former will be characterized by an integration of the production of high-tech goods and services with those of the household economy. This information economy will be one in which services such as banking and medical diagnosis will be delivered to homes via cable, satellite or Prestel – while those employed by the banks and health services will increasingly work from their homes using the same interactive technology. In contrast, the casual economy will be one characterized by an increasing overlap between declining low-tech industries and residual economic activities confined to the black economy and concentrated among poorer households.

The increasing importance of the home in people's lives is a critical assumption behind this scenario. The PSC data described in this chapter, together with changes in the overall nature of the economy and society lead us to believe that this scenario has a significant probability of being realized in Britain. But the rising importance of the home in people's lives is a result not just of the development of the economy and technology, but also of specific characteristics of society that are peculiar to Britain. These include:

1. The rapid rise in home ownership and aspirations for home ownership – Such a rise tends

to greatly increase the investment of both money and time in the home. It is debatable as to whether increased demand for private ownership is an inevitable result of economic development and rising affluence.

    2. Attitudes to service — Historically, personal service in Britain has been associated with servility. This has tended to make both the

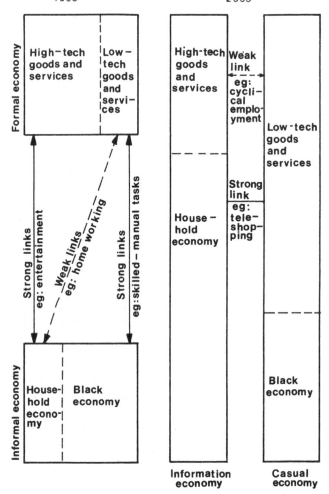

Figure 10.6   The changing economy — a projection for the future

server and the person being served uncomfortable in modern society. This may account for why the desire for self-service has been so strong in Britain. This situation contrasts sharply with the United States, for example, where service has tended to be associated with marketing rather than servility. Offering personal service does not therefore have 'demeaning' connotations in the United States to the extent it can have in Britain.

3. Concern about Safety - It is clear that for many people concern about safety significantly alters their behaviour in a way that increases the use of the home. Again it is unclear that this concern is an inevitable result of development. In Britain, as in other places, there is a perception of the phenomenon, only some of which would appear to be related to development.

4. Rising Individualism - This tends to raise the use of the home as it is one of the most convenient places to undertake , individualistic activities and to do things that positively contribute to self-expression. Again, the relative decline in collective behaviour in Britain may well be the result of cultural factors, such as the more 'reserved' nature of many segments of British society relative to, say, their south European counterparts.

Clearly, considerable research is still required on these and other issues, both to confirm the findings of PSC in relation to the development of the household economy and to determine which factors in the rising importance of the home are likely to apply to all countries as opposed to being unique to Britain[2].

NOTES

1. The Henley Centre for Forecasting, 2 Tudor Street, Blackfriars, London EC4Y OAA, England.

2. We wish to thank Clem Tisdell and our discussants at the 4th World Congress of Social Economists for their many helpful and encouraging comments on our research into the household economy.

REFERENCES

Becker, G. (1981) **A Treatise on the Family**, Harvard University Press, Cambridge, Masschusetts
Brown, C.V. (1982) 'Home Production for Use in the Market Place', in B. Thorne and M. Yalom

(editors), **Rethinking the Family**, Longman, London

Gershuny, J. (1983) **Social Innovation and the Division of Labour**, Oxford Unversity Press, Oxford

Pahl, R.E. (1984) **Divisions of Labour**, Blackwell, Oxford

Toffler, A. (1983) **The Third Wave**, Pan, London

Chapter Eleven

TELECOMMUTING, WORK FROM HOME AND ECONOMIC CHANGE

P.H. Hall

INTRODUCTION

Advances in information technology have led commentators in recent years to predict a significant shift in the location of work from downtown offices in central business districts to the home.

Many members of the labour force have always worked from home anyway, either wholly or in part. In the futuristic scenarios painted by commentators such as Toffler (1980) and the Research Group on Human Life in the Information Society (1983), however, this body of workers is envisaged to expand rapidly. In this chapter an effort is made to assess the prospects for the growth of telecommuting - of work done remotely, by assumption in the home, on the basis of directives given and output transmitted over the telecommunications network. Clearly such work is confined to inform- ation-processing tasks, but these are potentially very numerous and span a range from the most repetitive and routinized of secretarial work to complex decision-making processes relating to new strategies for business direction.

Commuting costs have played an important role in the literature which has addressed this question in the past (Niles, 1976), as has the recognition that firms could save themselves real estate and office operating costs. While such costs cannot be ignored, and are incorporated in the analysis here, we wish to argue that other factors may not have been sufficiently emphasized. In particular, the relative advantages of remote and centralized work, as viewed by the household have often been under- played, as has direct attention to questions of supervision and monitoring costs by firms.

Telecommuting and Work from Home

These questions are incorporated in the analysis here. Evidence on the phenomenon of telecommuting is as yet sparse. There has been a tendency to point to rising costs of office space and business travel, increased female participation in the labour force and pressures for greater flexibility in working arrangements - and then to infer that everything points to a trend towards remote work. (See, for example, Friedman, 1981; Handy, 1980; and Olson, 1983.) Yet it is clear that movement in this direction is proceeding more slowly than some futurologists had expected (Olson and Primps, 1984).

ANALYSIS

In the analysis that follows, a terminological simplification is used. The market for informa-tion-processing services has on its supply side the providers of such services, characterized as households. On the demand side are the users of these service, characterized as firms.

We look in turn at decision-makers on each side of the market and in a final section consider the implications for the organizational aspects of work generated by efforts to relocate the performance of tasks to a decentralized location.

HOUSEHOLDS

Single Individual Households
Assume initially that households comprise a single individual and consider utility maximization in terms of the leisure-consumption diagram, Figure 11.1. A is unearned income; T is a constant rep-resenting the hours in a period available for allo-cation to work or leisure; h represents hours of work; and c (equal to zero in the early part of the analysis) is commuting time. An exogenously fixed wage rate, w, is represented by the slope of EB.

As it stands this framework is not of much help in focussing upon our problem. To do that two modifications will now be made.

1. Assume that employment can be taken only in an indivisible multiple of hours deno-ted h (say eight successive hours a day).
2. Assume that c > 0.

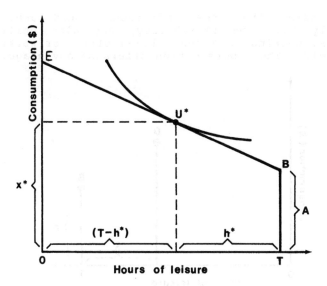

Figure 11.1: Constrained utility maximization for an individual with consumption from unearned income of A and complete flexibility in dividing time between work and leisure

On its own, assumption (1) implies that the consumption-leisure diagram must now be redrawn as Figure 11.2. Income from employment is now exogenously set at wh (where w is the hourly wage rate), and maximum consumption constrained to (A + wh). The individual is constrained to choose between point B, with consumption of A and leisure of T hours, and point D, with consumption of (A + wh) and leisure of (T - h). As long as D and B do not lie on the same indifference curve, one of these points will maximize constrained utility. Assuming that w is the same in each case, one supposedly attractive aspect of remote work can now be illustrated. From a point like D or B many individuals could in many cases increase their utility if they could attain some intermediate point between D and B or to the left of D. It has sometimes been suggested that if individuals work remotely on work channelled to them from a central computer, they can then do as much or as little work as they choose, and hence raise their level of welfare. But the argument is incomplete. If work was in infinitely elastic supply at a given wage, irrespective of where done, and commuting costs

were zero, then the individual could achieve
exactly the same flexibility, and also utility
levels, working in a centralized office or working
remotely. The remote option offers no advantage.

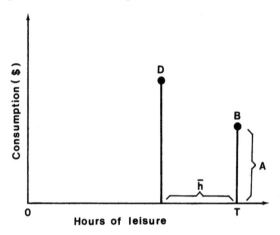

Figure 11.2: The budget constraint under a
fixed-hours employment contract

The flexibility argument on its own therefore
seems to offer little clue as to why work would be
done remotely. The same flexibility-enhancing
technology can be applied in either location. Only
if flex-time working were not available in a
central office but were available to remote workers
could the argument be brought to bear. This is
essentially an organizational issue.
If households can enjoy the same flexibility
in either location then for clues on whether the
new technology would induce household pressure for
remote work, we must look at other factors related
to the perceived costs and benefits of working in
one location compared with the other. A
potentially significant cost in working at a
central office rather than home is the sum of time
and resources devoted to commuting. It may be
helpful here to think of commuting costs as an
element of the transaction costs involved in
exchanging labour for goods: until the individual
has arrived at an appropriate location, the
employment contract cannot be activated. Assume
such costs are positive and are borne entirely by
the household. Assume for simplicity that all
households face the same fixed commuting costs

which have a time element $c = \bar{c}$, and a non-time resource element, $\bar{a}$.

If flexible working arrangements are available at a centralized office as well as in a remote location, the impact of the fixed commuting cost can be seen in Figure 11.3. In the absence of commuting, $T = (24 - b)$ where b is minimum necessary leisure-time, but when $c > 0$, the maximum time which could be devoted to work (or leisure) falls to $T' = (24 - b - \bar{c})$. The impact of the fixed, positive, non-time resource cost of commuting can be conveniently represented by reducing the value of unearned income A by the amount $\bar{a}$ to $A' = (A - \bar{a})$. In the presence of costly commuting, the household's budget set is OE'B'T'; in its absence the set expands to OEBT. Removing the need to commute will generate an unambiguous welfare gain for households, although in achieving a new utility maximum a household may choose to work either longer or shorter hours if it no longer commutes. The same argument applies if only time costs are incurred in commuting, but now the negatively sloped portion of the budget frontier springs from B".

It would seem that we have identified here an important reason why households would prefer remote work to travelling to a central office. However, what this analysis really does is to guide us to seek answers to further questions.

First, physically commuting to a central office will in the remote alternative have to be replaced by telecommuting. The time involved in establishing a telecommunications link will be positive but very small and we shall ignore it. Other time-denominated transaction costs might be greater in relation to remote work than when the work is done in a centralized office. It may take longer to interpret and clarify the nature of a job on a remote basis than in a situation where orders are given in the same office. If the information employee were made to bear the costs of clarification the situation in which clarification were more difficult to achieve would be at a relative disadvantage. For the moment, however, we assume no locational asymmetry in this respect.

Telecommuting is also potentially costly in non-time resource terms. Relevant capital equipment must be acquired and charges met for use of the telecommunications network. If the household must bear any of these costs, they may be viewed as resource costs akin to fares or petrol costs associated with physical commuting. But there is a

243

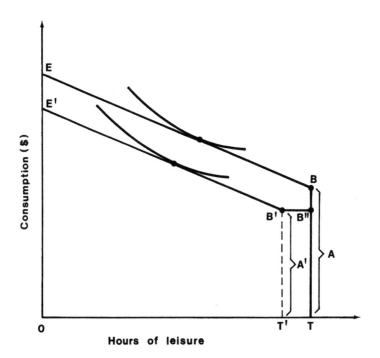

Figure 11.3: The budget set with and without commuting. The horizontal distance TT represents commuting time. The vertical distance BB'', equal to A - A' = $\bar{a}$, represents the non-time resource costs of commuting.

difference. If the household rents or owns information-processing equipment, the rental (actual or imputed) paid for it is a fixed cost which must be borne in order to do this type of work at all. This is analogous to the daily fare. But the more jobs that are done, the more telecommunication charges will have to be paid for transmission. There is thus a variable cost element to be considered. This difficulty will be accommodated by assuming that any reduction in net receipts per hour from labour employment ("the wage") occasioned by telephone charges will be exactly compensated by the purchaser of the service. Thus the slope and positions of B'E' and BE are unaffected by transmission costs. Whether the remote-work budget frontier now lies above or below B'E' will depend upon the fixed rental cost element.

244

As is illustrated in Figure 11.4, the budget
set expands eastwards because potential leisure (or
work) time now rises from T' to T. If rental costs
were zero, unearned income could again be left
unmodified at A, and the relevant budget set would
be OEBT. Positive rental costs could be illustrated by reducing the height of the eastern
vertical boundary of the budget set to levels of
less than BT. If rental costs were equal to the
non-time resource cost of commuting, $\bar{a}$ = BB", and
the potential welfare gain would still be unambiguous. If rental costs exceeded $\bar{a}$ by an amount
represented by B"B''', the household could at least
be not worse off by working remotely, but if rental
costs exceeded $\bar{a}$ by more than B"B''', then the household would unambiguously prefer centralized work.
    Normally, we would not expect information/
processing operatives working in a central office

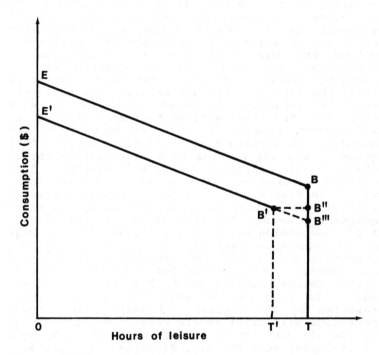

Figure 11.4: The budget set for a telecommuter
with a fixed rental to pay for computer use. The
budget set is unambiguously larger than that for a
worker who physically commutes so long as rental
charges are less than BB'''.

to have to make any contribution to the cost of
their equipment. This is a reflection of an
implicitly assumed employer-employee relationship
in which the employer provides the relevant
capital. So long as remote workers continue to
operate in an employer-employee relationship,
therefore, it seems that remote work would appear
relatively attractive to households under the
assumption made here. Only if centralized work
implied no cost bearing for equipment while remote
work necessitated cost bearing for equipment
greater than physical commuting costs would
centralized work appear relatively attractive.

This directs attention to other issues. It
might appear that all we have to do is compare
physical commuting costs with equipment rental
costs and reach the (fairly obvious) conclusion
that so long as rental costs are small relative to
commuting costs remote work will be preferred by
households. Technological advances which reduce
equipment prices should steadily increase the
proportion of households which have this preference
implied for any given spatial distribution of
population, and hence implied distribution of
commuting costs. On the other hand, operating
within the employer-employee relationship employers
might be reluctant to allow employees to work
remotely at the given wage on equipment provided by
the employer because of perceived supervision and
co-ordination difficulties - and hence concern that
equipment was not working in a way which maximized
return to the employer or firm's owners. This
could be tackled by offering. remote workers lower
wages. In Figure 11.5, households maximize utility
at U* at the initial wage, not commuting and using
equipment provided for them at no capital charge.
At U^A, households maximize utility at the same wage
on the assumption they physically commute. At U^B,
households attain the same utility as at U^A, but
work remotely on equipment for which they face no
capital charge, but for which they are paid a lower
wage. So long as the wage lies between rates
presented by the steeper and less steep slopes,
households will refer remote work. The actual wage
will be the outcome of bargaining between employer
and employee, more broadly, of market conditions.

Changing the wage is not, however, the only
possibility. If households rented or bought the
equipment themselves the information provided would
be put in a different relation to the buyer of
information services than that found in the

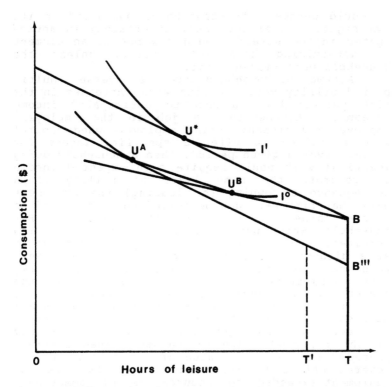

Figure 11.5: The less steeply inclined slope of the budget set boundary springing from B represents the lowest wage a household could accept, without loss of utility, if it were asked to accept reduced earnings in exchange for being permitted to work from home. Equipment rental charges are assumed to be zero.

employer-employee relationship in most offices. Unless the equipment were hired from the user of the services on the explicit condition that it be used exclusively for the information user's work, the information provider would acquire rights of ownership or use in the equipment which would generate a degree of freedom permitting it to be used on work for more than one client. Whether or not a household wished to avail itself of that freedom its position would nonetheless have changed significantly. It would have to decide <u>whether</u> to seek new markets for its information-processing services and, if so, would have to recognize that

247

it would become a "cottage-based business" in its own right. In either case, uncertainty in anticipated income streams would now become an element in determining household utility, unless the household were risk-neutral.

Assume the household were risk-averse. Multiperiod utility would decline with increases in the risk perceived to attach to anticipated income streams. Assume that a job in the employer-employee relationship using employer-owned capital were perceived to offer a specified income for certain over a given period, then a household doing identical work would require high expected income to generate the same level of utility if a consequence of owning (or leasing) the equipment were that risk were now perceived to be attached to income earned in providing the service. For households which perceived that remotely providing services, even to a previous employer, might put it at a disadvantage compared with direct employees, this could be sufficient to discourage remote work. Such disutility might be magnified if the household, in addition, were unsure of its managerial and accounting skills in running a small business. Clearly the argument could go either way, but would unambiguously favour remote work only if the expected value of income earned remotely exceeded the expected value of income earned in a central office by more than the rental cost of equipment exceeded the resource cost of commuting.

We argued earlier that at given rates of employment and remuneration, remote work might be favoured over centralized under zero commuting costs if it were possible to spread the work more flexibly in a remote situation (but that this was an organizational matter alone). In light of the subsequent discussion, we can now see that even if work is flexibly available remotely but not centrally, households might choose to work centrally. In order for that to be the case, it is clear that at any given hourly wage rate w, the rental cost of equipment r must exceed $\bar{a}$.

As we have set the problem up, a great deal hinges on the relative values of commuting costs and the rental costs of equipment used remotely in order to permit telecommuting. We have seen, however, that there is more to it than that. Because remote use of equipment may permit the equipment to be used for purposes of clients other than those of a direct employer, the purchaser of information services might be unwilling to allow a machine which he himself made available at zero cost to be used remotely, or may only permit remote work at a discounted wage potentially unsatisfactory to the household. Because of the reductions in expected income and utility which this generates for households, the centralized option associated with using an employer's machine may remain relatively attractive.

We have ignored the utility associated with location _per se_. Many operatives may prefer to work at a centralized office because of the company, camaraderie and opportunity 'to get out of the house'. Others may prefer to work away from home, although not necessarily at a central office, because they derive more satisfaction from work when it is not interrupted by the demands of domesticity. For the one-person household, the attractions of company are likely to be relatively great and the appeal of remote work relatively diminished as a result.

Finally, notice that physical commuting may not be a utility-neutral activity.

The rock-bottom model of the household we have adopted is indeed too bare to capture all of the nuances which arise in relation to the question we have posed. Among other things it is partial (it says little about interactions with other households and firms which underpin determination of the wage); it is comparatively static (it says nothing about transitional problems which might arise in moving towards equilibrium under the new technology); and it says nothing about decisions within a household or more than one person. These are serious shortcomings and yet even with this very simple model it has become apparent the mere fact that technological change has opened up the possibility of remote work is not a guarantee that this option will be widely adopted.

Households of More than One Person
In the preceding paragraphs, it was asserted that some individuals might prefer to work in one location rather than another because of utility associated with location _per se_. While this is plausible as it stands, it takes on more substance if the household is recognized to comprise more than one person. In that case, working remotely at home may have implications that office work would not have, while the costs associated with commuting

may be different for an individual earner-within-family than for an individual earner living solo.

For the individual working remotely, at home, a constraint which was formerly imposed upon the family group is now removed. If an individual goes to an office, that individual is physically prevented from participating in household activities in his or her absence. This reduces household utility if certain tasks can be done for others in the household only by that individual and only at a time when he or she is constrained by office work to be absent. But this is a polar case. Some substitute person can usually be found to perform tasks (e.g., a child-minder to care of children after school) and some tasks could be done in alternative time-slots. The critical question is, once again, one of costs and benefits.

Considering first substitute persons, the parent-child relationship is most likely to give rise to conflict. Not all parents would consider child-minders (or even grandparents) as perfect substitutes for themselves in caring for children, full-time in pre-schooling years, or after school in later years. Even under zero financial costs of child-minding, therefore, centralized office work might imply some loss of utility compared with that of parent availability at home. If the children are themselves detrimentally affected by child-minding, and/or if child-minding has a positive financial cost to the household, utility is further reduced. We must take care to adopt the correct benchmark for comparison, however. If a parent works at home, he or she will be physically available but may not be able to do the job of parenting at all, or at least as well as a child-minder because of the demands of work. Furthermore, the parent's utility may be substantially reduced by manifest conflicting demands. Assuming that a workforce participation decision has been made in the first place, there would seem to be no overwhelming reason to expect parents to prefer to work at home rather than at an office.

This, of course, begs a question: What determines participation? If we restrict the question to considering the decision of a potential second worker in a household the sort of answer usually given is that it will depend upon the income of the primary earner, unearned income, debt-servicing commitments and commitment of time to children (Deaton and Muellbauer, 1980, pp.273-5).

The introduction of the potential for remote

work has implications for this type of analysis. First, it may mean that the persons occupying the role of primary and secondary earner could change places. Secondly, it is often assumed in participation analysis that the hours worked by the primary earner are institutionally fixed. Use of the new technology makes it more difficult to sustain this assumption. If the new technology were used to facilitate great flexibility in the use of individuals' time, whenever they did their work, then households could co-operate to allocate time with less constraints than before, especially if more than one member were in information processing.

Consider finally the household allocation of tasks to time slots. If a household gains more utility by doing housework on Wednesday mornings than Saturday afternoons (because leisure complements are more plentiful at weekends), then it makes sense to allocate the mid-week time slot to housework rather than paid employment and devote Saturday to leisure if the utility gain resulting outweighs the sacrifice in lost income. So long as such a decision can be implemented by any individual in the household just as easily in the centralized mode as in the remote, the remote work option has no special advantage beyond those noted earlier in relation to commuting costs.

Household Life-cycle Considerations

The analysis to this point has proceeded essentially in a comparative static framework. A more ambitious model would recognize that life-cycle considerations may be important.

Childrens' development may lead to switches between participation and non-participation over a parent's child-rearing years. Over a longer perspective, it should also be recognized that working remotely might be regarded by members of the household as placing them at a career disadvantage. This is an irrelevance for employment lacking any career structure or for individuals devoid of ambition. But for many information processors neither of these conditions holds. For remote work to appear relatively attractive to centralized office work the lifetime net benefits, appropriately discounted, would have to be positive. This would require employees to believe:

1. that employment opportunities would be at

     least as potentially attractive if remote
     work were undertaken on a permanent or
     temporary basis.

  2. that firms giving undertakings in support
     of (1) could be relied upon to keep their
     word.

Given that many information processors are themselves at the managerial levels in firms, it is
difficult to believe that such individuals would be
so persuaded. Many other information workers
(e.g., publishers, editors, advertising copy-
writers, management accountants, etc.) might also
feel that their work actually required personal
interaction at a central location in order to
achieve sufficient quality in their work to merit
promotion.

FIRMS (INFORMATION USERS)

We have said a great deal from the perspective of
the household but assuming the wage to be given and
relevant work to be in infinitely elastic supply at
that wage, have not been able to make a conclusive
case that households as information suppliers would
prefer to operate remotely rather than in central
offices. Yet firms as households' clients in
purchasing information services clearly have an
important role in determining outcomes.
  First, if firms are prepared to reflect any
excess of physical commuting over telecommuting
costs in wages, then the incentive for households
to work remotely is reduced significantly.
Secondly, if firms are also prepared to allow
information providers to use the technology with
the same degree of flexibility when used centrally
as when used remotely, then the perceived
advantages to households of working remotely would
be diminished yet further. Turning the argument
around, if firms perceived it to be in their best
interest to encourage central office attendance,
then the new technology would certainly not prevent
that objective being achieved. But if firms felt
there was anything to be gained by having part of
its workforce operate remotely, then it would
recognize that wages and working conditions were
potentially open to bargain in achieving that too.
Assume firms are profit-maximizers. Then they will
also be cost-minimizers. For any given level of
demand, they will attempt to minimize the sum of

capital, labour and other input costs:

$$TC = \rho K + \omega L + vX$$

where ρ is explicit or imputed rental costs on buildings and equipment, K the stock of such capital, ω the wage cost, L labour hired, and v and X the price and quantity of other inputs. Transferring work from a central to a remote location offers the attraction of reducing K as less office space needs to be occupied downtown and (possibly) as information providers supply their own equipment; and of lowering ω as telecommuters will not require compensation for physical commuting and, if remote workers are part-timers or non-payroll workers, of relieving the firm of non-wage 'on costs' for labour.

Notice, however, that these potential gains rely upon a variety of subsidiary conditions:

1. While less office space needs to be rented in town, space is still needed for the work to be done - space in the home which could be put to some alternative use. If the household is in a strong position to bargain with the firm, perhaps because its skills and firm-specific human capital are valued highly, the household may be able to incorporate imputed rental on its house space in its wage as a measure of compensation for inconvenience.
2. If information providers supply their own equipment, they may (and in a perfect market would) be able to command rental on that machine equivalent to what the firm would have had to pay had it owned the machine itself. Again, the strength of the bargaining position is important.
3. 'On costs' disappear only if remote workers are not on the regular payroll. It is by no means impossible that some remote workers might remain on the regular payroll, especially if their integration into and commitment to the firm is regarded as important to the firm.

From these arguments, it is apparent that the benefits of reducing costs by employing remote workers are most likely to be found in relation to those tasks where information service suppliers have least bargaining power because their skills are of the most widely available form and their degree of commitment to the firm is regarded as unimportant to the successful completion of tasks allocated to them. Another way of looking at this is to say that if some task could be performed by a potentially wide range of information service suppliers, competition for the work should not only keep the wage down but also provide a discipline on the quality of the work so that commitment to a firm is unnecessary. This argument would suggest that remote work would be sought by firms in relation to the simpler, more standarized or routine tasks of secretarial and accounting work.

Notice, however, that a quite different argument may lead to a similar outcome. Information processors with significant bargaining power have that power because they are highly regarded and/or have considerable firm-specific knowledge: they are typically higher-level managers or system analysts. Assuming such individuals have sufficient motivation and commitment not to require the discipline of a competitive market to drive them to efficient performance, then firms may permit them to work remotely too, even at a salary equivalent to what they would earn if working centrally.

Many information-processing skills fall between these polar cases, however. Information service providers may have sufficient firm-specific knowledge to insulate them from competitive pressures, at least to an extent, and hence have a degree of bargaining power if working remotely which might enable them to raise their wage until it incorporated at least some elements they would enjoy as central office workers. Furthermore, in the absence of the commitment found among high-level managers, they might require costly supervision or alternatively perform less effectively than if working centrally. In such cases, it is unclear whether firms would minimize costs by employing individuals remotely or centrally.

Hidden in the last few paragraphs has been the question of supervision or monitoring. At this point we suggest a simple framework for combining that element with those already noted. Assume that an efficiency index can be calculated for the performance of any information provider. The more efficient the provider, the less costly are his or her services to the firm. Efficiency of performance is related to three factors: individuals' internal motivation or commitment, external market pressures upon individuals, and supervisory monitoring applied by the firm. In Figure 11.6 we assume that for a given task, efficiency increases at a declining rate as 100% efficiency is approached, as exposure to market force increases. The less exposed to threat from the market an individual is, the lower is his or her efficiency. However, if individuals are highly motivated or committed then even at low levels of threat from market forces, their productive efficiency is higher than for individuals with low levels of internal motivation.

Now, for jobs in which the market can be used as a discipline, levels of internal motivation become irrelevant or almost so: all information providers must perform efficiently at a market-determined wage or will be dispensed with rapidly. Supervision costs for the firm here are minimal,

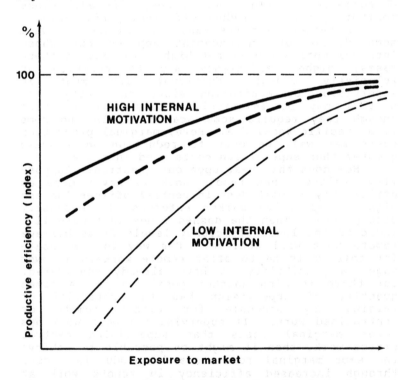

Figure 11.6: Variation in the level of productive efficiency achieved by workers from home under varying degrees of exposure to market pressure and with different levels of internal motivation.

wages competitive and efficient performance guaranteed.

At the other extreme, some tasks may only be done by individuals whose position is entrenched because of scarce skills or firm-specific knowledge. If they are lowly-motivated individuals, substantial gains in efficiency may be available to the firm if such individuals are supervised and monitored closely - achieving reductions in marginal costs through increased productive efficiency which are greater than the marginal costs incurred by the supervision itself. However, individuals with scarce skills and/or specific knowledge may well also be highly motivated. If so, then the marginal costs of monitoring may well outstrip the reductions in marginal production costs achieved by any small gain in efficient performance. (In such cases, indeed, close monitoring may even reduce efficient performance.)

In between lie the many individuals for whom some degree of entrenchment applies but whose internal motivation is not high. In many of these cases, higher efficiency may be achieved at relatively modest additional investment in supervision or monitoring since the tasks they perform may be relatively easily assessed even though they require some scarce skills and some firm-specific knowledge. Here, marginal production costs may well be open to reduction on a scale greater than supervision costs need increase.

How does this bear upon our question? Suppose firms believe that remote work is never done as efficiently as work done in central offices (unless highly competitive market enforces the necessary discipline). Then the dashed lines in Figure 11.6 indicate the lower efficiency levels firms believe remote work will achieve. One way to compensate for this would be to offer remote workers a lower wage, a possibility we have already considered. But there is also another possibility. A given quantity of supervision has the potential of raising any schedule for either remote or centralized work. If supervising remote work has lower marginal costs than supervising central office work, then it might be possible to achieve the same marginal reductions in production costs through increased efficiency in remote work at lower marginal supervision costs than those associated with centralized work. In this case, firms would favour remote work. In fact, the new technology would seem to have reduced the potential supervision and monitoring costs in <u>both</u> locations, and many firms may still believe supervision, however operated, to be less effective in increasing the efficiency of remote work compared with central- ized. Particularly for tasks where information workers have only modest internal motivation, therefore, the remote option would not be favoured automatically by firms. Lower wages for remote work would seem to be needed as an inducement to firms.

One point which emerges from this discussion is that the potential for remote work may well depend on the contractual relationship between information provider and information user. As an obvious example, firms which could call upon the services of self-employed information workers using their own equipment in a competitive market might well expect to achieve lower costs than if they used the same operator on an employment contract basis. This is because self-employed external operators can be used for defined tasks of specified content and/or duration and paid on a per-task basis whereas direct employees must be paid for a determined working day, irrespective of how it is filled. Even taking account of overhead costs which might have to be paid to self-employed operators, the total costs to the information users could thus fall below the cost level associated with an employee's wage cost, including non-wage 'on-costs'. Different institutional arrangements may, however, be associated with different incen- tive structures — a matter which deserves separate discussion.

CONCLUSION

In this chapter we have attempted to analyze the factors underlying the potential rate of increase of telecommuting given a technological change which permits information-processing work to be done remotely. It has become apparent that remote work might not always be utility-maximizing for infor- mation providers at a rate of remuneration (wage) equal to that offered for centralized office work and that firms may not always find it satisfies their objectives to best effect to have information work done remotely. Much will depend upon the type of information-processing work to be undertaken. We have seen that the flexibility argument must be treated with caution. Any technology which permits work to be done remotely in whatever quantities and at whatever times the household wishes must also permit it to be done under those conditions at a central office. It is therefore logically incomplete to argue that the new technology necessarily favours remote work on flexibility grounds. This would be so only if the technology were put to work with less organizational flexibility in a central location than when used for remote work. Beyond that, the perceived costs and benefits of remote and centralized work must be brought into play. Clearly, if physical commuting costs are positive, flexible use of the technology at a centralized location might be achievable only at heavy costs in terms of time and non-time resources: the more often during one period a journey must be made to use a centralized base of capital equipment, the more costly flexible use becomes. It is in that context then, that the supposed flexibility advantage of the remote option must be viewed: work can be done for chosen periods of long or short duration within any 'working day' without having to incur physical commuting costs as a transaction cost on each occasion.

But this is not the end of the story. The physical commuting costs associated with centralized work must be compared with the telecommuting costs of remote work. Such costs may include rental and transmission charges for information-processing equipment; sacrificed living space, or the cost of creating new work space; reduction of utilities associated with work itself through the absence of personal contact with colleagues, and the potential for domestic interruption; and reduction of utility associated with leisure taken domestically when pressures of work are so much more easily perceived. There is evidence (Olson and Primps, 1984) that these factors are potentially significant, though they are likely to apply in different degrees to different households at different stages of the life-cycle.

Whether the technology is used remotely is not purely a matter of household choice, however. Firms as buyers of information services may well have reason for preferring work to be done in one location rather than another which in turn may restrict households' freedom of action. In particular while remote work offers firms potential costs savings in some direction, they may perceive that remote work will, in some cases, be associated with less efficient performance. Much will depend

upon the nature of the task, which in part also
determines the internal motivation of the individual to perform it satisfactorily and defines the
exposure of individuals to external pressures.
While it seems likely that information users will
find that the balance of such factors might favour
the remote performance of tasks which are either
routinized or, at the other extreme, engage the
specialized services of the heavily committed,
there remains a substantial middle ground in which
our analysis suggests that the outcome is far from
clear.

REFERENCES

Atkinson, J. (1984) 'Manpower Strategies for
    Flexible Organisations', **Personal Management**,
    16, 8, pp.28-30
Baran, P. (1971) **Potential Market Demand for
    Two-Way Information Services to the Home
    1970-1990**, Institute for the Future, Menlo
    Park, California
Bonus, H. (1973) 'Quasi-Engel Curves, Diffusion and
    the Ownership of Major Consumer Durables',
    Journal of Political Economy, 81, pp.655-677
Deaton, A. and Muellbauer, J. (1980) **Economics and
    Consumer Behaviour**, Cambridge University Press
Friedman, B. (1981) **The Second Stage**, Cambridge
    University Press
Handy, C. (1980) 'The Changing Shape of Work',
    Organisational Dynamics, Autumn, pp.26-34
Niles, J.M., Carlson, F.R., Gray, P. and Hanemann,
    G.G. (1976) **The Telecommunications-Trans-
    portation Tradeoff: Options for Tomorrow**,
    Wiley, New York
Olson, M.H. (1983) 'Remote Office Work: Changing
    Work Patterns in Space and Time', **Commu-
    nications of the A.C.M.**, **26**, 3, pp.182-187
Olson, M.H. and S.B. Primps (1984) 'Working at Home
    with Computers: Work and Non-Work Issues',
    Journal of Social Issues, **40**, 3, pp.47-112
Research Group on Human Life in the Information
    Society (Chairman, Yonegi Masuda) (1983) **The
    Information Society and Human Life**, Social
    Policy Bureau, Economic Planning Agency of the
    Japanese Government, Tokyo
Toffler, A. (1980) **The Third Wave**, Morrow, New York

Chapter Twelve

ATTITUDES OF BANK EMPLOYEES TO TECHNOLOGICAL CHANGE:
A SURVEY OF THE SOUTH AFRICAN BANKING INDUSTRY

Hazel T. Suchard

INTRODUCTION

Technological change can be taken to mean any
change in the methods or context of work which is
associated with the use of new machinery. New
technology affects all workers ranging from those
who work with machines in industries such as motor
and engineering to those who work with word-
processing and data-processing technology in the
clerical sector. It concerns, for example, the
introduction of automatic teller machines in the
banking industry.

In recent years, technological change and its
effect on employment have become an issue of
concern in industrialized countries. At the 7th
World Congress of the International Industrial
Relations Association (1986) in Hamburg,
technological change and labour relations were
considered a major topic for discussion.

In many countries, unions have been active in
formulating policies about the introduction of
technological change and its impact on employment
and what the role of unions should be.

In Britain, since about 1978, a large number
of unions, especially white-collar unions, have
organized special committees and working parties to
look at the effects of new technology on their members, and union departments have produced reports
about new technology. Few employers have tried to
involve unions or employees in decisions concerning new technology, and unions have not been very
successful in trying to influence the introduction
of new technology via collective bargaining. In
Australia, the union movement has evidenced concern
with regard to the effects of new technology.
However, as in Britain, management has tended to

have the major say as far as technology is concerned. Trade unions in Norway, Sweden and West Germany have been far more successful. For example, union representatives in Norway and Sweden have the legal right to obtain all information about proposed new technology and can present the union's point of view to company boards of directors. Moreover, if marketplace changes adversely affect job safety and health the unions have the power to veto these changes.

Bamber and Lansbury (1986) have however argued that in countries with adversarial traditions in industrial relations (such as most English-speaking countries) unions are more likely to oppose technological change than their counterparts in countries with recent traditions of social partnership in industrial relations (such as West Germany and the Scandinavian countries).

Conflict has arisen over the negative (for example, unemployment) effects versus the positive (for example, benefits to business) effects of the new technology and attempts have been made to ascertain the views and attitudes of employees to new technology. For example the results of a study in Australia (Anon., **Tradition in Transition**, 1981) appear to indicate a somewhat negative attitude on the part of banking employees to technological change.

In South Africa, a country where white trade union groupings generally have had non-adversarial, good working relationships with employers, the available statistics on banking and building societies make no connection between technological change and employment. The issue was considered sufficiently important by the banking union SASBO (South African Society of Bank Officials) to be the subject of a special survey on the attitudes of banking and building society employees to technological change. The refusal of the major banks to cooperate in any way with the study both made a survey the more necessary and dictated that the survey be conducted through the unions rather than the employers.

It originates from a Australian survey (Anon., **Tradition in Transition, Technological Changes and Employment in Banking**, 1981) of a similar nature, carried out a few years ago, and was done with the object in mind of comparing the South African attitudes with those of the Australians and to collect data on South African banking employees' attitudes.

Bank Employee Attitudes to New Technology

Questionnaire items were developed in two different ways. Firstly, items were taken from the Australian study and these represent issues as well as perceptions of union and management people involved in the use of technology on a daily basis. Further items were added which were theoretically and empirically derived in an eclectic fashion, but no single model was used. The interest was not in demonstrating the validity of the underlying domain but in gathering the initial data. Both developing the underlying dimensions and formulating and testing the model are future issues.

Although both the BSOA (Building Societies Officials Association) and the in-house unions of Volkskas and Nedbank took part in the survey, only certain of the results applicable to the banks will be discussed here and only some tables are shown. Additional tables can be found in Suchard (1986).

THE SURVEY

As of the date of sample selection, December 1984, members of SASBO totalled 29,519, BSOA 16,267, VAV (Volkskas Amptenare Vereeniging) 10,000 and Nedbank 4,253 - a total of 60,000 members. A list of members was made available and a sample of 15,000 was obtained by selecting every fourth name. The questionnaire was discussed with senior officials of SASBO and was also considered by its union committee, which suggested some minor amendments. Following pilot testing, the questionnaire was dispatched during January 1985. By the end of March 1985, 3,634 useable replies had been received, a response rate of 24.23%.

Although this response rate affects the randomness of the sample, a follow-up of the non-respondents in order to improve the response rate was rejected, as the proportion of respondents in each category was fairly close to the proportions of the population. The results obtained from the questionnaire are largely regarded as illuminative, where trends in the industry are highlighted. SASBO felt it important to have some knowledge of the attitudes of a significant number of its members with regard to technological changes in the industry, and 3,634 members were regarded as a significantly large number. The results that follow are thus reported from the sample of 3,634 respondents. Of this number, 2,536 were banking respondents.

Bank Employee Attitudes to New Technology

Much of the information described below under the distribution headings is of value as some of the actual statistics on the population are unavailable.

DISTRIBUTION OF RESPONDENTS BY CATEGORIES

Distribution of Respondents by Union Grouping, Race and Age

In terms of the distribution of respondents by union grouping, the number of SASBO respondents was larger, the number of VAV respondents roughly the same as in the actual population. The proportion of Barclays and Standard bank respondents were the highest; however, they did compose the major membership of SASBO. The proportion of male respondents was considerably greater than might have been expected from their proportion in the union membership, where females greatly outnumber males. Why this should be so is not clear. It is possible that male staff are especially enthusiastic about answering questionnaires or that female staff are simply more apathetic.

By far the largest percentages of respondents were white. The percentages of Black, Coloured and Asian respondents were higher than in the actual population.

The largest percentages were in the 21-27-year-old age groups, males or females. Below age 21 and after age 60, the percentage declined dramatically. More female respondents fell into the younger age ranges (under 27 years) than did males. Contrary to expectations, that female respondents would comprise a small percentage of the 28-40 age groups as they have left the work-force to have and look after children, they did not comprise a small percentage of the 28-40 age group.

Distribution of Staff Duties of Respondents in Terms of Branches, Head Offices and Data Centres

The sample was heavily biased towards branches (81.20% of the respondents worked in branches) rather than head offices and data centres.

Distribution of Respondents by Educational Qualifications and Earnings

The vast majority of bank employees left school

263

after standard 10, but the greater percentage did not go on to achieve higher educational qualifications. While only 19.96% of banking respondents had higher academic qualifications, 39.56% were currently enrolled in a higher educational institution. Part-time employment did not appear to be significant in the banking industry.

An interesting observation was the tendency for females to earn less than males. This is clearly shown in the survey where for example, 57.97% of females earned under R899 as compared to 24.62% of males. The fact that females earned less than males could be due to the fact that they still occupy the less skilled categories. For example, 31.27% of the male bank respondents were managers as compared to 2.10% of the females; 13.21% of the male bank respondents were accountants as compared to 4.38% of the females.

Salary was looked at in terms of position, according to sex. More female trainees than male trainees are found in the lower salary scales. More female sole tellers than male sole tellers are found in the highest salary scales. More female senior clerks are found in both the lowest and the highest salary ranges and more male accountants are found in the higher salary ranges than female accountants. With regard to managers, a larger percentage of females than males are found in the highest salary range. More male than female clerks are found in the lowest salary ranges and more females are found in the highest salary range. Larger percentages of male computer operators than female are found in the higher salary ranges. More male than female supervisors are found in the higher salary ranges.

Distribution of Respondents by Occupational Category, Region and Banking Experience

The sample was biased towards managers (17.85%) and specialized clerks (13.98%). It is not possible to say whether this was because respondents in these categories were particularly enthusiastic about answering questionnaires or whether they occupy a large proportion of the banking workforce, as the latter figures could not be obtained. Computer operators, programmers and systems analysts made up only a small percentage of respondents. A breakdown of duties by age and sex reveals that a large proportion of the females in the youngest age category (15-20 years) were trainees. In all age categories, female trainees outnumbered males. Rather than a new career-minded attitude on the part of women, the results may indicate a willingness on the part of banks to train more women. Women are, however, still predominant in the traditional occupations such as typist. In the younger age group, under 28 years, the percentages of males who were tellers or sole tellers are greater than females.

The sample is heavily biased towards the Transvaal, where 54.6% of the respondents worked. It is not possible to say whether this result conforms to the original distribution of union members as these statistics are unavailable.

The concept of career advancement through banking experience appears to be still valid for the majority of employees, most of whom would have joined the banking industry straight from school, and many have worked with the same bank throughout their employment in the banking industry. Of those presently working in banks, only 2.34% have had building society experience. Any transfer that takes place appears to be from banks to building societies and not vice versa.

ATTITUDES OF RESPONDENTS (EMPLOYEES) TO THE BANKING/BUILDING SOCIETY INDUSTRY AND TO TECHNOLOGICAL CHANGE IN THE INDUSTRY

Contact with New Technologies

Much has been said about the effect of new technology on banking employees, but did the respondents in fact have much contact with new technologies?

As far as contact with new technologies is concerned, 84.30% of bank employees stated that they had direct contact. However, there was little contact with specific new technologies (Table 12.1). The new technology most likely to be encountered by respondents was on-line terminals; 50.46% of employees frequently came into contact with them and 26.89% occasionally. The other technologies which would then be likely to be encountered were ATMs, automatic teller machines, (frequent by 28.01% of respondents), visual display (frequent by 25.59 of respondents) and microfilm (frequent by 21.53% of respondents). CEMTEX (Centralized Electronic Magnetic Tape Exchange) was

265

seldom encountered. Only 4.89% of respondents had frequent contact with CEMTEX. Off-line terminals are not encountered by the majority of respondents; 60.71% do not encounter them. Word processors are not encountered by 73.60% of the respondents.

Table 12.1: Contact of Respondents in Banks With Specific New Technologies, South Africa, 1985

Technology	Frequently		Occasionally		Not at all	
	Nos.	%	Nos.	%	Nos.	%
Word processors	252	11.98	343	15.22	1659	73.6
On-line Terminals	1143	50.46	609	26.89	512	22.6
Off-line Terminals	320	14.22	564	25.07	1366	60.71
CEMTEX	110	4.89	191	8.49	1949	86.62
Mini/Micro Computers	281	12.46	345	15.30	1629	72.24
SWIFT	333	14.75	483	21.39	1442	63.86
Micro Film	484	21.53	606	26.96	1158	51.51
ATM'S	629	28.01	584	26.00	1033	45.99
Visual Display	575	25.59	561	24.97	1111	49.44
Other	92	4.12	32	1.43	2107	94.44

Source: SASBO Survey, 1985

That there are so many employees still involved in jobs which do not involve contact with new technology suggests that there is still considerable potential for technological change. The result suggests that the simple money transaction process is still dominant and that it is in this process that the majority of employees are engaged.

Effect on Career
A job can be distinguished from a career in that a job is of a short-term nature and its worth is in terms of immediate benefits. A career is long-term and offers personal advancement and growth. Do the respondents have a career in banking and has new technology improved their career prospects?

Respondents were asked whether they felt that they had a career rather than a job in banking. Banking does appear to be a career for the majority of women. 61.33% of female employees felt that they have a career rather than a job in banking. This feeling is more marked among male employees than female employees (76.13% as compared to

61.33%), but it is not possible to say that banking is not a career for the majority of women. The tradition of banking employment appears to be one of the secure and dependable career. Overall approximately two-thirds of respondents regarded banking as a career and one-third considered it to be a job. However, this tendency is less predominant among Blacks and Asians. 52.94% of Black male respondents and 59.09% of Asian male respondents felt that they have a career as compared to 78.82% of White male respondents and 62.50% of Coloured male respondents. 56.25% of Black female respondents and 38.24% of Asian female respondents felt that they have a career as compared to 62.42% of White female respondents and 60.32% of Coloured female respondents.

Banking employees were asked whether they felt that the new technology introduced by the banks had improved their career prospects. As indicated in Figure 12.1, 41.11% felt that their career prospects have been improved while 39.23% felt that their prospects have not improved. Large percentages of males and females in the younger age categories felt more positively about their career prospects. The percentages feeling that new technology had improved their career prospects decreased with age - this characteristic being more

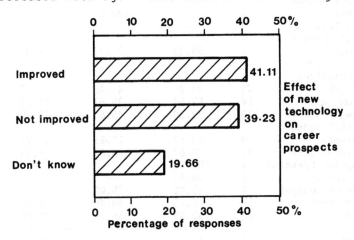

Figure 12.1: Percentage distribution of responses of bank employees in South Africa, 1985, to the question of whether new technology has improved their career prospects (Source based on SASBO Survey, 1985).

pronounced for males than females. The response was also broken down by job category (See Tables 12.2 and 12.3). As far as bank branch staff are concerned the majority of accountants and managers felt that their career prospects had not improved while the majority of computer operators, ledger examiners and typists felt that their career prospects had improved. Apart from senior clerks, managers, supervisors and others, the majority of bank head office staff thought that their career prospects had improved. As can be seen from Table 12.3, generally those in the higher echelons were

Table 12.2: Response of Bank Head Office Staff to Effect of New Technology on Career Prospects, South Africa, 1985

Job Category	Number	Career Prospects Improved %	Career Prospects Not Improved %	Don't Know %
Trainee	14	50.00	21.43	28.57
Machine Operator	4	50.00	25.00	25.00
Typist	16	56.25	18.75	25.00
Ledger Examiner	1	100.00	–	–
Teller/Junior Clerk	1	–	100.00	–
Sole Teller	0	–	–	–
Teller/Senior Clerk	12	58.33	33.33	8.33
Senior &/or Specialized Clerk	44	34.09	45.45	20.45
Accountant	14	57.14	28.57	14.29
Manager	125	39.20	45.60	15.20
Clerk/Process Worker	9	66.67	11.11	22.22
Training Officer	24	66.67	25.00	8.33
Computer Operator	1	100.00	–	–
Programmer	1	100.00	–	–
Systems Analyst	4	75.00	25.00	–
Supervisor	13	46.15	38.46	15.38
Other	109	52.29	36.70	11.01
Total	392	47.96	37.24	14.80

Source: SASBO Survey, 1985

268

less positive about the consequences of technological developments for their career prospects.
Most (68.48%) of bank data centre staff felt that
their career prospects had improved.

Respondents were also asked what effect they
thought specific new technological developments
would have on their job or career prospects. The
new developments chosen included those with recent
introduction (ATMs and on-line facilities) and
those about which a considerable amount has been
written (telephone banking), but have not generally

Table 12.3: Response of Bank Branch Staff to Effect of New
Technology on Career Prospects, South Africa, 1985

Job Category	Number	Career Prospects Improved %	Career Prospects Not Improved %	Don't Know %
Trainee	152	48.03	26.97	25.00
Machine Operator	21	47.62	38.10	14.29
Typist	86	52.33	30.23	17.44
Ledger Examiner	72	51.39	30.56	18.06
Teller/Junior Clerk	99	43.43	33.33	23.33
Sole Teller	69	40.58	33.33	26.09
Teller/Senior Clerk	179	37.99	39.11	22.91
Senior &/or Specialized Clerk	267	39.70	43.07	17.23
Accountant	192	25.52	51.56	22.92
Manager	281	24.20	55.52	20.28
Clerk/Process Worker	50	48.00	30.00	22.00
Training Officer	5	80.00	–	20.00
Computer Operator	14	64.29	28.57	7.14
Programmer	0	–	–	–
Systems Analyst	0	–	–	–
Supervisor	46	43.48	47.83	8.70
Other	215	38.60	39.07	22.33
Total	1748	38.16	41.08	20.77

Source: SASBO Survey, 1985

been used. Their response was analyzed by age and sex. In all age categories, the response to complete on-line facilities, ATMs and electronic fund transfer was positive. More bank employees under age 34 view the effects of automatic clearing as being beneficial than those who feel that they will be affected. Larger percentages of older people than younger people thought they would not be affected. Younger employees appeared to view telephone banking more adversely than older ones. The general indication is that employees did not view the effect of specific new technologies on their job or career prospects as being adverse. However, as Table 12.2 indicates there was a high degree of ignorance about how automatic clearing would affect job/career prospects. A high degree of ignorance was also evident for other technological developments.

Response was also broken down by job category. The largest percentages of respondents who viewed complete on-line facilities as being beneficial to their jobs or careers were systems analysts, training officers, programmers and clerks. As far as

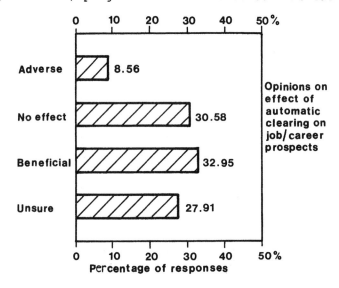

Figure 12.2: Percentage distribution of opinions of responding bank employees in South Africa, 1985, about whether automatic clearing has adversely or beneficially affected their career prospects (Source based on SASBO Survey, 1985).

ATMs are concerned, relatively large percentages of
bank machine operators (24.24%), junior clerks
(24.00%) and sole tellers (32.35%), viewed ATMs as
being adverse, although relatively large percentages also viewed ATMS as being beneficial - machine
operators (33.33%), junior clerks (50.00%), sole
tellers (50.00%). The majority of bank employees
who were machine operators, junior clerks and sole
tellers did not know how their job/career prospects
would be affected by POS (point of sale transfers).
The majority of programmers thought that their
prospects would be beneficially affected and a
large percentage (46.75% of managers) did not think
that they would be affected at all. Adverse
reactions were few, the largest percentage being
13.43% of the sole tellers. A general conclusion
here would be necessity for more information on the
effect of POS. As far as telephone banking is
concerned, fairly large percentages of sole tellers
were either adversely disposed (31..34%), or did not
know its effects (37.31%). A lack of knowledge
was also shown by junior clerks, machine operators
and clerks.

The majority of programmers and systems
analysts viewed telephone banking as being
beneficial to their job/career prospects. As far
as electronic banking is concerned, the largest
percentage of adverse reactions to electronic
banking by bank employees were shown by sole
tellers (22.39%) and computer operators (28.00%),
although fairly large percentages in both categories also thought that their prospects would be
beneficially affected. The majority of bank
training officers, programmers and systems analysts
were beneficially disposed towards electronic fund
transfer and a large percentage (42.42%) of machine
operators did not know how they would be affected.
Percentages in the thirties were shown here also by
ledger examiners, junior clerks, sole tellers,
clerks and systems analysts. As far as automatic
clearing is concerned, largest percentages of
adverse reactions were from bank computer operators, and largest percentages of most favourable
reactions were from programmers, training officers
and clerks. In all categories, ignorance was shown
as to how job-career prospects would be affected
and this was particularly so for machine operators.

The results were also broken down in terms of
staff duties. Those people working at the head
office and data centre were more beneficially
disposed to the effect of complete on-line

facilities than were those working at the branch, while those working at the head office were the least adversely disposed. As far as ATMs are concerned, more bank data centre people were beneficially disposed than either branch or head office people. With regard to POS, head office bank people were most beneficially disposed and data centre people most adversely disposed. Head office building society people were most benefic- ially disposed to POS and branch people most adversely disposed. The largest percentage of bank staff beneficially disposed toward telephone banking worked in data centres and the largest percentage adversely disposed worked in branches. More people working in branches did not know how they would be affected than those working in head offices and data centres.

The largest percentage of bank employees adversely disposed towards electronic fund transfer (13.08%) worked in branches and the largest percentage beneficially disposed worked in data centres (42.55%). The largest percentage of those who did not think that they would be at all affected worked in head offices (37.18%). Those bank employees most adversely disposed towards automatic clearing worked in branches and those most beneficially disposed worked in data centres. Again, those who worked in head offices constitute most of those who did not think that their prospects will be affected.

The data was broken down in terms of schooling and qualifications. Level of schooling did not appear to make much difference to how bank employees viewed complete on-line facilities. However those with academic qualifications did appear to be more beneficially disposed.

Those with higher levels of schooling and academic qualifications appeared more inclined to think that their prospects would not be affected. With regard to bank employees' views on telephone banking, those with academic qualifications were more inclined towards a 'beneficial response'. As far as electronic fund transfer and automatic clearing is concerned, this latter statement also applies to respondents.

Respondents' opinions were also analyzed in terms of race. With regard to complete on-line facilities and ATMs, a large percentage of respondents of all races gave their answer as 'beneficially' but Whites and Asians were more inclined to do so. Fewer Whites as compared to the

other race groups answered: 'don't know'. Large
percentages of Blacks, Coloureds and Asians did not
know how POS would affect their job/career
prospects and a fairly large percentage of Whites
(32.27%) did not think their job/career would be at
all affected. With regard to telephone banking, a
similar trend could be discerned, although not as
marked as with POS and the same is the case with
electronic fund transfer and automatic clearing.
Why this should be so is not clear unless mainly
members of the White group are coming into contact
with the new technologies.

Effect of New Technology on Work
Although the majority of respondents had actually
encountered few of the technologies in question,
the majority of respondents chose to express an
opinion about the effect of new technology on their
work. Figure 12.3, for example, shows that the
majority of respondents agreed that the new
technology made jobs easier. Response was analyzed
in terms of age and sex and in terms of job
category.
    The majority of all age groups of both sexes
agreed that the new technology made jobs easier.
This view is not quite as strong for males over age
51 and below age 20. The majority of respondents
of all age groups and both sexes were convinced
that jobs have become more interesting, although
the conviction is not held as strongly by females
over the age of 41 and males and female over the
age of 51. The majority of respondents under age
20 and females aged 34-40 and a large proportion in
other categories seemed to think that the new
technology made their current work more repetitive.
The percentage is not as great for males aged
34-40. The majority of all age groups of both
sexes felt that their work had become more
responsible. While the majority of respondents
aged under 20 felt that the new technology had made
their current jobs more secure, this feeling was
not quite as positively held as was the case with
other effects on current work, by respondents in
other age groups, particularly females over age 51
and males aged 34-40 years and 41-50 years. Except
for those aged over 51, where percentages are in
the forties, the majority of bank respondents felt
that the new technology had made their work more
satisfying. The same trend is shown with regard to
skill in their job. The vast majority disagreed

273

with the statement that new technology made no difference to their jobs. There is no ascertainable difference between women and men, except with regard to women over age 50 where 32.56% felt that the new technology had made no difference.

When one looks at the response by job category, the majority in all job categories agreed that their current work had been made easier. This view is not held quite so strongly by machine operators. The majority in all job categories also agreed that their current work had been made more interesting. This view is again not held quite as strongly by machine operators or tellers and sole tellers. In spite of this trend, large percentages (mostly in the forties) of respondents in all job categories, did, however, think that their work had

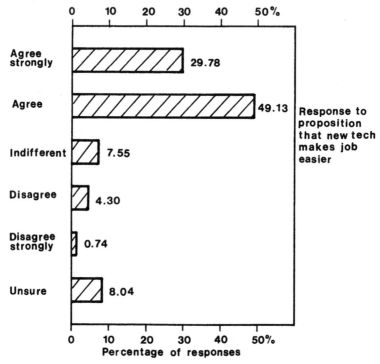

Figure 12.3: Percentage distribution of reactions of responding bank employees in South Africa, 1985, to the statement that the introduction of new technology has made their banking work easier (Source of data is SASBO Survey, 1985).

been made more repetitive. This view is not held as strongly by managers and systems analysts. Apart from machine operators, the majority of employees also thought that their current work is now more responsible. The feeling of more security, as compared to the other effects, was not held by as great a percentage of employees, except for computer operators and programmers. Except for machine operators (48.46%), the majority of employees also felt more satisfied. The majority in all job categories thought that they are now more skilled and only small percentages in all job categories felt that they were no different.

Effect of Introduction of New Services on Current Work

The effect of the introduction of new services on the current work of respondents was analyzed by job category. The majority of respondents in all job categories, except machine operators, agreed or agreed strongly that their work had been made more interesting, not more than approximately 13% in other categories disagreeing. A large percentage of machine operators (33.33%) answered: 'don't know'. The majority of respondents in all job categories except machine operators, typists, accountants, clerks and others thought that they had become more skilled.

With regard to the introduction of new services bringing about more customer contact, bank employees in most job categories appeared to be more or less equally divided as to whether there was more customer contact or not. A small percentage of machine operators and programmers agreed/agreed strongly that there was more customer contact. A large percentage of training officers disagreed or disagreed strongly. Fairly large percentages, although not the majority, thought that the introduction of new services has led to better prospects. The largest percentage of those who disagreed or disagreed strongly were accountants (37.32%) and the largest percentage who didn't know were machine operators (33.33%). The majority of bank employees in all job categories except machine operators and clerks agreed or agreed strongly that new services had led to more variety. The highest percentage of those who disagreed or disagreed strongly are machine operators (27.27%). Of those who were indifferent the largest percentage (24.21%) are those who are

275

accountants (18.66%) and senior clerks (18.55%).

Large percentages, although not the majority in all categories, agreed or agreed strongly that new services had led to more satisfaction. Of those bank employees who were indifferent, the largest percentages were senior clerks (35.02%) and managers (35.27%). The largest percentage of those who disagreed or disagreed strongly or did not know are machine operators. In all job categories, there are large percentages of those who disagreed or disagreed strongly that the introduction of new services had no effect. Typists were more or less equally divided as to whether there was an effect. A large percentage of machine operators (21.21%) did not know if there would be an effect or not.

View as to the Fitting of Counter Terminals, Refilling of Cash Machines, Availability of Home Banking Services and Change in the Number of Banks and Building Societies

Respondents' views as to the fitting of counter terminals in other places were ascertained. The response was overwhelmingly positive. Respondents were also asked for their views as to whether shopworkers should be able to refill cash machines in stores. The majority of respondents felt that they should not do so.

Respondents were also asked as to when they thought that home banking services would be available. The major proportion (49.53%) thought that the likely dates would be 1987-1990. Many of the respondents thought that there would be no change in the number of South African banks by 1990, then there were those who thought that there would be a decrease and then those who thought that there would be an increase. As far as bank branches are concerned, the largest percentage thought that there would be an increase by 1990. They are followed by those who thought that there will be a decrease and a small percentage who think that there will be no change. A large percentage of respondents thought that the number of South African building societies would decrease by 1990. They are followed by those who thought that there would be no change and a relatively small proportion who thought that there would be an increase. An overwhelming percentage of respondents (72.28%)

thought that ATM transactions would outnumber teller transactions by 1990.

VIEWS AS TO COMPUTER LITERACY, JOB SECURITY AND MANAGERIAL AND UNION ACTIONS

Most bank respondents thought that they either were computer literate or had some knowledge, but expressed a need for more specialized training. Most (66.92%) also thought that they were receiving insufficient training to enable them to cope with the new technology. Only 26.08% said they were receiving enough training and 7% did not know. Respondents were also asked to say which bank or building society was most ahead vis-a-vis the new technology. The majority of those who worked in banks thought that either Standard Bank (50.23% of banking respondents), or Barclays Bank (24.43% of banking respondents) were ahead.

Respondents were also asked to give their views as far as their own job security was concerned. The majority of respondents (65.97%) felt that their job was safe. The majority of respondents in all job categories except trainees, machine operators, clerks and sole tellers felt that their job was safe, but even with regard to these categories, high percentages in the forties are seen. The largest percentage of respondents who felt that their job was safe are programmers. Fairly large percentages (20-30% range) of trainees, machine operators, tellers, sole tellers and clerks did not know.

Respondents were asked to give their views as to the importance of certain actions that can be taken by management. Most respondents felt that there should be early notification of change. The percentage favouring good retrenchment terms is also large. The same applies to retraining, maintenance of interesting work, guarantees of job security and notification of staff prospects, natural wastage. However, the percentage ranking reduced working hours as important, quite important and important was not so great. This was also the case with early retirement.

Respondents were questioned as to whether unions were sufficiently active vis-a-vis the introduction of new technology. Figure 12.4 shows that respondents were divided in opinion with 36.61% stating that they were sufficiently active and 35.50% stating that they were not. 27.88% did

277

not know. As far as health-related problems caused by the new technology are concerned, most respondents (67.95%) thought that there were no problems. As far as specific problems are concerned, 28.16% experienced eye strain, 16.04% experienced general fatigue, 13.92% experienced back-related problems, 11.78% noise problems and 9.67% other problems.

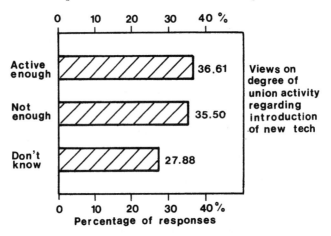

Figure 12.4: Percentage distribution of opinions of responding bank employees in South Africa, 1985, as to whether unions are active enough in relation to the introduction of new banking technology (Source of data is SASBO Survey, 1985).

CONCLUSIONS

With regard to the distribution of respondents by earnings, there is a tendency for females to earn less than males. As far as technological change is concerned, there is still considerable potential for technological change. Banking is still regarded as a career for the majority of respondents but respondents are divided on whether technology has or has not improved their career prospects. Younger respondents are more positive than older ones and accountants and managers tend to be negatively disposed. Employees did not view the effect of specific new technologies on their job or career prospects as being adverse. There is a need for more information on the effect of POS and automatic clearing. Machine operators, in particular,

278

did not know how their job or career prospects would be affected by automatic clearing. While level of schooling did not appear to make much difference to how bank employees viewed complete on-line facilities, those with academic qualifications did appear to be more beneficially disposed. As far as the effect of new technology on work is concerned, large percentages of all age groups of both sexes were beneficially disposed towards the new technology, except insofar as their work had been made more repetitive. There is a need for more specialized training in computer literacy and general training to enable them to cope with the new technology. The majority of respondents felt secure in their jobs although fairly large percentages, in the 20-30% range, of trainees, machine operators, tellers, sole tellers and clerks did not know. The majority of respondents were in favour of actions that can be taken by management such as guarantees of job security. Respondents were divided in opinion as to whether unions were sufficiently active or not in relation to technological change and most respondents did not experience health-related problems, physical or otherwise, from the introduction of new technology into banking.

NOTE

1. I would like to thank Mr. D. Young of the Department of Statistics, University of the Witwatersrand, for assistance with statistics and computerization of data and Professor B. Gordon, Department of Economics, University of Newcastle, Australia for the valuable comments made when acting as Congress discussant.

REFERENCES

Anon (1985) 'Special Survey on Top Companies', **Financial Mail**, May 24 and June 28, Johannesburg

Anon (1981) 'Tradition in Transition: Technological Change and Employment in Banking', **Working Paper No.33**, Department of Economics, University of Queensland, St. Lucia, Qld.

Bamber, G.J. and Lansbury, R.D. (1986) **International and Comparative Industrial Relations**, Allen and Unwin, Sydney

Bank Employee Attitudes to New Technology

Barclays Bank (undated) **The Clearing Banks, Their Role and Activities,** Barclays Bank, London

BIFU (undated) 'New Technology in Banking, Insurance and Finance' Publicity Department, BIFU (Banking, Insurance and Finance Union), London

BIFU (undated) 'Microelectronics', Briefings Nos. 1 and 2, Publicity Department, BIFU, London

BIFU (undated) 'Microtechnology: A Programme for Action', Publicity Department, BIFU, London

IFCCTE (1977) 'Rationalization, Automation and Employment Perspectives in European Banking', IFCCTE (International Federation of Commercial, Clerical and Technical Employees), Geneva

IFCCTE (1978) **Proceedings FIET Conference on Computers and Work,** International Federation of Commercial, Clerical and Technical Employees (IFCCTE) Velu, Austria

Suchard, H.T. (1985) 'Trade Union Response to Technological Change: Some Reflections on the International Scene', **South African Journal of Labour Relations,** 9, 1, pp.4-15

Suchard, H.T. (1986) 'Technological Change in the South African Banking Industry: Results of a Survey' paper presented at Fourth World Congress of Social Economics, Toronto, Canada, 12-15 August.

TUC (1979) **TUC Report on Employment and Technology,** Trade Union Congress, London

Chapter Thirteen

SOCIOECONOMIC IMPLICATIONS OF NEW TECHNOLOGY IN BANKING: SOME AUSTRALIAN AND NEW ZEALAND EVIDENCE

Rae Weston and Alan Williams

INTRODUCTION

It is widely and popularly believed that the major impact of new information technology on the banking industry will act to shift institutions from a labour-intensive to a capital-intensive mode of operations. This assumption is based upon the availability of electronic systems that permit services to be offered outside the normative and traditional pattern. This chapter will argue the case that such assumptions about the employment effects of new technology must take into account factors relating both to the capital investment involved, and to the managerial infrastructure that will emerge from such developments. Further it will be argued that confusion of cause with effect has and is occurring, and that the speed with which such changes will be put in place has tended to be exaggerated. It will also raise some of the major labour market issues that surround the subject of new technology in the banking industry.

THE NEW TECHNOLOGIES IN BANKING

Electronic banking may be described in simplistic terms as the application of advanced technological systems to the agency-client relationships that are the primary focus of banking activity. In fact, the various systems that will be described below have one thing in common, they allow users in the external physical and operational environment of commercial and private banking requirements to initiate transactions, which are then duly processed through the internal system of the agency being employed. In essence, the electronic system operates dual functions, linking external locations to internal processing. The key point at this juncture is that such systems do not constitute products or services in their own right. They are not economic goods per se, but rather transmission mechanisms.

AUSTRALIAN DEVELOPMENTS

In Australia, transactions have been moved through the use of magnetic tapes since the middle of the 1970s when trading banks implemented CEMTEX, the Central Magnetic Tape Exchange. Each bank produced a magnetic tape incorporating its direct credits from or debits to all other banks and sent the tape to the CEMTEX operator bank in the state. Here all tapes were amalgamated, and one tape was produced for each bank containing its transactions from all sources. In 1984 this system was superseded by a new procedure which had each bank producing a tape of transactions for each other bank, and exchanging them daily after trading. This has led to an increase in the number of tapes created, and is seen as an intermediate step, toward their super-cession by electronic images, which will signal that full electronic payments have finally arrived.

A much more dramatic shift, at least on the surface, has been the development of systems where-by the consumers electronically communicate instructions to financial institutions. It is clear that Automatic Teller Machines (ATMs) have become internationally accepted, though much of the public relations surrounding their introduction tend to disguise the fact they represent only a partial utilization of the new technology. While this particular consumer-machine interface might be capable of extended functional usage in a variety of additional areas such as travel booking and accommodation arranging it cannot be claimed that ATMs represent the full potential of the of the new technology (Bjorn-Anderson et al., 1979).

It should also be noted that the development of ATMs represents a consumer-driven initiative, since continued demand signals that the convenience of the services offered outweigh the learning difficulties involved in utilizing the equipment.

NEW ZEALAND DEVELOPMENTS

The introduction of standardized controls over inter-bank transactions through the conjointly owned Databank system, reflects the high degree of system integration and common sharing of the costs of introduction by New Zealand trading banks. The major institutions rely on a standardized means of electronic control over both single bank and multiple bank transactions. The only differences between bank cheques, for example, is to be found in the house preferences for logos and other symbols of individual ownership. Otherwise, all technical requirements for processing follow standard formats. It must be said that consumer response in a country that generates a high volume of such transactions, to what is in effect a national system of electronic clearances, has been highly appreciative of the innovation (Brockelsby, 1984).

THE QUESTION OF THE NEWER TECHNOLOGIES

It is less easy to find demand or consumer-driven justifications for two further developments at the customer interface, which are about to be introduced in depth in both Australia and New Zealand, EFTPoS (electronic funds transfer at the point of sale) and home banking. By definition, EFTPoS is a delivery system which communicates by an electronic message switching network between the point of sale and individual consumer bank accounts, allowing direct debits to be made. The value to the consumer of EFTPoS appears to be ambiguous. Payment in the conventional way by cheque or credit card allows the benefit of a float before funds are actually withdrawn from an account although the consumer may be delayed while a retailer verifies his or her credit rating. But EFTPoS actually transfers payment at the moment of sale, so that the purchaser's bank account is instantly debited.

This characteristic while of somewhat dubious value to the consumer, is of critical importance to the retailer, and only slightly less so to the banks. Retailers obtain the speed and certainty of payment, but to date these advantages appear to be somewhat offset by operational costs which banks appear not to have completely specified. It would appear that in order for EFTPoS to be readily adopted by consumers, suppliers must signal that there are cost advantages to be gained from use of

283

the system over and above those currently offered by cheque and credit card facilities. To the present time, those offering such services have been unable to establish that the volume of such transactions can in fact justify the costs of the investment in the technology.

The third element of the electronic interface is home banking. Apart from the social issues of consumer privacy, the primary intention of the banks in terms of the motivation for introducing such a system lies in the assumption that the existence of a direct link between the retail user and the bank's processing system will substantially reduce the high cost of manually or semi-manually processing large volume/low value individual transactions. In other words, the efficacy of such a system depends on the willingness of consumers to meet both the operational costs of servicing, and the front end cost of the installation of a telephone modem. From the evidence thus far, it would appear that banks have had only limited success in persuading customers that the costs of home banking outweigh the benefits, an issue to which discussion will return in a different vein later in this chapter.

ELECTRONIC BANKING AND THE INSTITUTIONAL CONSUMER

In Australia prior to 1983, there was little demand for and consequently little supply of, electronic banking services to corporations. Attempts by overseas banks to sell such programmes as account reporting systems had no real success. In 1983, Banklink was introduced (using a GEISCO Mark III Network) by three Australian banks. This enabled client users to access accounting data from their in-office terminals. But with an operational cost of $400-$500 per month, most companies preferred to pay the price of a telephone call to access such information.

Now corporate electronic funds transfers service both in country and offshore are being offered by at least two major Australian banks. Despite this the core of corporate resistance remains, as observed by Chapman (1986), who lists unwarranted concerns over information security by various corporate boards as a main cause.

The fact remains however, that the process of innovation in Australasia is still supplier-driven rather than demand-determined. For the banks this has enormous implications for future policy, in which they must grapple for the first time with the concept of a consumer regime.

THE QUESTION OF CONSUMER RESPONSES

The essentially supplier-led nature of bank policy toward the new technology has to be seen against their traditional roles as agencies often restraining credit supply below a level demanded by the community, as often as not under the larger direction of governmental monetary policy. But the failure of the community at large to accept in the necessary overwhelming numbers the electronic services now offered, has forced banks to come to terms with the need to market services in a consumer-dominated rather than a supplier-dominated environment. Unfortunately, with an enormous and exposed investment in technology now at risk, banks are also having to face the fact, that supplier-driven introduction of electronic technology has had quite different results to those expected.

This places the banks in the position of having to come to terms with major socioeconomic implications of technological change, by dropping some fundamental original assumptions concerning the consequences of new technology.

Within existing bank policies, it was assumed that capital-labour substitution would occur as a reaction to strategies designed to reduce costs. In reality, it would appear, that where substitution has occurred, and it can be argued, that the employment effects of change are as yet indeterminate, it has tended to occur at the lower end of the operational spectrum. In other words, occupations such as clerical worker or teller, have been considerably modified, but banks have had to take on board new and expensive specialists to operate the new system. The full implications of this will be considered in more detail below.

While ATMs have increased the level of transactions by making individual access to funds easier, there is a real need for banks to market a wider range of services if they are to cover the costs of the total investment in new technology. At this point problems of considerable magnitude occur. As Chapman (1986) has observed, clients may now have access to a very wide range of information services which are of benefit particularly to corporate users. But their actual complexity is not without problems, since the effective marketing of such services is the only key to increased use, and such services are not easy to sell given their technological nature.

In turn a new set of problems emerges, involving information control in a system increasingly vulnerable to the possibility that the technologists running the machines will emerge as a managerial elite. Apart from the enormous consequences for a traditionally hierarchical management system, there may thus emerge the need to create appropriate networks, or "buffer groups" to translate information for all employees, because in the new order, knowledge is power.

In a complex electronically-based system, no individual or small employee group can be allowed to become dominant thus creating a situation where only technicians have such knowledge. The ultimate point here is the paradox that a policy of technological innovation by banks ostensibly based upon a shift to a cost-saving capital-intensive technology, might well have the opposite effect by creating the need for a technologically-based labour force, in addition to rather than instead of the traditionally based organizational structure.

One further comment remains to be made about problems now inherent in the marketing of the new services. The fact that home-based banking facilities will have to compete against developments in areas such as retailing, where the customer now sees shopping as a function of a total social milieu. Malls, and facilities based upon attracting customers into the High Street, have an equally important role in terms of the social behaviours of the elderly, and the geographically isolated who see shopping under such circumstances, as much a social as an economic event. To alter such a socioeconomic pattern of behaviour will require stronger arguments than have been heretofore put forward by the banks.

Consumer responses are made increasingly indeterminate from a marketing point of view for another important reason. The fact that none of the devices specified as forming the EFT revolution are monopolized by banks alone. Non-banking financial intermediaries encouraged by developments to de-regulate financial and related markets, are quite prepared to be in the vanguard of new technology in order to build new client networks. De-regulation of competition in countries like New Zealand for example means that banks will have to compete with an increasing number of alternative institutions all seeking the consumer dollar.

The focus of this contribution now shifts from discussion of the broad themes already raised to specific labour market issues. The question of employment effects and consequences, as specified by the original policy intention to substitute capital for labour will be raised first in general terms. Consideration will then be given to current research findings based on Australasian studies which have attempted to evaluate the human resources consequences of technological change.

THE LABOUR MARKET CONSEQUENCES OF NEW TECHNOLOGY: SOME CURRENT ISSUES

In most popular studies of the development and application of electronic technologies in industrial settings, critics have tended to focus attention upon three assumed outcomes. These are the effects of technology on employment, the consequences for traditionally defined skills and occupational classifications, and employee responses.

In terms of the first issue, scenarios range from the pessimistic to the optimistic. Thus Heineke (1984) argues that massive unemployment and attendant socioeconomic dislocation will take place. Conversely, Schwartz and Mieker (1983) raise the countervailing view, that the market-driven dynamic of technological change carries within itself a corrective mechanism, in the sense that new employment will be created by shifts in productive emphasis as new industries emerge.

Both parties target the same basic cause of change, chip technology. In turn both arguments according to Sadler (1980) are in danger of overstating technological consequences. Taking an aggregate view, he suggests that large-scale shifts in traditional sources of employment linked to structural changes in market economies may have more to do with current levels of unemployment than arguments based on the impact of new technology.

Estimates of employment outcomes, by critics of either persuasion, would appear to hold to a common assumption, that the introduction of technology is by definition both a constant variable and an exponential factor in the investment strategy of organizations. In other words, as the

287

pace of technological development increases, the entrepreneurial drive to invest in such new technology also increases. In fact, the evidence does not support such an assumption, given the sheer capital costs of such entrepreneurial activity.

The reality more closely approximates earlier analyses that deal with customer responses to new technology. Thus Fisher (1979, p.37), remarking upon the ultimate vision of banking theorists driven to flights of fancy, said:

> Great promise was held out for the introduction of an electronic payment system and the resultant cashless chequeless society. It not only has not happened, there are experimental results that suggest it will not happen...

The reasons for such a conclusion are to be found in earlier discussions and will not be reviewed here, save to remark that pessimism has replaced optimism.

SOME FINDINGS

A recent British study by Shaw and Colbeck (1983) has predicted that one consequence of possible bank retrenchment as the exposed investment in technology continues to fail to make an adequate return over time, will be a 12% fall in banking employment by 1990. This view is supported by a similar study on behalf of the Clearing Banks Union, which targets clerical workers, administrative and mid-career staff as suffering a 10% to 12% job loss in the same period.

Another important trend is reported by Ragan (1984) who observes that the career streams in banking and related industries are becoming increasingly differentiated, with the career stream requiring more intensive human capital investment through training, and the non-career stream, mainly married women in their thirties and forties, supplying an increasing component of part-time workers carrying out routinized tasks.

He goes on to further assert that while technological change is creating specialist positions, within banking administration, training for senior positions is becoming, and needs to be, increasingly broad spectrum, and based upon human resource-communication skills.

Socioeconomics of New Banking Technology

Predictive consequences become more indeterminate when attention is focussed upon specific occupational classes. For example, Wilman and Cowan (1984) found that as a consequence of the large-scale introduction of ATS, the employment effects have been positive and not negative, and concluded that either banks had failed to take up the savings from planned redundancy, or business had expanded to encompass the displaced staff through transfer rather than dismissal. They cautiously concluded that in the medium term job losses had not been significant in the teller group, the focus of their research.

Other studies have come to somewhat similar conclusions. Perhaps the largest attempted, that of Bjorn-Anderson, et al. (1979), which sampled employment effects of technological change in five major banks located in four European countries, found that it was virtually impossible to estimate either negative or positive effects even for the same operational parameters between the different banks in the sample. In a more recent report, Kendall et al. (1983), who tried to correlate changes in the quality of working life with the new technology that caused such changes, found that while new technology required a reduction in work autonomy regarding task priorities and the sequence in which work should be planned as a function of machine programming, most respondents in the sample did not mind this, and expressed preference for the new systems. Overall however, they found the same methodological problems which faced the earlier study cited above impeded judgements as to the relationships being analyzed.

In industrial relations terms there is overwhelming evidence that the process of technological innovation went on apace in most countries with little or no input from employee organizations. Trade union roles have to date been reactive rather than proactive with a notable Australian exception that will be discussed later.

Such unilateral actions did not escape the attention of the world body to which bank employee unions belong. In a major report at its annual congress, the International Federation of Commercial, Clerical Professional and Technical Employees, (FIET, 1980), the world group called for bi-lateral discussions not only on the costs and benefits of the new technologies, but also for consultation between employers and unions when a given bank acted to introduce such processes.

Socioeconomics of New Banking Technology

The report reflected in a real sense the
essential weakness and conservatism of bank
officers organizations. At no point was the
concept of electronic banking challenged; rather,
the unions simply signalled a reaction to decisions
that had already been made and implemented. The
overall impression as the 1980s unfolded is of
employees organizations being carried along in the
wake of an employer-driven technological shift.
Discussion will now turn to the Australasian
context, where the general pattern of events
already described reflects a basic similarity to
global experience.

BANKING IN AUSTRALIA AND NEW ZEALAND

The industry in both countries is dominated by a
strong tradition of branch banking, suitably modified to meet the different needs of each national
system. In Australia, banking is divided into four
main elements: trading banks, saving banks, the
Commonwealth Banking Corporation (CBC) and the
Reserve Bank. Since New Zealand does not have a
federal political structure, there is no equivalent
to the CBC, though the Bank of New Zealand is in
fact government-owned. In both countries the
industry reflects large changes, not least of which
is the movement toward deregulation of the market,
which has already occurred in Australia and is
scheduled to do so during the term of the current
Labour administration in New Zealand.
In terms of new technology, New Zealand has
enjoyed some degree of advantage from having a
smaller and more homogeneous system, both physically and organizationally. According to Hogg
(1981) the Databank system, described above, has
inbuilt facilities for expansion, that make it
feasible to build a full EFT (electronic funds
transfer) capacity onto the existing network. At
the moment of writing, the BNZ, Westpac and ANZ
have made on-line EFTPoS available and the National
Bank is introducing a telephone-based home banking
service.
By contrast, the sheer size and organizational complexity of the Australian banking
market, mitigated according to Griffin (1982),
against the rapid introduction of new technology
into branches. In fact it took from 1964 until
1973 to establish on-line technology to cover total
needs.

The resultant employment effects seem in general terms to reflect the experience of other countries already reported in this chapter. After describing the introduction of ATMs, Griffin (1982) concluded that technological change has not been reflected to date in higher levels of redundancy. The private sector of the banking industry has verbally guaranteed no job losses but has refused to formalize such an arrangement through appropriate collective agreement.

From the New Zealand perspective, the same general results are assumed to obtain. Thus the New Zealand Employers Federation in a special report, **Change for the Better** (1980, p.171), observed that aggregate employment in banking after the introduction of the Databank system in 1967 saw an initial drop in employment from 10,196 down to 9,942 in 1970. Employment then rose steadily during the next decennial period to 14,983 in 1980. On the basis of available data at this point in time, we are left with the corroborative assumption that the employment effects of new technology as adopted by the Australasian industry over the last several years, reflect indeterminate consequences in the aggregate, at least in the medium term.

Unfortunately, aggregate employment effects tell us nothing about the more complex (internal) changes going on within the industry, with regard to such matters as occupational role changes, and the overarching quality of working life.

Such work as has been done in Australasia reveals some important directions for future research, rather than mature conclusions based on detailed studies. In one specific case, Brockelsby (1984) attempted to test the de-skilling thesis of the labour process as attributed to Braverman, in the New Zealand industry. The results were indeterminate in the sense that while changes were reported at the junior levels in terms of job content, there was no evidence that progressive and large de-skilling had occurred.

The researcher's task in this case was compounded in terms of difficulty by a number of important events in the overall labour market, which have coloured the national scene thus far during the 1980s. The national government imposed a three-year moratorium on wage and salary movements from 1982, which was only lifted with the Labour administration accession to office in 1984. Large-scale industrial volatility has been a feature of the national industrial relations scene

since that time, as the current government searches
for a reformist programme. In this period white-
collar militancy has been a marked feature, and a
number of major banks have experienced direct
industrial action. In this milieu any attempt to
abstract specific technological issues from within
a larger framework of mainstream industrial
relations concerns within the industry is made
extremely difficult. But the study did point to an
important labour market effect of new technology,
which was later identified in the Australian
industry, by the work of Hill, Birrell and Cooke
(1985). Both research studies revealed that as a
consequence of technological input, banks are
recruiting EDP specialists into the industry on a
direct entry basis. The result it is argued is an
emergent two-tiered labour market.

Such policies have a clear and detrimental
consequence for the overarching assumption discussed earlier, that the primary intention of EFT
development is based upon cost-saving capital
interventions. That assumption is now under
serious pressure from two major directions. In the
first instance, banks must compete by definition,
in a suppliers market for available EDP staff,
either as organizational members or in a consulting
capacity. Market signals for Australasia indicate
considerable tightness in the matter of available
human resources, which means that banks as
employers or as users, must therefore bid against
each other in terms of remuneration packages.
Labour-saving costs are by definition lost in these
circumstances.

This situation is compounded organizationally
by the fact that banking is traditionally a hierarchical, seniority-based service industry, in
which authority moves vertically upward. But
increased technological innovation shifts organizational power toward those who control the information systems upon which the organization relies to
give it machine-led directions. Of equal importance
is the fact that professional specialists who enter
the industry by such direct means, do not share the
common ethos of tradition and career-based,
service-orientated activity, that motivated more
conventionally recruited personnel. They are, in
other words, not organizationally committed.

These developments give rise to a scenario
that has already been discussed in general terms
earlier in this chapter. The fact is since the
imperatives of competition require that banks

292

continue to develop electronic technology as a means to maximize net efficiencies, there could be important consequences for traditional management practices. Those in what might be termed the information technology segment of the occupational labour market could well become the arbiters not only of efficiency, but of corporate policy in the long term.

INDUSTRIAL RELATIONS AND EMPLOYEE RESPONSES

Before beginning the examination of employee responses to technological changes in the banking industry, it is necessary to observe that the industrial relations system of Australia and New Zealand reflects a long tradition of legally based and centralized procedures, based on the rules of compulsory conciliation and arbitration. While there are differences based essentially upon the fact that Australia has a two-tiered state-federal tradition, the general principles hold for both countries.

This allows private sector unions access to industrial awards and related collective agreements, which lay down minimum levels of remuneration, and a variety of rules and other requirements for a discrete term. The system has had an interesting side effect in Australia, where the CBC staff as quasi-public servants, enjoys employment conditions based on those relating to the private sector.

In both countries the call for consultation before innovation has mostly fallen on deaf ears. In fact, the bank unions have demonstrated a chronic inability to influence technological change in the least degree.

This brutal reality is given point in the New Zealand experience by the fact that in 1984, a conjoint banking project team drawn from the five trading banks field-tested on selected sites an EFTPoS system which will be locked into the existing Databank network, and which was signalled for operational introduction in late 1986.

In terms of bank employee responses, the issue has tended to be somewhat overshadowed by conventional industrial relations matters. One point of significance has recently emerged, however, the fact that in line with a 1985 directive of FIET, the New Zealand union will now view new technology as an industrial imperative consequential upon

increases in competition from nonbanking financial
agencies.   In sum only the CBC in Australia has
developed and sustained a consultative approach to
new technology.   At the same time it must be
remembered that as a federal agency, the managerial
ethos of the CBC reflects more a public service
that a private sector tradition.
   In both countries the history of union responses to new technology is littered with pious
resolutions, that have had no effect upon the
employer-driven initiatives of the large private
sector banks. How far a more aggressively competitive environment will change this, as banks are
forced to retreat from a somewhat paternalistic
employment policy, and verbal guarantees of continued employment it is hard to estimate. What cannot
be guaranteed of course is the possibility that
bank staff up to middle management will not face
technological redundancy as the full weight of
technological change is put into place on a managerial and organizational structure that is not
designed to accommodate it.

SOME TENTATIVE CONCLUSIONS

This chapter has attempted to isolate and examine
the available evidence on a number of selected
issues that face the industry as a consequence of
decisions to introduce electronically based technological change.   It confirms in part the belief
emanating from the evidence currently available
that changes have neither been as revolutionary nor
as widespread as popular arguments about electronics technology would have us believe. It would
appear, and the Australian evidence such as it is
also supports the view, that the human resource
consequences implicit in a manifest shift from
labour-intensive to capital-intensive operations
are at least in the medium term indeterminate in
outcome.
   This view gives further support to the contention of Peitchinis (1983) that in most industries, the age of the machine has not yet given way
to the age of the complete network. Effectively
this means that the ultimate model of a banking
system based upon a total system of EFTs has yet to
emerge.
   Further unforseen problems seem to have
arisen, not least of which is the consequential
development of a more freely competitive market as

the consequence of governmental decisions to de-regulate the monetary and fiscal services. This means that those who direct the future of the industry are now faced with the task of accommodating consumer-driven requirements in a highly competitive market to original concepts of costs and benefits emerging from early decisions to move toward EFTs. How to protect the massive existing and exposed investment already made in such technology also figures largely on the agenda for the 1990s.

In the total context of technological change, it would appear that the socioeconomic effects of the decisions already made might not only change the shape of the industry per se, but also, the very cultures which have determined the nature of organizational growth and development since banking was first conceived as a function of socioeconomic evolution.[1]

NOTE

1. The authors wish to thank Professor Barry Gordon of the University of Newcastle for valuable criticism of the original manuscript. Gratitude is also expressed to colleagues at the Fourth World Congress of Social Economics, where the paper that forms the basis of this chapter was first presented. Errors of omission and commission remain the authors' own.

REFERENCES

Bjorn-Anderson, N., Hedberg, B., Mercer, D., Mumford, E., and Sole, A. (1979) **The Impact of Systems Change in Organisations: Results and Conclusions,** Sijthoff and Noordhoff, the Netherlands

Brockelsby, J. (1984) 'Technological Change and the Labour Process: Toward an Analysis of Computerisation in New Zealand Trading Banks', **New Zealand Journal of Industrial Relations,** 9, 3, pp. 314-325

Chapman, G. (1986) 'The Impact of Electronic Banking on Cash Management', **Massey Journal** of **Asian and Pacific Business,** 2, 1, pp.33-37

FIET (1980) **Bank Workers and the New Technology: An International Trade Response,** International Federation of Commercial, Clerical Professional and Technical Employees, Geneva

Fisher, F.F. (1979) 'The Decade of the 1980s: New

Concepts of the World of Banking', The Bankers' Magazine, 162, 1, p.37

Griffin, G. (1982) 'Managing Technological Change: Industrial Relations in the Banking and Insurance Industries', Journal of Industrial Relations, 24, 1, pp.53–83

Heineke, I. (1984) Electronic Illusions, Penguin, Harmondsworth

Hill, J.V., Birrell, R.J. and Cooke, J.P. (1985) 'The Industrial Relations Attitudes of Australian Private Bank Employees', Journal of Industrial Relations, 27, 3, pp.310–328

Hogg, G.H.J. (1981) 'Payment Systems in New Zealand' Journal of Bank Research, Winter, pp.219–222

Kendall, P.M.H., Malacki, A.M.J., Alexander, W., Wallace, A.S. and Wheatley, T.F. (1983) The Impact of Chip Technology on Conditions and Quality of Work, Ministry of Social Affairs, the Netherlands

Mills, C.P. and Sorrell, G.H. (1975) Federal Industrial Law, Butterworths, Sydney

New Zealand Bank Officers Union (1984a) Chequemate, No. 55

New Zealand Bank Officers Union (1984b) Chequemate, No. 57

New Zealand Bankers' Institute (1984) New Zealand Bankers' Review, 4, 2

New Zealand Employers Federation (1980) Change for the Better

Peitchinis, S.G. (1983) Computer Technology and Employment: Retrospect and Prospect, Macmillan, London

Ragan, A. (1984) New Technology and Employment: IMS Special Report, Gower Press, Aldershot

Revell, J.R.S. (1983) Banking and Electronic Funds Transfers, OECD, Paris

Sadler, P. (1980) 'Welcome Back to the Automation Debate', in T. Forester (ed), The Microelectronic Revolution, Blackwell, Oxford

Schwartz, G.G. and Mieker, W. (1983) The Work Revolution: The Future of Work in Post-Industrial Society, Rawson Associates, New York

Shaw, E.R. and Colbeck, N.S. (1983) United Kingdom Retail Banking Prospects in the Competitive 1980s, Staniland Hall, London

Wilman, P. and Cowan, R. (1984) 'New Technology in Banking: The Impact of Auto Tellers on Staff Numbers', in M. Warner (ed.), Microprocessors, Manpower and Society, Gower Press, Aldershot

Socioeconomics of New Banking Technology

Woods, N.S. (1963) **Industrial Conciliation and Arbitration in New Zealand,** Government Printer, Wellington

Chapter Fourteen

SOCIAL DETERMINISM, TECHNOLOGY AND ECONOMIC
EXTERNALITIES

Jacobus A. Doeleman

RAPID HISTORICAL CHANGE AND THE QUESTION OF FREE
WILL

To say that the twentieth century way of life is
subject to unbridled forces of change may safely be
described as a platitude. As the saying goes: the
future is not what it used to be. A consensus
prevails that human history has, so to speak, been
caught up in the fast lane. It is widely accepted
also that the cause of this acceleration in the
pace of our times lies, directly and indirectly, in
the numerous applications of an increasingly rapid
expansion of the body of human technological knowledge. In the event, our natural and man-made
physical environment as well as our social environment and psychological, cultural and spiritual
values are all subject to an unprecedented
multitude of pressures. These pressures have not
necessarily been intended.
    One wonders whether such rapid and profound
developments are desirable and whether, on the
whole, modern history signifies progress or decline
in the standing of the human species. Moreover,
one might ask: whether, and to what extent,
individual decision making and political processes
are capable of exerting control - if so wanted -
over the speed and direction of said dynamics of
history.
    Regarding the first issue, that of progress or
decline of humankind in recent and imminent
decades, suggestive evidence and strong arguments[1]
have been put in the support of either contention.
Given the range of opinion, it would be prudent to
claim that social scientific judgement has been and
remains divided on this issue. The fact that
developments making for progress coexist and

298

interact with developments making for decline, is complicating the matter. Being caught up in the fast lane, we are perhaps poorly placed to resolve whether the balance of the forces of historical change is positive or negative. Positive or negative by which comprehensive index? Measuring the realization of sustainable prosperity, security, humanity, happiness...? And - in an unequal world - for whom? Which countries and which living and unborn generations? For the purpose of this chapter, however, it is sufficient that agreement exists on the extraordinary magnitude of modern socioeconomic historical change. Likewise, agreement may exist on the extraordinary magnitude of the welfare effects brought about by unremitting surges of change even though the sign and order of the net result of such historically imposed welfare effects is not well understood.

The second question posed above concerns the control that can be exerted by the political process, or by individuals directly, over the rapid changes to which our times are subject. In this respect, the mainstream literature in economics (including social choice theory) appears to be strongly influenced by an optimistic and perhaps naive emphasis on 'free will'. Accordingly, economic or political agents are modelled to exploit their environments by maximization or optimization, be it of income, consumer/voter satisfaction, commercial profit or electoral advantage. Scant attention is paid to the interaction between agent and environment; and, in particular, to the projection of the agent as a product - if not a captive - of the environment.

So much has optimism prevailed with regard to the ability of households, enterprises and governments to dominate the economic interaction with their environment, that the question of reaction, especially the wider and long-run aggregate reaction to our exploits, has been all but dismissed by the dogma of laissez-faire. Laissez-faire dictates that maximization or optimization should be undertaken selfishly, with a minimum of collective interference and with no regard per se for the greater well-being of present or future society other than, of course, any opportunistic concern for the welfare of others.

Following mainstream neoclassical economics, the greater well-being of society is thus supposed to take care of itself from below - albeit not entirely without welfare-theoretical reservations. In the words of Adam Smith, an invisible hand will arrange for the wealth of nations, provided intervention-free competitive self-advancement is made to form the cornerstone of economic policy. Implicit in this Smithian line of thinking hide two appealing thoughts. First, there is an inherent belief that the socioeconomic future can be left unplanned, based, presumably, on an optimistic interpretation of the notion of progress. Secondly, there is the thought that people themselves know best what is good for them. This is the liberal view – supported in what may be described as 'free will' market economics. Market economics advocates an institutional framework of 'small' government, which, inter alia, protects personal freedom (equality) and property rights (liberty). Within this legal framework, people are permitted to pursue freely the dictates of their sets of personal preferences. Personal preferences then are made to be the ultimate source of economic behaviour.

Surprisingly, however, the discipline of economics has shown little interest in the processes that govern the formation of personal preferences. Perhaps it is felt that preferences are mainly of interest to the moralist and philosopher. Alternatively, it could be held that preferences have been created in the Garden of Eden and as such are the concern of religion. Or it might be thought that the study of personal preferences and the variations therein properly belongs to the realm of biology, psychology and/or anthropology. In any case, for the purposes of market economic analysis, it is customary to begin by 'assuming' some well-behaved preference function, thereby treating preferences as 'given' or as exogenous.

DETERMINISM OF INDIVIDUAL PREFERENCES

By determining preferences exogenously, economics dismisses an integral part of its subject matter. It does this in a way that happens to bolster significantly the attractiveness of the 'free will' case. To assume preferences in a vacuum, as if supplied **deus ex machina**, invokes in effect the denial of any 'deterministic' interpretation of socioeconomic interaction. Admittedly, economists could be excused for not being qualified where the formation of preferences touches upon matters biological, moral, divine, psychological or anthropological. However, there is no excuse in so far as economic life itself plays a systematic role in the development of personal preferences from one situation to the next.

Preferences may ultimately derive substance from biological reality (nature). We are the prisoners of our genes. But it would be trite to deny the validity of the concept of 'free will' on this basis. The point is that the expression of that genetic source in terms of actual preferences appears to be dependent to a significant extent on the environment (nurture). The economic factor in the environment, which interacts with moral, social and cultural factors, appears to have become more dominant in modern times. Its influence on preference formation can be readily illustrated by noting that only in recent times do people buy refrigerators, automobiles, television sets, antibiotics, etc.... Only in prosperous economies do consumers demand airborne tourist packages or do producers have an appetite for transnational commercial expansion. And so on. Clearly, the changing economic environment has a strong bearing on choice across a wide spectrum, be it in fashion in clothing or buildings or, more generally, in lifestyles, commercial trends and political movements. Indeed, economics may set the mood of the country or the tone of a decade.

The relevance of the environment, i.e., of geographical and historical coordinates, applies at the individual level as it does for society as a whole. Thus the individual's preference function is shaped by changing local circumstances; by personal history; by socio-financial position; etc. It is also shaped by the forces affecting society's preferences. These forces are expressed in politics and derive from collective experience and expectations, not to mention the active manipulation of preferences by political demagoguery or commercial public relations. Society's preferences relate to technological change; to workplace developments; to trends in income distribution; to demographic change; to environmental change; and more.

Preferences, for these reasons, cannot be treated as strictly exogenous. In part at least they are endogenous to comparative and dynamic economic analysis. To the extent that this is so, the notion of 'free will' or sovereign choice loses validity. Correspondingly, this notion requires to be supplemented with that of determinism. Given 'free will', economic agents are controlling their circumstances to maximum advantage. Determinism signifies the reverse. People are being controlled by their circumstances. It seems that both these views are compatible with reality.

Naturally, the idea of determinism has been promoted before. Yet in the discipline of economics, acknowledgement of it is sporadic. It is not to be found in mainstream neoclassical economics but in the so-called institutional literature. A deterministic point of view is, for instance, provided by Fred Hirsch's book: **Social Limits to Economic Growth** (1967). A further example can be found in an interesting anthropological study on consumer behavior by Mary Douglas and Baran Isherwood (1978). A number of other contributions in economics deserve to be cited: amongst them John Kenneth Galbraith (1977), Ezra Mishan (1981) and Tibor Scitovsky (1976). However, for a thorough appreciation of the extent of determinism in socioeconomic behavior one must look beyond incidental insights provided by institutional economists and consult other social disciplines including the contributions of French social philosophers, for instance Claude Levi-Strauss (1968) and Louis Althusser (1975) - the latter having gone so far as to claim that: 'history is a process without a subject'. The roots of their views, in turn, can be traced to the theories of Emile Durkheim (social determinism), Karl Marx (historical determinism) and Sigmund Freud (biological determinism). **Nous sommes que les autres.**

Two factors related to an endogenous treatment of preferences call for special attention. One derives from the perceived urgency of our material needs as reflected in the market rate of interest and the short time horizons typical of private, commercial and political decision making. This apparent urgency has remained surprisingly strong even in prosperous economies. The second factor concerns the mentioned philosophical leaning against planning and in favour of laissez-faire. In part, this leaning against planning reflects political distrust of state control. In part, it rests on an ideological commitment to the perceived relative economic virtues of the market mechanism. This last opinion, however, is fallacious on the ground that the market mechanism can be conceived as a major instrument of planning implementation.[3]

How are these factors connected to an endogenous or deterministic unfolding of time? Assuming idealized market conditions are met by approximation, it is conceded in Western-style economies that the grass-roots freedom of unplanned market choice may result in economic decision makers getting the pragmatic best (or second best) out of a given set of circumstances confronting them. The phrase 'the pragmatic best' refers to efficient or Pareto-optimal behavior but also to the qualification that decision makers at the microeconomic level can be observed to maximize or optimize their interests in narrow selfish or local terms and against said short time horizons. Generally, they do not of their own volition take into consideration how the long run and aggregate consequences of their decisions might affect a future given set of circumstances. This may hold true even when the long run or aggregate consequences are recognized as distinctly undesirable. It follows, therefore, that individuals, enterprises and governments too, could find that the choice over the circumstances that confront them has already been preempted. To the extent that this is the case, determinism is dictating market choice and reducing the relevance of 'free will'.

The apparent contradiction between freedom of choice and determinism is thus explained in that the aggregate of choices and actions designed to make the best of a given short run and local set of circumstances in turn carries substantial and often misunderstood or overlooked consequences which will take effect further afield and in the medium and long term, thus shaping circumstances for others elsewhere and in the future. In the absence of effective long run planning, guiding or targeting, these wider and longer-term consequences - good and bad - arrive by default. The bad wider consequences will act to constrain choice. Both good and bad wider consequences will, as we will see, contribute to determinism.

VOLUNTARY FUTURE OR THE AVOIDABILITY OF ECONOMIC GROWTH

In the unmitigated deterministic view, unforeseen or unaccounted consequences of short-horizon decision making are so paramount that indeed the

subjects of modern history are reduced to a
helpless tinkering at the edges while matters of
progress and prosperity, of culture, of war and
peace are decided by historical forces beyond
control. Which is not to say that historical
forces are independent of human decision making and
particularly not of the introduction of new
technologies. Rather, it says that society is
acting out what is largely inevitable. Taking this
deterministic line highlights once more the problem
of whether the future has been 'determined' for the
better. If the river of time is supposed to be
transporting communities and societies downstream
like leaves, it would be natural to reflect on the
rapids and falls as well as the brilliant lakes
that may lie ahead.

A deterministic interpretation of history
contrasts with the ready opinion that government
and business decisions wittingly control and shape
a better future for all (or some). This is perhaps
to be expected because the concept of a deterministic history cannot be a popular one. Determinism
creates scope for fear and pessimism. Pride in the
remarkable technological achievements of modern
civilization is being challenged by the suggestion
that the human predicament of survival has remained
tenuous. It is unpleasant to acknowledge that in
spite of technology, a spectre of widespread
poverty, of environmental disasters, of threatening
mega-violence, mars the outlook on what is and what
may be.

The deterministic view may also be unwanted on
account of being fatalistic. However, fatalists
are extremists among determinists. Come decline,
fatalists would argue, in resignation, that efforts
to affect the course of history are futile. On the
other hand, a moderate position on determinism
could be allowed by the division between pessimistic pessimists and optimistic pessimists. The
optimistic pessimist may try to promote an appreciation of the failure of control over the dynamics
of our age as a necessary step in coming to grips
with that failure.

In economics, the problem of coming to grips
with the spillovers of human activities on the
natural environment has been underlined by the
debate of the seventies concerning the limits of
growth. A pessimistic case has been put that
continued economic and demographic growth will
threaten human survival by pollution and exhaustion
of natural resources, affecting flora and fauna,

the soil, its minerals, the water systems and the atmosphere. This case has been answered as follows: the promise of ongoing advancement of technology will deliver 21st-century society from the prospect of fatal alienation of the biosphere.[4] Yet, curiously, technological advance is at the very roots of economic and demographic momentum.

Noteworthy therefore is that the long-run societal implications of a hopeful technological rescue have not been spelled out analytically. Indeed, one might have to rely on science fiction writing. Admittedly, however, a number of studies dealing with post-industrial society have presented constructive and hopeful trends and ideas. Alvin Toffler (1981) provides a noted example. Nevertheless, a credibility gap remains as politics does not address itself deliberately to the long-run future. Technology is not therefore being designed to ensure the realization of progress. Rather, it is being designed to fill what gaps arise with time. As argued, this amounts to accommodation of the circumstances that confront society and not to shaping of those circumstances.

It could be said that the technocratic optimists — finding a willing ear in business and government circles dependent on growth (the 'dynamus quo') — have constructed their position in the negative as it were.[5] The optimists have explained why the environmental doomsayers would be wrong on the issue of the feasibility of continued economic growth. Many new and miraculous inventions are to come to society's aid as the need, and thus the incentive, will arise. However, the optimists do not make a positive contribution in presenting a vision of the overall merits of an ongoing 'technologization' of society other than to point out that technology (human inventiveness) is society's insurance of coping with present and future contingencies. Hence, it seems that doubt must be sustained. If it is not doubt on the adequacy of the proposed insurance, doubt still applies with regard to the agreeability of the technological future implied.

Apart from concern about undue technological optimism regarding the feasibility of continued growth, the literature presents an independent case against its desirability in the rich economies.[6] For these reasons, it seems trusting, if not wishful to accept the belief in a technocratic fix and to persist with the currency of the view that the future requires no planning or that growth requires no control. Nevertheless, the seventies debate on the feasibility and desirability of continued economic growth has left no apparent policy impact. Quite the opposite. The rhetoric of economic decision makers of the recessed eighties' calls for more growth as if this panacea to multiple economic ills had never been challenged.

Perhaps, therefore, the explanation of the absence of plans or measures aimed at a no-growth, sustainable economy, must be found in an under-estimation of the deterministic nature of history. Even if convinced of the case against the desirability and/or feasibility of continued growth, how can responsible decision makers in business and in government be expected to re-organize socioeconomic and political reality and by what means of transition? What vision and what control have the decision makers really got? Put differently, the analytical questions of feasi-bility and desirability are less than difficult as compared to the largely overlooked problem of the avoidability of continued growth.

GROWING RELEVANCE OF ECONOMIC EXTERNALITIES

As a first approximation, economic externalities, colloquially referred to as spillovers, may be described as unintentional welfare effects enjoyed or suffered as a consequence of choices enacted by third persons. Economic externalities constitute economies (benefits) or diseconomies (costs) which are conferred on (unsuspecting) parties by economic agents who are typically not accountable for doing so and who, therefore, are not held to consider such benefits and costs in private rationalization. External benefits and costs are also known as social - as distinct from private or internal - benefits and costs.

The importance of the concept of economic externalities is attributable to the two pro-positions developed above: (1) that rapid socio-economic historical change imparts on every person and institution welfare effects of considerable magnitude; and (2) that the welfare effects of our changing times contain a significant component that is involuntary in character. This involuntary component equates with both the incidence of externalities as well as with the notion of deter-minism. Consequently, to gauge the importance of the phenomenon of externalities is close to the

306

heart of this contribution. Economics, and even environmental economics, seems to neglect the complexity and magnitude of the incidence of externalities and commonly treats cases of externality as minor market imperfections that often do not warrant correction because of uneconomic levels of correction cost. Perhaps, however, this unappreciative view in economics is a view in transition. This could be so because the phenomenon of externalities may have been spreading and building up rapidly in recent times.

Fifteen to twenty years ago one would have been hard-pressed to find a reference to the phenomenon of externalities in an English-language textbook on economics. Around that same time, however, the neglect was ended in a definitive way by Mishan's book **The Costs of Economic Growth** (1967). Mishan showed how pervasively the spillovers of economic growth affected our prosperity, how these effects had strong negative elements (external diseconomies) and how they put in doubt the impression of material progress until then so convincingly suggested by GNP growth figures.

Decades earlier, A.C. Pigou (1932) had pioneered the notion of externalities by distinguishing between social costs and benefits on the one hand and private costs and benefits on the other. Yet the many examples in his work hint more at academic curiosity about the theoretical niceties of misallocation and maldistribution than at concern about an issue of possibly great societal consequence. Among Pigou's examples are those that refer to the damage by rabbits suffered on one country estate as a result of negligent control measures on neighboring estates; or to the uncompensated locomotive spark damage to vegetable crops along the lines of British rail. Even the more grave subject of air pollution in industrial centres such as Pittsburgh and Manchester, is considered in limited terms such as the cleaning-up costs of extra scrubbing and more frequent washing of clothes. In the fifties, a similar impression of political triviality is still gained from James Meade's (1952) marginal analysis of the reciprocal externalities between apiarist and orchardist.

Western economics following World War II did not recognize the problem of externalities as one of substance or challenge. Following the Keynesian revolution, the 'remaining' challenges were widely perceived to present themselves in three areas mainly. In macroeconomics, John Maynard Keynes' work required to be extended into a dynamic or growth model of the economy in an attempt to understand and control the business cycle. Secondly, decolonialization underlined the need to formulate a theory of economic development capable of dealing with the specific problems of Third World countries. And, finally, in microeconomics, monopolistic practice presented itself as the central shortcoming of the market system and an important field of analysis.[10] The rise in the late sixties and seventies of a branch called environmental economics was entirely unanticipated. So was the sudden and widespread interest around the same time in the externalities associated with pollution and, some years later, the interest in the externalities of resource exhaustion.

Milton Friedman's extensively read **Capitalism and Freedom** (1962) was published before this upsurge of interest in environmental problems and such problems barely rate a mention in his book. Yet, Friedman acknowledges explicitly that externalities are a fundamental cause of market failure. However, he too considered this flaw to be of minor consequence; much less than the market failure entailed in monopolization. His book recommends no intervention to combat either problem. But an exception applied. This exception relates to the external diseconomies generated in a complex modern society by people who cannot read or write. In this case, Friedman advocated the enforcement of compulsory primary education.[11]

What these samples from the literature make out is that, in the past, amongst economists a degree of oblivion has prevailed on the subject of externality. Since the seventies, however, in the footsteps of writers such as Ezra Mishan, Kenneth Boulding and others, an opposite view is emerging. This view rates social and natural environmental externalities as a disturbing source of malfunctioning of the market; one which should take a foremost position in any critique of the free market ideology.[12] As has been inferred by the environmental pessimists, externality departures from the market ideal may, accumulatively and with the passing of time, prove far more significant – if not vital – to the welfare of society than the conventionally acknowledged monopolistic losses. A net negative balance of externalities raises the very debate over historical progress and can be viewed as an indicator of a possible decline in the quality of life in the face of improvements in economic quantity.

The juxtaposition of an emphasis on the phenomenon of externalities with more dated economic preoccupations could invite an accusation of smugness. It could be considered smug to suggest that recent contributors, in a fashion of enlightenment, are advancing the insights of earlier scholars who failed to assess fully the importance of externalities. This need hardly be so. Rather, it demonstrates the premise of the institutional strand of economics which accepts that theory cannot be universal but needs continuous adaptation while the reality to which it applies is subject to historical change or geographical difference. Thus a recent appreciation of the importance of the phenomenon of externalities is not so much a function of enlightenment but reflects on the developments of our time. Environmental problems in particular have multiplied in recent decades. In the main, science has responded to these problems only after they have become more apparent.

What should be done about externalities? The answer which dominates the environmental literature is that externalities, where realistic, should be internalized. However, before elaborating on the concept of internalization, a point of definition needs to be cleared up. The point is that so-called Scitovsky or pecuniary externalities are ruled out in the present discussion. Mishan's literature survey of externalities (1971) clears up this issue. In an economy in which, in principle at least, all movements in quantities and prices are interrelated, one person's economic choice would have a bearing on the economic conditions faced by all other persons. Therefore, it would be normal for third parties to experience an infinite number of unsolicited welfare effects for which they are not responsible, e.g., the price of petrol goes up or down, the exchange rate varies, etc. These pecuniary welfare effects emanating from the market, however, differ from externalities proper - such as arise in environmental spillovers. The difference is that pecuniary externalities are functional in the allocation and distribution processes of a market economy and need not call for policy measures.

Policy measures, on the other hand, appear in order if one is to avoid the costs of external diseconomies proper.[13] Policy designed to force external diseconomy-generating parties to take account of these diseconomies are said to internalize an externality. For such policy to be economic, the implementation costs of internalization measures must be outweighed by the benefits of gains in efficiency and equity.[14] Internalization can take many forms. In the case of environmental externalities, economic forms of internalization include schemes providing for taxation of spillovers or the marketing of spillover licenses. In practice, bureaucratic, legal and political means of internalization are more common. These means range from legislative and regulative enforcement of what are considered to be politically acceptable levels of environmental pollution or depletion; the use of zoning in town and land planning; the recognition and protection of amenity rights; to merger or centralization designed to encompass the interests of externality-generating and externality-affected parties.[15]

An increased incidence of externalities may thus be expected to involve government in a variety of internalization measures. Accordingly, government departments – frequently newly formed – can be seen trying to cope with the modern complexities posed by social and environmental spillovers. Externalities, one might speculate, may have contributed significantly to the dramatic growth in the establishment of civil servants witnessed in many countries. Likewise, the production of law and statute may have been caused to expand greatly. The growth of the government sector has been strong also in countries with a non-intervention, anti-state tradition. But of course only an impressionistic link is being presented between the growing complexity and interdependency of society on the one hand, and the growth of externalities together with an expanded role of government, on the other.

The case of a growing influence of externalities can be outlined in more detail following the distinction of four categories. These are: (1) contemporaneous spillovers affecting the natural and man-made environment (leaving aside here the non-anthropocentric welfare effects); (2) contemporaneous spillovers affecting the social environment; (3) dynamic or long-run external effects; and (4) cross welfare effects arising from activities that are public or collective in nature. Modest attention has been paid by economists to the first three classes. These three classes will be

discussed briefly in the remaining two sections of
this chapter. As for the last category, this
concerns the provision of public goods (or the
prevention of public ills). Public goods entail
external benefits to 'free riders' and public
economics teaches that unless internalization by a
(compulsory) sharing of costs can be worked out, a
suboptimal supply of public goods will result.
However, issues of public economics do not seem
immediately relevant in the present context.

GEOGRAPHIC AND SOCIAL EXTERNALITIES

Spillovers affecting the natural and man-made environment - one might call these geographic spillovers - can be subdivided as follows: (1) pollution, manifesting itself over a broad spectrum,
with new and sometimes disturbing forms and interactions being 'discovered' with regularity; (2) exploitation and conceivable exhaustion of natural
resources - both renewable (e.g., timber) and non-
renewable (e.g., minerals, fossil fuels, ozone);
(3) land transformation, in which natural ecosystems are being eroded or replaced by agriculture
or by urban-industrial development; (4) congestion,
e.g., overpopulation, high-rise urbanization and
traffic congestion.[16]
     The first and fourth mentioned group of exter-
nalities lend themselves more easily to economic
analysis on account of their 'flow' character.
That is to say, pollution or congestion can be
viewed as continuous processes for which, in theory
at least, environmental economics offers a prescription known as the optimal level of pollution or
congestion.
     'Stock' externalities such as those of the
second or third group involve a once-and-for-all
change in status. In these cases, questions of
what is optimal decision making are more difficult
on account of the high level of time preference
applying in commerce and in politics. A high level
of time preference, as measured by the rate of
interest, signifies a high propensity to consider
the present before the future. This propensity
facilitates the processes of change by subjecting
variations in the status quo to pragmatic criteria
only. Pragmatism, we argued, celebrates the
immediacy of results at the expense, if necessary,
of what has been inherited from the more distant
past or what may affect the longer-term future.

Social Determinism and Technology

A visual illustration of stock externalities relates to our architectural heritage. This effect can be gauged from historic photographs of one's town or village of residence. Old pictures reflect the starkness of an accumulation of changes that by themselves may have gone more or less unnoticed. Examples of stock externalities are not restricted to the aforementioned categories of resource depletion and land transformation. Notably, pollution also carries important stock implications, as instanced in the pollution from long-life radioactive materials, or as in the allegedly dangerous build-up of carbon dioxide in the atmosphere. Unlike flow externalities, therefore, stock externalities might not merely pose losses and risks for the present but they may continue to do the same in the future.

Summarily, entertain also the incidence of social externalities. Mindful of the key role played by technology in changing the social environment, we find society and its way of life being altered from decade to decade and now profoundly different from the nineteenth century. Telecommunications, modern transport, computers, medical technology and so on are responsible for this ongoing process of transformation. There can be little doubt that many of these technologies have delivered major contributions to economic, if not spiritual well-being. On the other hand, reservations of substance have been expressed about less desirable spillovers.

Foremost amongst such reservations is the incremental external insecurity of nations that is believed by many to have arisen from the advance of military technology. Also fears have been expressed with respect to the internal security and privacy of citizens as a result of new technologies in the field of surveillance. Furthermore, much has been written about the dehumanization and alienation effects of technology in modern society. For instance, working with machines can be repetitive and devoid of meaning. Also, machines are capable of causing obsolescence in what Joseph Schumpeter has aptly labelled "creative destruction". Obsolescence does not merely affect investments already locked in place, but competent and skilful people are being made superfluous.[17] At another level, apprehension has been expressed about astounding rates of urbanization and human mobility in general. This is unravelling the character of life-long personal associations

312

typical of small rural communities. Without
romanticizing rural community life, ample scope
exists to be critical of city life for the million-
plus masses of relative strangers. Lastly, and
against an international background, technology
which has 'opened up' the world, is also closing it
in, by way of reductionist pressures on cultures
and languages to conform to the demands of international integration.[18]

DYNAMIC OR HISTORICAL EXTERNALITIES

More intractable than current, immediate, syn-
chronic or contemporaneous external effects are the
long-run, diachronic or dynamic spillovers that
result from the introduction of new technologies;
from ensuing economic and demographic momentum;
from social and physical infrastructural change;
and so on. Dynamic externalities are historical in
that they impinge on intergenerational welfare.
Historical spillovers or 'forward effects' act both
by widening opportunities and choice as well as by
limiting or, sometimes irreversibly, closing off
options. Such externalities intersect with the
categories of geographic and social externalities
in so far as these contain significant stock
elements. However, the notion of historical
spillovers goes beyond foreseeable stock effects.
It reaches into an uncertain realm of consequences
that are no longer predictable and that will not
necessarily iterate to nothing.

It would seem impossible to anticipate and
isolate scientifically the various long-run consequences, direct and indirect, of major technical
revolutions such as are being witnessed at present
in the widespread adoption of micro-computers or in
the area of genetic engineering. Likewise, it
would have been impossible to scientifically
predict the dynamic externalities affecting the
welfare of generations following the introduction
of the steam engine, the motor car, the telephone,
the television and so many other revolutionary
ideas. At best an understanding could have been
sketched using artistic license.

This raises the question of how dynamic
externalities are recognized and experienced when
they arise. And how do these economic welfare
effects relate to social determinism? The short
answer to the second question is that, over time,
positive dynamic externalities will widen choice,

open up opportunities and thus create room for 'free will', whereas negative dynamic externalities have the opposite effect. Both types contribute to the measure of determinism because their effects have been unaccounted for. The same assessment would apply contemporaneously for static or concurrent externalities.

Concern with determinism stems from the dynamism or turbulence of recent human history. It has been suggested that this dynamism has brought a high incidence of externalities because social and economic history is essentially unplanned.[19] People experience the dynamics by having to adapt – sometimes willingly, sometimes relentlessly – to the changing requirements of society. In this adaptation process lies a measure of determinism. When people are observed to behave conformatively in any one given period and to adapt alike when moving to the next, then herein a test of determinism has been employed.

What is not tested is the question whether people are, or should be, happier having adjusted to the requirements of modernity. Also, it is not clear how long the present dynamic phase of history will persist and where it might lead. On this last point, major socioeconomic upheaval has affected humankind before, some ten millennia ago, when nomadic societies of hunters and gatherers adopted a pattern of settled agricultural production. However, no parallels exist in known history that would compare with the post-medieval dynamic build-up that has become apparent since the days of the Industrial Revolution. If anything, dynamics are still intensifying as new technology – the acknowledged engine of the dynamics – is being developed rapidly with no technological plateau in sight.

Newly developed technology, naturally, is adopted, after its commercial viability will have been scrutinized. But this scrutiny would not necessarily have covered contemporaneous external effects while dynamic external effects almost certainly would have been ignored. Dynamic spillovers are not only difficult to predict, they are difficult to recognize when actually experienced. The point is perhaps best illustrated by specific example. Consider the technology of locomotion by internal combustion as commonly applied in the private motorcar. The reliance of advanced economies on this invention of but a hundred years ago is outright phenomenal. Everywhere the urban environment has been transformed beyond recognition to cater this now ubiquitous machine. Lifestyles have come to revolve around the automobile to a very major degree. And for good reason.

The car has given mobility to thousands of millions of people. It has extended the horizon of the community. It has created opportunities to exercise choices previously unattainable. It could be a monument to 'free will' as it permits us to move as we please. Yet it has brought adverse dynamic spillovers too. So, could it be imagined that determinism forces people against their best interests to drive their cars? Surely, no person is taken to a car dealer at gun point, or is normally barred from walking, cycling or making use of public transport. Presumably, if people voluntarily buy cars, they do so because they feel better off with the purchased mobility. Freedom of choice is of course central to the rationale of market exchange. It is this· freedom which guarantees implicitly that both buyer and seller are better off in the market place.[20]

Unfortunately, the reasoning is flawed by determinism. As concluded in an earlier section, choices made in the present shape the circumstances of the future but do so largely without design. This is the essence of dynamic externalities. It means that free choices are not made in a vacuum. People make choices to deal as best they can within a set of circumstances over which they do not have control. For this reason, a family living in a twentieth century Western city may have little choice as to whether a car is acquired. In the circumstances, the car may well be a necessity with an urgency not far behind that for clothes or shelter. That is to say, a car is then purchased not because of the positive utility inherent in its use, but because of the disutility associated with not having a car. Thus there are dynamic external effects as a consequence of countless micro-motoring decisions which in the end have made society increasingly car-dependent. Free choice has been eroded accordingly. Choice, in fact, may no longer be about acquisition but merely concern secondary decisions such as whether the car shall be Japanese, white or blue, automatic, prestigious, second-hand, etc.

Society, in being geared to the use of cars, can be seen to penalize those who cannot afford this requirement. In turn this means that although voluntary choice in favor of private motorcars guarantees an advantageous outcome from each individual's point of view, this is so only because a prior penalty is being avoided. Therefore there can be no guarantee that society is better off because of the revealed preference for this mode of transport. Indeed there is an impressive body of contraindications relating to death and injury, to pollution, to congestion and to the destruction and erosion of urban amenities. Regrettably, the deterministic factor in society's reliance on motorcars appears to go unnoticed by the free motoring public at large. All the same, it remains unusual, by historical or biological comparison, for two-legged creatures to move on wheels.

A predisposition of a typical Western consumer household to possess a motorcar is not unlike its similarly predictable propensity to watch TV, to subscribe to the telephone network, to enjoy packaged holiday tours, to undergo coronary bypass operations and to partake in more of the range of goods and services so unique to modern advanced economies. Thus citizens consume in a fashion that is dependent on the parameters of the country and the era. Likewise, they work according to the conditions of the day. They live, as the case may be, in stereotype city apartments or in the suburban sprawl. They share similar interests, norms and attitudes. All these parallels, it seems, arise because that is how life happens to be determined. Regardless of active encouragement of individualism, there is perhaps but a small margin of choice.

It should be stressed that such an anti-free picture need not necessarily be unappealing. The good sides of progress are abundantly in evidence and future generations are unlikely to protest having their lives determined by telephones, articulated water, sewage works, electricity, high standards of education and medical care, etc. Dynamic externalities can be liberating externalities. However, it is when dynamic externalities have the effect of varying the circumstances of future generations negatively - often not because of technology's inherent fault but because no appropriate supplementary socioeconomic controls are being enforced to manage its development and introduction - that determinism becomes a threat. As we have seen, this threat is materializing on the environmental and other fronts.

Negative static externalities are being approached by means of economic, legal, bureaucratic and political internalization techniques. The control over negative dynamic externalities is virtually overlooked. To counter their adverse impact on the environment would involve the need for preventative planning, principally aimed, I would guess, at curtailing demographic growth and sectors of economic growth.[21] The justification of planning lies in the real possibility that the balance of externalities is determining the long-run future adversely. A continuation of the policy of laissez-faire could be seen as preempting freedom in the future, in exchange for the maintenance of freedoms currently enjoyed. If freedom is paramount, however, then also the future should be voluntary. A voluntary future may ensure sustainability, if not progress.[22]

NOTES

1. Compare, on the one hand, authors such as Wilfred Beckerman (1972, 1974), Jacob Bronowski (1973), Herman Kahn and Anthony Weiner (1967), John Maddox (1972) or Julian Simon (1981), with, on the other hand, Charles Birch (1975), Barry Commoner (1971), Herman Daly (1980), Meadows et al., (1974), Mesarovic and Pestel (1974), or Michael Stewart (1983). For an overview, see Christopher Freeman and Mary Jahoda (1978).

2. John Bury's work (1955) demonstrates how difficult it is to pursue the validity of judgements about progress.

3. Oskar Lange and Fred Taylor (1964) have provided the classic demonstration on this point. Besides, the wealth of supportive comparative economic systems that evidence the use of the market mechanism to control environmental spill-overs is discussed by, for instance, Clem Tisdell (1983).

4. For both pro- and anti-growth positions see again Freeman and Jahoda (1978) as well as note 1. The OECD Interfutures study (1979) is a further prominent contribution on the side of growth and technology.

5. E.g., Beckerman (1972), Kahn and Simon (1984), Simon (1981).

6. See for instance, Daly (1980), Hirsch (1967), Mishan (1967, 1981), Scitovsky (1976).

7. Recessed because of unemployment, not lack of growth.

8. Welfare effects can be experienced due to acts of nature, e.g., earthquakes, disease, etc.

Social Determinism and Technology

Although external, these effects, if not caused or facilitated in association with the economic activities in society, are not presently of interest.

9.   Paul Samuelson's popular and comprehensive **Economics** (1967) did provide an exception. But although the technical concept of externalities is raised in a number of instances, any great environmental and social significance goes overlooked.

10.   Major contributions in these respective areas were made by R. Harrod and E. Domar, by A. Lewis and by E.H. Chamberlin. See also Joan Robinson (1964).

11.   Of course, the collective provision of goods and services is generally justified by the need to manage external welfare effects. The question is to what extent education is a private or public good.

12.   One should hasten to add that competing economic systems are seen to experience comparable difficulties in coming to grips with external spillovers.

13.   There is a dichotomy between the requirement for intervention in the case of external diseconomies and the case of external economies. In both cases it may seem that the collective interest that would be served by intervention in the external effect and the party suffering the effect are in conflict, whereas the second case of external economies is one of harmony. A policy to combat external diseconomies will therefore require political direction from above. By contrast, external economies can be exploited by initiative from below, consistent with the liberal principle of freedom of commercial initiative.

14.   Where the latter criterion is relevant in terms of distribution as well as in terms of incentives.

15.   Desirable as internationalization measures are, there is evidence to suggest that these measures, in themselves, will merely address the symptoms of historical change. This view has been developed by Doeleman (1985).

16.   For details on spillovers, consult Ehrlich (1970), IUCN (1980), U.S. State Department (1982), or Vester (1972).

17.   The external human obsolescence effect of the introduction of new technology could be internalized by institutionalizing severance payments to be shouldered by those who stand to profit from the implementation of new technology. Within reason,

people threatened by skill and/or job severance might be allowed to reject severance compensation they believe would make them worse off on the whole.

18. For detailed treatment of these summarized points, see for instance, Illich (1973) or Toffler (1981).

19. The same applies in the planned economies in so far as plans deal merely with short-run allocational and distributional solutions.

20. Cf. Milton Friedman (1962).

21. The anti-growth position does not necessarily attack new development. It seeks to redefine a mechanical path of exponential expansion into organic growth. Organic growth is a term used by Mesarovic and Pestel (1974) and relates to growth of a biological organism which on passing through its juvenile stage will stop growing in size but may continue to grow in terms of maturity.

22. I would like to thank my colleague John R. Fisher for his helpful suggestions. Shortcomings are of course my responsibility.

REFERENCES

Althusser, L. (1975) **Reading Capital**, Vesso, London
Beckerman, W. (1972) 'Economists, Scientists, and Environmental Catastrophe', **Oxford Economic Papers**, 24, pp. 327-345
Beckerman, W. (1974) **Two Cheers for the Affluent Society – In Defence of Economic Growth**, Jonathan Cape, London
Birch, C. (1975) **Confronting the Future: Australia and the World the Next Hundred Years**, Pelican, Harmondsworth
Boulding, K.E. (1966) 'The Economics of the Coming Spaceship Earth', pp.3-14 in H. Barrett (ed.), **Environmental Quality in a Growing Economy**, John Hopkins University Press, Baltimore
Bronowski, J. (1973) **The Ascent of Man**, BBC, London
Bury, J.B. (1955) **The Idea of Progress**, Dover, New York
Commoner, B. (1971) **The Closing Circle**, Knopf, New York
Daly, H.E. (1980) **Economics, Ecology, Ethics**, Freeman, San Francisco
Doeleman, J.A. (1985) 'Historical Perspective and Environmental Cost-Benefit Analysis', **Futures**, 17, 2, pp. 149-163
Douglas, M. and Isherwood, B. (1978) **The World of**

Social Determinism and Technology

Goods: Towards an Anthropology of Consumption, Allen Lane, London

Ehrlich, P. R. and Ehrlich, A.H. (1970) **Population, Resources and Environment,** Freeman, San Francisco

Freeman, C. and Jahoda, M. (1978) **World Futures: The Great Debate,** Martin & Robertson, London

Friedman, M. (1962) **Capitalism and Freedom,** University Press, Chicago

Galbraith, J.K. (1977) **The Age of Uncertainty,** Hutchinson, London

Hirsch, F. (1967) **Social Limits to Economic Growth,** Harvard University Press, Cambridge, Massachusetts

Illich, I. (1973) **Tools for Conviviality,** Calder & Boyars, London

International Union for the Conservation of Nature and Natural Resources (IUCN) (1980) **World Conservation Strategy: Living Resource Conservation for Sustainable Development,** Glands, Switzerland

Kahn, H. and Simon, J.L., (1984) **The Resourceful Earth: A Response to Global 2000,** Blackwell, Boston

Kahn, H. and Weiner, A.J., (1967) **The Year 2000** Macmillan, New York

Lange, O. and Taylor, F.M., (1964) **On the Economic Theory of Socialism,** McGraw-Hill, New York

Levi-Strauss, C. (1968) **Structural Anthropology,** Penguin, Harmondsworth

Maddox, J. (1972) **The Doomsday Syndrome,** Macmillan, London

Meade, J.E. (1952) 'External Economies and Diseconomies in a Competitive Situation', **Economic Journal, 62,** pp. 54-67

Meadows D. et al. (1974) **The Limits to Growth: A Report for the Club of Rome,** Universe Books, New York

Mesarovic, M. and Pestel, E. (1974) **Mankind at the Turning Point,** Dutton, New York

Mishan, E.J. (1967) **The Costs of Economic Growth,** Praeger, New York

Mishan, E.J. (1971) 'The Postwar Literature on Externalities: An Interpretative Essay', **Journal of Economic Literature, 9,** pp. 1-28

Mishan, E.J. (1981) **Introduction to Normative Economics,** Oxford University Press, New York

OECD, (1979) **Interfutures – Facing the Future,** Organization for Economic Cooperation and Development, Paris

Pigou, A.C. (1932) **The Economics of Welfare,** 4th

ed., Macmillan, London

Robinson, J. (1964) **Economic Philosophy**, Pelican, Harmondsworth

Samuelson, P. (1967) Economics, 7th ed., McGraw-Hill, New York

Scitovsky, T. (1976) **The Joyless Economy**, Oxford University Press, New York

Simon, J. L. (1981) **The Ultimate Resource**, Princeton University Press, Princeton

Smith, A. (1950) **The Wealth of Nations**, Methuen, London

Stewart, M. (1983) **Controlling the Economic Future**, Harvester Press, Brighton

Tisdell, C.A. (1983) 'Pollution Control and Policies Proposed by Economists', **Journal of Environmental Systems**, 12, pp.363-380

Toffler, A. (1973) **Future Shock**, Pan Books

Toffler, A. (1981) **The Third Wave**, Pan Books

U.S. State Department and Council on Environmental Quality (1982) **The Global 2000 Report to the President: Entering the Twenty-first Century**, Penguin, Harmondsworth

Vester, F. (1972) **Das Uberlebensprogramm**, Kindler Verlag, Munchen

Chapter Fifteen

TECHNOLOGICAL ADVANCE: UNRAVELLING THE STRANDS

R. J. van Wyk

INTRODUCTION

For many years economists have tried to describe
and measure the effect of 'technological advance'
on the economy.   The orthodox literature in this
field adopted either a macro-approach, such as
economic growth accounting, or a micro-approach,
involving case-study-like procedures to analyze the
impact of innovation.

The   economic-growth-accounting   approach
created much interest and encouraged a widespread
awareness of the importance of technological
advance.   However it also emphasized the limitations of the methodology.   Because of the
uncertainty about the forces contributing to
'technological advance' (sometimes referred to as
'increased productivity') many authors refrained
from specifying the magnitude, preferring to refer
to it in more generalized terms such as 'the third
factor' or 'the residual', that is the entire set
of inputs over and above the inputs of labour and
capital that can be explicitly measured.

The micro-approach produced a wide variety of
fascinating and well-focussed contributions.   Much
experience was gained from descriptions of the
application of new technology in particular
settings, and a wealth of quantitative evidence was
amassed highlighting the significance of technological advance in each.

By and large however, the two approaches
differed significantly, each adopting a unique
methodology.   Reconciliation between the two proved
extremely difficult and well nigh impossible.

It would be unproductive to attempt a review
of the relevant literature in an article such as
this.   Two excellent review articles have appeared

in the eighties and provide the backdrop to the present venture (Nelson, 1981; Majer, 1985).

Both these authors came to the conclusion that present approaches had reached a 'dead end' and that a 'new departure' was called for. In this chapter one possible approach to such a new departure is suggested. It is based on a fresh intellectual discipline, increasingly referred to as 'the general theory of technology' in which an attempt is made to describe the phenomenon of technology in broad outline, and deals with the dynamics of the technological totality that is becoming known as the 'technosphere' (Martin, 1984, p.33).

This field of enquiry seems to be extremely powerful and may quite well do for the study of technology what macroeconomics did for the study of the economy. However the field is still very much in its infancy and much remains to be done before it emerges as a comprehensive and commonly accepted field of analysis.

In this chapter the early work describing and measuring technology, using orthodox economic analysis, is briefly reviewed. The alternative approach using the concepts of the general theory of technology is then introduced and its application discussed.

TECHNOLOGY IN ECONOMIC ANALYSIS

Macroeconomic Analysis

One particular approach to macroeconomic analysis holds that the aggregate level of economic activity in a nation is determined by three inputs, namely: labour, capital and technology. These three may be combined into an aggregate production function, such as the well-known Cobb-Douglass function, in the following way:

$$Y = aL^{\alpha} K^{\beta} T$$

where Y is a measure of aggregate economic activity such as gross domestic product

L is a measure of the input of labour such as people-days worked

K is a measure of capital inputs as measured by the value of the stock at a given time

α and β are elasticities representing the relative weights of the contributions of L

and K. In the base year of calculation
$\alpha + \beta = 1$
a is a scale factor
T is the level of technology.

This production function may then be restructured to have the following format:

$\delta Y/Y = \alpha \delta L/L + \beta \delta K/K + \delta T/T.$

where δ denotes change and the various terms thus represent weighted rates of growth for given periods.

In practice the calculation of the various inputs for historical periods involves the calculation of $\delta Y/Y$, $\delta L/L$, and $\delta K/K$, the weighting of the latter two terms with chosen values for α and β, and the calculation of $\delta T/T$ from the formula:

$\delta T/T = \delta Y/Y - \alpha \delta L/L - \beta \delta K/K.$

The influence of technology is not therefore calculated directly but as the difference between the measurable growth in aggregate economic activity and the measurable effect of labour and capital inputs.

This indirect method of calculation means that the value of $\delta T/T$, or technology, reflects not only that which it is meant to reflect but a whole host of other factors as well, including all the errors in calculating α, β, $\delta Y/Y$, $\delta L/L$ and $\delta K/K$. No wonder that the value of $\delta T/T$ became known as 'the third factor', the 'residual' and the 'measure of our ignorance'.

Notwithstanding the uncertainty surrounding this factor it became an important statistic in many economic analyses. In a now classic book, Denison attempted to break down this third factor – or aggregate measure of technology – into a number of constituent components (Denison, 1962, p.266). A summary of the various growth forces identified by Denison in a study of the United States economy is shown in Table 15.1.

From this analysis it follows that increases in labour inputs ($\delta L/L$) accounted for 30.7 units out of 100 units of growth, increases in capital inputs ($\delta K/K$) for 14.7 units of growth, and the third factor ($\delta T/T$) for 54.6 units. The latter category was further broken down into: 'Education and advance of knowledge', 'Economies of scale' and 'other factors', each contributing a share as outlined in Table 15.1. In the original text the latter three categories were broken down even further.

Table 15.1: Allocation of Growth Rates of Total Real National Income of the U.S.A. Among Various Sources of Growth, 1929–57

Sources of Growth	Growth Rate in Percentage Points %	Index of Relative Contribution to Growth (2.93%=100)
Increased employment (net effect of more man-years, shorter hours, changes in the composition of the labour force)	0.90	30.7
Increased use of capital	0.43	14.7
Education and advance of knowledge	1.25	42.7
Economies of scale	0.34	11.6
Other factors	0.01	0.3
Overall Growth	2.93	100.0

Some authors attempted an international comparison of the importance of the third factor (Aukrust, 1965, p.19; Bruton, 1967, pp.1103–1104). Denison himself undertook an interesting comparative study of the third factor and its constituent growth forces in nine countries (Denison, 1967, pp.298–316). And there were many others (Nelson, 1981).

By and large these studies of the effects of the third factor had a great impact on our understanding of the subtler forces of economic growth including the impact of technology. On the whole, however, healthy reservations were expressed about the various methods employed and about the validity of the results obtained. Apart from the fact that technological advance was a catch-all concept incorporating a great variety of influences, more fundamental objections were raised. For instance, its magnitude can only be calculated if economic growth is positive, that is if $\delta Y/Y > 0$. The impact of subtle technological forces that help avoid a decline in economic activity cannot be calculated.

In addition to this, many observers were per-
plexed by the strange way in which the various
contributory forces were classified. Some of them
seem to be far removed from actual production
arrangements and their influences are extremely
difficult to visualize. As Nelson so aptly puts
it: 'Everybody knows that the residual accounts
for a hodge-podge of factors, but these are difficult to sort out. If this 'measure of our ignorance' is not completely mysterious, it certainly is
not well understood' (Nelson, 1981, p.1035).
        Professor Helga Majer of Stuttgart arrives at
very much the same conclusion: 'Contemporary theory
of technical progress seems to have reached a dead
end' (Majer, 1985, p.335).

Microeconomic Analysis
A review of the treatment of technology in micro-
economic analysis is a far more difficult undertaking than a review of the treatment of technology
in macroeconomic analysis. First there is no
central and unifying theory as there is in the case
of macroeconomic analysis, and second the variety
of studies is so great as to prohibit logical
generalizations.
        Many aspects have been addressed in the
literature, ranging from the nature of organizations, intra-industry differences among firms
and potential causes of productivity differences.
Once more the reader is referred to an excellent
review (Nelson, 1981).
        On the whole these studies provide ample
evidence of the significance of technological
advance but contribute very little to a complete
description thereof.

CONFRONTING TECHNOLOGY DIRECTLY

The General Theory of Technology
While economists battled bravely on in their
attempts to disaggregate the third factor or
combine the effects of many economic benefits
measured at the micro-level, others interested in
the phenomenon of technology followed their own
routes of enquiry.
        Technological forecasters, a very pragmatic
group of analysts, continued in their attempts to
describe the evolution of given technologies and to

chart their future courses (Bright, 1978; Martino, 1972; Jones and Twiss, 1978). By the late seventies the technological forecasters broadened their gaze. Instead of limiting their focus to given technologies they asked the question: What is the general thrust of technology? (Van Wyk, 1979).

In the meantime, a specialized breed of philosophers turned their enquiring minds to the phenomenon of technology. These philosophers noted with some alarm, 'But it is an astonishing fact that the commonly accepted and carefully investigated philosophy of science has not yet found its counterpart in an established philosophy of technology' (Rapp, 1974, p.vii). By the mid-seventies, new thought structures were being formulated providing the student of technology with simple yet robust concepts for understanding complex technological phenomena.

Another source of inspiration for the broad understanding of technology was general systems theory (GST). The creation of abstract models for understanding various kinds of systems contributed to the intellectual tool-kit for handling complex technological systems (e.g., Miller, 1978).

These influences led to the suggestion that what was needed for the proper understanding and management of technology was a 'general theory of technology' or, as it was formulated in German, 'eine allgemeine Technologie'. In 1979, such a systems theory of technology was formulated and published (Ropohl, 1979).

This emphasis elevated the study of technology to a new independent level, placing it in a similar theoretical plane to descriptive sciences such as biology and geology. The main objects of study are artefacts, that is those independent depositories of skill created by people to facilitate human endeavour.

Within the general theory of technology a subfield has emerged concerned with developing quantitative procedures for analyzing technological phenomena at both the macro- and micro-levels. This subfield may be referred to as 'technological analysis' and is based on a particular set of analytical tools (Van Wyk, 1984, 1985). Another, closely related and theoretically well-rooted field is called 'technometrics' (Sahal, 1985). While a third related endeavour refers to the 'functional approach' to the measurement of technology (Majer, 1985). A synthesis of these approaches appears possible and would seem to hold

327

great promise. Unfortunately this cannot be attempted here.

For the purposes of the present chapter one approach only is introduced and explored further, namely that of technological analysis.

Tools of Technological Analysis

Technological analysis as it is used at present employs four analytical tools:

1. A classification of technological artefacts
2. A standard set of technological trends
3. A chart of technological limits
4. A socio-technical preference profile.

Two of these are particularly important to the problem at hand. The first is a simple classification of all artefacts and the second a standard set of trends describing the patterns of change experienced by these artefacts in the long run.

The system of classification employed here is one developed by Continental philosophers of technology. Artefacts are classified in terms of two characteristics, the nature of their output and the manner of handling the said output. Outputs can be Matter (M), Energy (E) or Information (I). The manner of handling can be Processing, Transporting or Storing. By combining these possible characteristics in a grid format a basic classification for technologies is found, called the nine-cell matrix. This is an extremely powerful approach – its simplicity belying its tremendous analytical and descriptive value. For the purposes of the present chapter, it is merely presented and not probed further. The nine-cell matrix is shown in Table 15.2.

Table 15.2: The Nine-Cell Matrix - A Basic Classification of Technological Artefacts

Output	Type of Manipulator		
	Processor	Transporter	Store
Matter (M)	.	.	.
Energy (E)	.	.	.
Information (I)	.	.	.

This system covers the entire spectrum of artefacts and acknowledges the inherently hierarchical nature of technology. Artefacts consist of subsystems and are themselves frequently linked into larger agglomerations. Thus an engine driving a sawmill is an E-processing artefact when viewed by itself. However, the sawmill as such is an M-processing device. The various components of the engine may be classified as M, E or I handling devices, depending on their particular function within the engine. The nine-cell matrix therefore allows for analysis at both the component and agglomerate level. This is an extremely important quality as it allows for aggregation and therefore a more or less uniform approach for both macro- and micro-analysis.

The second tool of technological analysis which is of importance to the study of technological change at the macro-level is a standard set of technological trends. If the analyst can identify a set of persistent and recurrent trends affecting all nine classes of artefacts, such a set could provide a convenient framework to search for and measure technological change.

The Standard Sixfold Classification of Technological Trends

The literature on technological analysis has addressed this issue and does provide us with such a simple classification. Six overriding technological trends are differentiated. Four of these may be described as _performance_ and two as _structural_ trends. These in summary are:

Performance trends: 1. Increasing efficiency
2. Increasing capacity
3. Increasing density
4. Increasing accuracy

Structural trends: 5. Increasing size range
6. Increasing complexity

We shall examine these trends in detail. However, in examining these trends two qualifications should be borne in mind. First, while they are extremely pervasive they do not always occur simultaneously in the evolutionary pattern of each and every artefact. Second, they may not adequately reflect the subtleties of the evolutionary process as it manifests itself in the case of unique and special artefacts. By and large however, they seem to provide a powerful grasp of the more persistent features of technological evolution.

(1) Increasing Efficiency. Increasing efficiency is one of the most persistent trends in technological evolution. Efficiency is characterized in terms of a ratio, the ratio of output to input. Successive generations of artefacts seem to evolve in the direction of greater efficiency.

Examples include the increase in the output of a product produced (output of M) per unit of raw material required, an increase in the volume of energy generated (output of E) per unit of fuel needed and an increase in the number of bits handled by a computer (output of I) per unit of some given input.

(2) Increasing Capacity. Another trend that seems to be almost as pervasive as the trend of increasing efficiency is the trend of increasing capacity.

Capacity is defined as the capability of an artefact to bring forth its designated output. Mostly it is characterized in terms of a ratio, the ratio of output in relation to the time required to produce, or keep, such an output.

Examples include the increase in steel production per hour in the case of blast furnaces; the increase of electricity generated per hour in the case of a generating plant; and the increase in bits calculated per second in the case of computers.

(3) Increasing Density. Many artefacts exhibited the phenomenon of increasing functional density from one generation to the next. In this context functional density is taken to mean the output that the artefact can achieve per unit of space required to do so.

Examples of increasing density include an increase in the amount of gas that can be stored in vessels of a given size, an increase in the amount of energy that can be stored in batteries of a given size; and an increase in the capability of computers of a given size.

330

(4) Increasing Accuracy. In the evolutionary histories of many artefacts a persistent increase may be noted in the accuracy with which their output can be controlled. In this respect accuracy may be characterized by the precision with which a given outcome is specified.

Examples include ever finer tolerances in the case of machined surfaces; more minute volumes of energy handled with precision; and ever better resolution in the case of image processing.

(5) Increasing Size Range. Successive generations of artefacts are exhibiting some quite startling scale characteristics. Some of them are becoming ever larger in size, that is, the size of the largest example is increasing, while others are becoming significantly smaller. Examples of increasing size include earthmoving equipment, buildings, ships and aircraft. Examples of miniaturization include drug delivery systems (that are implanted into the human body) and modern electronic circuits.

(6) Increasing Complexity. Many of the trends describing improved performance can be linked to better structured artefacts. In this respect, the phenomenon of increasing complexity describes the growing list of capabilities that successive generations of artefacts are expected to possess.

A fairly consistent pattern is for artefacts to start off their evolutionary trajectories as simple passive devices, that is, merely an M system. In time a motor is added to drive the artefact, that is, the system becomes an M+E system. Finally information handling capability is introduced leading to an M+E+I system.

Examples of this 'M,E,I succession' include the evolution of aircraft from simple gliders, for instance the Lillienthal glider that resembled many of the hanggliders in use today was no more than a passive M device. The aeroplane used by the Wright brothers had an added feature, namely an engine, or an E processing system. Modern aircraft are extremely well endowed with I processing systems. The progression from M to M+E to M+E+I is frequently observed in technological evolution.

In practice of course these four trends are closely linked. They all influence each other and it is not possible to arrange them in a hierarchy implying that one is more important than the other.

Having reviewed the standard set of technological trends the question that now needs to be answered is: Can they be measured and, if yes, how?

MEASURING TECHNOLOGICAL CHANGE

Basic Units

This section is, of necessity, somewhat technical. The serious student of technological analysis is recommended to study it thoroughly. For the cursory reader the section Basic Units would suffice.

As may be inferred from the previous section, the measurement of technological change focusses on changing values for the performance parameters and to an extent structural parameters rather than on changing configurations of artefacts. Configurations are more difficult to describe systematically than functional features.

The parameters referred to remain reasonably constant for a given period of time, depending on the rate of technological evolution, and then undergo certain changes as the artefact is improved upon. What do these parameters look like?

Historically technological forecasters were not very explicit in dealing with technological parameters. It was realized that parameters had to be chosen to reflect adequately the true capability of an artefact, but no simple framework existed that could serve as a menu of available parameters. However, with the creation of a standard set of technological trends this relatively unstructured approach could now be advanced a little further. Based on the standardized set of trends a standardized framework of parameters could be created. Such a framework is suggested below and is discussed for each of the types of trend identified. But first a word about units.

If technological parameters are to be measured they have to be expressed in quantifiable units. Five basic units are used. These are presented in Figure 15.1 in diagrammatic form - a diagram that may be called the technological pentagon.

The use of these units in measuring the various technological trends is explained below.

332

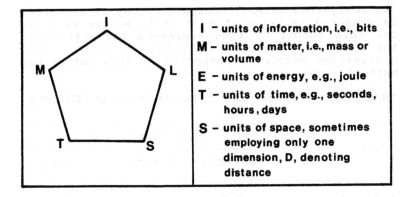

Figure 15.1: The technological pentagon

Measuring Individual Trends

(1) Measuring Efficiency Trends. Efficiency is defined in terms of a ratio of output to input. **Output** is always expressed in terms of units of M, E and I depending on whether the output is of matter, energy or information handling.

Similarly **input** is also measured in terms of M, E or I. The denominator is M if the emphasis is on the efficiency of using matter, the denominator is E if the emphasis is on the efficiency of using energy.

On the role of I as an input the situation is a little more difficult. More often than not savings in M and E are effected by investing more heavily in I, in other words the impact of information inputs is to reduce the inputs of M and E. When this is the case it would be futile to expect a reduction in the ratio of output to input. At times a reduction in the input of I would make sense, namely where one is working with information handling equipment. In this case an increase in the ratio of I_0/I_i could be expected, for instance in the case of more efficient algorithms requiring less computer memory required to merely run the system. Table 15.3 provides a summary of the parameters employed in measuring efficiency.

(2) Measuring Capacity Trends. Capacity reflects the sheer ability of the artefact to bring forth

its designated output. **Output**, as may be expected, is measured in terms of M, E or I, as the case may be. This output is then expressed in relation to the time (T) required to bring it forth. The generalized measure of capacity is thus output per unit of time.

Table 15.3: Parameters Used to Measure Trends in Efficiency

Output	Type of Manipulator		
	Processor	Transporter	Store
Matter (M)	M_0/M_i M_0/E_i	$M_0.D/M_i$ $M_0.D/E_i$	M_0/M_i M_0/E_i
Energy (E)	E_0/M_i E_0/E_i	$E_0.D/M_i$ $E_0.D/E_i$	E_0/M_i E_0/E_i
Information (I)	I_0/M_i I_0/E_i I_0/I_i	$I_0.D/M_i$ $I_0.D/E_i$ $I_0.D/I_i$	I_0/M_i I_0/E_i I_0/I_i

Notes: In this Table M, E, I, are defined as they have been previously.
D=Measure of distance
The subscript $_0$ refers to outputs and the subscript $_i$ to inputs.

This general measure is fine as far as **processors** of M, E and I are concerned. In the case of **transporters**, it is customary to introduce a measure of distance into the numerator, such as in the ratio passenger-kilometres per hour. In the case of **stores** the sheer bulk that can be contained, as expressed simply in units of M, E or I, is usually an adequate parameter. Parameters used to measure capacity are summarized in Table 15.4.

(3) Measuring Density Trends. Density refers to the intensity with which an artefact functions per unit of space required to do so. The numerator in the ratio is M, E or I as the case may be, and the denominator is S. A system of parameters is summarized in Table 15.5.

334

Table 15.4: Performance Parameters Used for Measuring Capacity Trends

Output	Type of Manipulator		
	Processor	Transporter	Store
Matter (M)	M/T	M.D/T	M
Energy (E)	E/T	E.D/T	E
Information (I)	I/T	I.D/T	I

T=Measure of elapsed time

(4) Measuring Accuracy Trends. Increasing accuracy implies increasing specification of output. Thus increased accuracy can be expressed in the number of bits required to express the output required. More traditional artefacts were required to meet reasonably rough specifications. A modern milling machine whose tolerances are so finely specified that it has to sense and correct for the passing of a vehicle or a person whose wake may cause a turbulence affecting its temperature and the distortions caused thereby, obviously requires many more bits of information to describe than a traditional machine milling to a 'few thousands of an inch'.

Table 15.5: Performance Parameters Used for Measuring Density Trends

Output	Type of Manipulator		
	Processor	Transporter	Store
Matter (M)	M/S	M.D/S	M/S
Energy (E)	E/S	E.D/S	E/S
Information (I)	I/S	I.D/S	I/S

S=Measure of space occupied

(5) Measuring Size Trends. The measurement of size usually offers few difficulties. The bulk may be

expressed in volume or mass units or, in special cases, by the dimensions of the most important operational part - such as boom length in the case of draglines, or bucket size in the case of trucks.

(6) Measuring Complexity Trends. The trend towards greater complexity may be measured in two ways, not mutually exclusive. In the first instance, it may be expressed in terms of the number of evolutionary steps that the artefact has taken towards complete automation.

Secondly, the more self-acting the artefact becomes the longer the algorithm required to govern its actions. So increased autonomy may be expressed in increasing length of algorithms, and once again the measure of number of bits becomes significant.

Comment

Using the tools of technological analysis it is possible to characterize the technological change that takes place in a given artefact from one generation to the next. This is done by describing change in terms of six dimensions which correspond to the standard set of technological trends.

Also, using the nine-cell matrix it is possible to 'unbundle' a given technology and then trace the effect of technological advance in each of its subsystems. This will help identify which subsystems contribute towards improvement in the artefact as a whole.

In theory, it is also possible to use this approach to study technological change at the macro-level. To do this it will be necessary to focus on agglomerations of technological systems at the broadest conceivable level of aggregation, for example, at the national level. Again the nine-cell matrix will help to identify the nine national technological systems while the standard set of trends will help identify changes in each of these. In this way a veritable tableau technologique could be created providing an overview of technological change for a nation as a whole.

Unfortunately, the tools of technological analysis are still very new and relatively untried at the macro-level. Empirical evidence of successful exercises in technological analysis at the macro-level is hard to come by. However, various authors have already undertaken technological

336

analysis at that level, using accepted technological parameters, but without the benefit of a comprehensive framework and without knowledge of the full range of tools available to the technological analyst. An exercise in technological forecasting dealing with system thermal efficiencies in a set of power plants belonging to a national utility provides an interesting case study (Pouris, 1985). There is encouraging evidence that a quantitative <u>tableau technologique</u> may be achievable.

While it would seem logical that most advances in technology along any of the trends identified will lead to an improvement in the value of $\delta T/T$ in the macro-production function, it would be very difficult if not impossible to establish a clear-cut line of calculation from individual artefact to the aggregate production function. However, bearing in mind the difficulties in calculating the third factor and considering the variety of influences forced together in that magnitude, a reconciliation between the table of technological achievement and the size of the third factor should not be seen as the final measure of approbation of the analytical approach suggested here.

There are a number of dangers inherent in the approach outlined above and these have to be clearly stated. First there is the danger of misplaced isolation. By focussing on artefacts in isolation, important social, historical and institutional links are ignored. Second, the analysis does not give sufficient explicit recognition to accepted techniques in technological analysis such as S-curves and substitution analysis. Third, the trends described make more sense at the micro-than at the macro-level. They cannot, for instance, reflect the increase in aggregate know-how in a nation. Finally, the analysis does not address soft (abstract) artefacts directly.

CONCLUSION

The conventional economic approach to the description and measurement of the impact of technology on the economy seems to have reached a dead end. The general theory of technology and more specifically the field of technological analysis may provide a fresh start.

The field of technological analysis provides

two useful tools for visualizing technological change: a classification of technological artefacts and a standard set of technological trends.

In theory, these tools should function at both the micro- and the macro-level. Because of their novelty, this contention has not yet been adequately investigated. Nevertheless, evidence does suggest that a macro-analysis leading to a type of tableau technologique mapping out the major thrust of technological change could be constructed.

Two major avenues for further research are indicated. First the refinement of the field of technological analysis. A powerful synthesis of the fields of technological analysis, 'technometrics' and the 'functional approach to technology measurement', seems desirable and could lead to a new level of understanding of technology and the measurement of its impact on the economy. The second area for further research would involve the empirical testing of the tools of technological analysis in a macro-setting.

This should lead to a new level of understanding of technology and the measurement of its impact on the economy.[1]

NOTE

1.   Herewith a note of appreciation to Professor Louis J. Fourie, Department of Economics, Univesity of South Africa, who shared his insight, perused a draft of the document and offered critical comment. Much was learned from the comments of Henry Briefs and Nripesh Podder who acted as discussants of the paper on which this chapter is based and introduced fresh perspectives. No delegation of responsibility is thereby implied. Thanks are also due to the Human Sciences Research Council and the University of Stellenbosh who both contributed to the cost of preparing and presenting this paper.

REFERENCES

Aukrust, O. (1965) 'Factors in Economic Development, A Review of Recent Research', **Productivity Measurement Review,** February 1965, No. 40, pp. 6-22

Bright, J.R. (1978) **Practical Technology Forecasting,** Industrial Management Center, Austin, Texas

Bruton, H.J. (1967) 'Productivity Growth in Latin

America', **American Economic Review,** 57, 5, pp. 1099-1116

Denison, E.F. (1962) **The Sources of Economic Growth in the United States and the Alternatives before Us,** Committee for Economic Development, New York

Denison, E.F. (1964) 'Measuring the Contribution of Education (and the Residual) to Economic Growth', in Study Group in the Economics of Education, **The Residual Factor and Economic Growth,** OECD, Paris

Denison, E.F. (1967) **Why Growth Rates Differ,** Brookings Institution, Washington, D.C.

Jones, H. and Twiss, B.C. (1978) **Forecasting Technology for Planning Decisions,** Macmillan, London

Majer, H. (1985) 'Technology Measurement: The Functional Approach', **Technological Forecasting and Social Change,** 27, pp. 335-351

Martin, M.J.C. (1984) **Managing Technological Innovation Entrepreneurship,** Reston Publishing Co., Reston, Virginia

Martino, J.P. (1972) **Technological Forecasting for Decisionmaking,** American Elsevier Publishing Co., Reston, Virginia

Miller, J.G. (1978) **Living Systems,** McGraw-Hill, New York

Nelson, R.R. (1981) 'Research on Productivity Growth and Productivity Differences: Dead Ends and New Departures', **Journal of Economic Literature,** 19, pp. 1029-1064

Pouris, A. (1985) 'Forecasting System Thermal Efficiencies in Technology Importing Countries', **Technological Forecasting and Social Change,** 28, pp. 335-350

Rapp, F. (1974) **Contributions to a Philosophy of Technology,** D. Reidel Publishing Company, Dordrecht

Ropohl, G. (1979) **Eine Systemtheorie der Technik,** Carl Hanser Verlag, Munchen

Sahal D. (1981) **Patterns of Technological Innovation,** Addison-Wesley, Reading, Massachusetts

Sahal, D. (1985) 'Foundations of Technometrics', **Technological Forecasting and Social Change,** 27, pp. 1-38

Van Wyk, R.J. (1979) 'Technological Change: A Macro Perspective', **Technological Forecasting and Social Change,** 15, pp. 281-296

Van Wyk, R.J. (1984) 'Panoramic Scanning and the Technological Environment', **Technovation,** 2, pp. 101-120

Technological Advance: The Strands

Van Wyk, R.J. (1985) 'The Notion of Technological Limits: An Aid to Technological Forecasting', **Futures**, 17, pp. 214–223

340

Index

342

For Product Safety Concerns and Information please contact our
EU representative GPSR@taylorandfrancis.com Taylor & Francis
Verlag GmbH, Kaufingerstraße 24, 80331 München, Germany